ANAPHORA AND DEFINITE DESCRIPTIONS

SYNTHESE LANGUAGE LIBRARY

TEXTS AND STUDIES IN
LINGUISTICS AND PHILOSOPHY

VOLUME 26

JAAKKO HINTIKKA

and

JACK KULAS

Department of Philosophy, Florida State University

ANAPHORA AND DEFINITE DESCRIPTIONS

*Two Applications of
Game-Theoretical Semantics*

D. REIDEL PUBLISHING COMPANY

A MEMBER OF THE KLUWER ACADEMIC PUBLISHERS GROUP

DORDRECHT / BOSTON / LANCASTER

Library of Congress Cataloging in Publication Data

CIP

Hintikka, Jaakko, 1929–
    Anaphora and definite descriptions.

    (Synthese language library; v. 17)
    Bibliography: p.
    Includes index.
    1. Anaphora (Linguistics) 2. Semantics (Philosophy) 3. Definition
(Logic I. Kulas, Jack. II. Title. III. Series.
P299.A5H48   1985   415   85-10776
ISBN 90-277-2055-X
ISBN 90-277-2056-8 (pbk.)

Published by D. Reidel Publishing Company,
P.O. Box 17, 3300 AA Dordrecht, Holland.

Sold and distributed in the U.S.A. and Canada
by Kluwer Academic Publishers,
190 Old Derby Street, Hingham, MA 02043, U.S.A.

In all other countries, sold and distributed
by Kluwer Academic Publishers Group,
P.O. Box 322, 3300 AH Dordrecht, Holland.

Contents

Jaakko Hintikka, Methodological Introduction   ix

Acknowledgements   xiii

PART I: Introduction to Game-Theoretical Semantics

1.   General   3
2.   Formal first-order languages   3
3.   Equivalence with Tarski-type truth-definitions   6
4.   Translation to higher-order languages   7
5.   Partially ordered quantifiers   8
6.   Subgames and functional interpretations   9
7.   Extension to natural languages   11
8.   Similarities and differences between formal
      and natural languages   14
9.   Competing ordering principles   18
10.   Atomic sentences   21
11.   Further rules for natural languages   22
12.   Explanatory strategies   27

Notes to Part I   31

PART II: DEFINITE DESCRIPTIONS

1.   Russell on definite descriptions   33
2.   Prima facie difficulties with Russell's theory   38
3.   Can we localize Russell's theory?   45
4.   Game-theoretical solution to the localization
      problem   47
5.   Anaphoric "the" in formal languages   50
6.   Applications   51
7.   Epithetic and counterepithetic the-phrases   53
8.   Vagaries of the alleged head-anaphor relation   54
9.   The anaphoric use of definite descriptions as a
      semantical phenomenon   56
10.   The quantifier-exclusion phenomenon in natural
      languages   59
11.   Inductive choice sets   63
12.   Other uses of "the"   64
13.   The Russellian use   66
14.   The generic use motivated   68
15.   Conclusions from the "pragmatic deduction"   69

Notes to Part II   75

PART III: TOWARDS A SEMANTICAL THEORY OF
PRONOMINAL ANAPHORA

Chapter I: Different Approaches to Anaphora   79

   1.   Approaches to anaphora in terms of the head
     relation   79
   2.   Recent Approaches to anaphora in terms
     of coreference assignments   81
   3.   Discourse anaphora. Anaphora vs. deixis?   84

Chapter II: A Game-Theoretical Approach to Anaphora   87

   4.   Anaphoric the-phrases as a paradigm case   87
   5.   Game rules for anaphoric pronouns   90
   6.   What is the logic of anaphoric pronouns?   94
   7.   Different kinds of pronouns   95
   8.   Consequences of the rules   98
   9.   Subgames and discourse anaphora   104
  10.   The nature of anaphoric pronouns and
     the concepts of sentence and scope   109

Chapter III: The Exclusion Principle   113

  11.   Partially exclusive interpretation needed   113
  12.   Peculiarities of pronouns   116
  13.   The Exclusion Principle and reflexive
     pronouns   119
  14.   The Exclusion Principle is semantical in
     nature   125

Chapter IV: General Theoretical Issues   129

  15.   Anaphoric pronouns and quantifier phrases   129
  16.   Pragmatic factors   133
  17.   Semantics and strategy selection   138
  18.   Irrelevance of the head-anaphor relation, and
     the semantical character of pronominal
     anaphora   145
  19.   Shortcomings of the notion of coreference   150

Chapter V: GTS explains Coreference Restrictions   157

    20.   Game rules and their order as explanation
           of coreferentiality restraints   157
    21.   Ordering principles and the Langacker–Ross
           restriction   161
    22.   The timing of rule applications   163
    23.   Rules for prepositional phrases   172
    24.   Don't try to anticipate the course of a
           semantical game   179
    25.   Surface vs. deep structure   182
    26.   Other intervening rules   187
    27.   Coreferentiality and special ordering
           principles   190
    28.   Different explananda   191

Chapter VI: Comparisons with Other Treatments   197

    29.   Comparisons: general perspectives   197
    30.   Comparisons: Chomsky   198
    31.   Comparisons: Reinhart   203
    32.   The Exclusion Principle is clausebound   208
    33.   The Exclusion Principle and different
           methods of identification   209
    34.   Apparent exceptions: pronouns of laziness   217
    35.   Apparent exceptions: syntactical control
           or not?   220

Notes to Part III   223

Bibliography   225

Subject Index   235

Name Index   249

Methodological Introduction

In order to appreciate properly what we are doing in this book it is necessary to realize that our approach to linguistic theorizing differs from the prevailing views. Our approach can be described by indicating what distinguishes it from the methodological ideas current in theoretical linguistics, which I consider seriously misguided. Linguists typically construe their task in these days as that of making exceptionless generalizations from particular examples. This explanatory strategy is wrong in several different ways. It presupposes that we can have "intuitions" about particular examples, usually examples invented by the linguist himself or herself, reliable and sharp enough to serve as a basis of sharp generalizations. It also presupposes that we cannot have equally reliable direct access to general linguistic regularities. Both assumptions appear to me extremely dubious, and the first of them has in effect been challenged by linguists like Dwight Bolinger. There is also some evidence that the degree of unanimity among linguists is fairly low when it comes to less clear cases, even in connection with such relatively simple questions as grammaticality (acceptability). For this reason we have tried to rely more on quotations from contemporary fiction, newspapers and magazines than on linguists' and philosophers' ad hoc examples. I also find it strange that some of the same linguists as believe that we all possess innate ideas about general characteristics of humanly possible grammars assume that we can have access to them only via their particular consequences.

This point applies especially poignantly to semantics. Chomsky and Chomskians seem to think that the proper representation of semantical structure is given by something like the customary formalism of quantificational logic. Do they claim that this formalism is a generalization from sample sentences and inferences couched in Queen's English? Even if some philosophers used to maintain that, I don't see that there is a shred of serious evidence to support such claims.

Even more importantly, the currently accepted ideas about the goals of linguistic theorizing depend on an antiquated and primitive conception of scientific explanation. In no theoretically sophisticated science are generalizations from data the end-all and be-all of theorizing. Rather, what the aim is, is a grasp of the underlying mechanism, i.e., a grasp of the several factors which together govern the phenomena to be studied. This aim is so crucial that, e.g., physical theories which right from the beginning were known to be only approximations have constituted major breakthroughs in physics, because they have offered insights into the *modus operandi* of the physical forces being studied. Both the Rutherford and the Bohr model of the atom were cases in point. Their importance is thus due, not to their accounting for the details of available data, but to their capturing some aspects of the mechanism which underlies these data. Such mechanisms – in the sense of complexes of interacting factors – are often not obtained as generalizations from data, but as outcomes of an analysis of the theoretical situation, usually resulting in a model which incorporates the different relevant factors. This model typically incorporates, not just empirical generalizations, but independently accepted general principles, which in the case of a physical theory might include, e.g., some of the general conservation principles. (They are not empirically established for each physical theory separately; they are assumed right from the outset in developing a theory for some class of physical phenomena.) In the case of our theory of anaphora, these general principles are those of game-theoretical semantics. They can be argued for – and have been argued for – independently of the particular phenomena of anaphora.

The conception of explanatory strategy I represent should apply even better in linguistics than in natural sciences. For since we are dealing with *our* language, we can expect to have keener insights into the theoretically relevant factors than in a study of external nature. Furthermore, the detailed data are likely to be much more complex in the case of a phenomenon which like language is a part of human life than they are in the case of physical reality. Hence the strategy of direct generalization from data is even less likely to succeed in linguistics than in physics, nothwithstanding the fact that few physicists think of it as a viable research strategy.

What we are trying to achieve in this book is a theoretical model of the semantics of definite descriptions and of (singular) pronominal anaphora. The model should not be viewed as a generalization from particular examples, even though it has to be tested in terms of such examples. For the role of examples is not just that of conforming or not conforming to a generalization. Their main function is to provide insights into the factors which govern the linguistic phenomena being studied.

What game-theoretical semantics provides is a theoretical model of the right sort. It is roughly comparable to such familiar frameworks of semantical representation as first-order logic. However, the earlier theoretical frameworks offered by contemporary logic are simply far too distant from the realities of natural languages to be what linguists really need. This fact will be illustrated repeatedly in the course of our study. In fact, our game-theoretical viewpoint quickly shows what the true logico-semantical mechanism is on which pronominal anaphora is based. It is here that the contrast between customary logical models and ours is particularly vivid. The true logical mechanism of anaphoric pronouns is not that of the bound variables of quantification, as it is usually taken to be, but (we shall argue) that of independently evaluated terms, roughly comparable to Hilbert's epsilon-terms or Russell's definite descriptions. It is not likely that this general idea could be obtained as a generalization from examples, even though suitable examples, such as Geach's "donkey sentences" (cf. below, Part III, sections 6 and 8), can yield important clues to the right choice of the overall model, and even though it has to be related to a wide variety of examples.

Ability to cover such examples is nevertheless not the only standard for measuring the success of a theory. Another one is the power of the theory to throw light on important concepts and theoretical issues. We shall apply our theory so as to illuminate, among other concepts, those of sentence (clause), scope, head (grammatical antecedent), coreference, and even the general concept of meaning. Moreover, we shall try to put the entire recent discussion of restrictions on coreference in a new context by considering such restrictions as consequences of the principles which govern the order of application of the rules of semantical games. In so far as these applications are successful, they speak for our theory even more strongly than its capacity of accommodating particular examples.

It is to be noted, moreover, that to have the right theory means primarily to have recognized the different theoretically relevant factors and the mode of operation of each of them. It does not always mean that one can predict the details of the interaction of the different factors. Once again it is completely unrealistic to require such a detailed predictability in all cases. Galileo correctly diagnosed the motions of freely falling bodies as resulting from constant acceleration independent of the falling body in question impeded by the resistance of the medium in which the motion takes place. While the mathematics of a motion with constant acceleration is clear, neither Galileo nor any subsequent physicist has given us a way of predicting in full realistic detail the actual motions of all and sundry freely falling bodies in a medium. In the same way, it is a false dream to hope to have a theory which predicts in one fell swoop the semantics of each and every sample sentence. We shall leave in this work more detailed loose ends hanging than is fashionable to admit that one is leaving. We do not think that any apology is needed for doing so.

If I were uncharitable, I would perhaps try to diagnose the popularity of the strategy of direct generalization as being due to methodological insecurity. It seems much easier to judge a purportedly exceptionless generalization than to estimate the theoretical value of a model which covers the known data only partially. I believe that the time has come to give theoretical considerations their due in theoretical linguistics and philosophy of language.

Jaakko Hintikka

Acknowledgments

The research reported here was made possible by NSF Grant # BNS - 8119033 (Linguistics), with Jaakko Hintikka as the Principal Investigator.

In writing this book, we have enjoyed the advice and criticism of Lauri Carlson. So many of his suggestions have made their way into our text that he should really be considered its co-author. For instance, the idea of strategic meaning (Part III, sec. 17) was inspired by discussions with Carlson. However, Lauri Carlson is not responsible for our mistakes and does not agree with everything we say.

Part II contains material which has been previously appeared in the following publications:

Jaakko Hintikka and Jack Kulas, "Russell Vindicated: Towards a General Theory of Definite Descriptions", *Journal of Semantics,* vol. 1 (1982), pp. 387–397.

Jaakko Hintikka and Jack Kulas, "Definite Descriptions in Game–Theoretical Semantics", chapter 6 of Jaakko Hintikka and Jack Kulas, *The Game of Language,* D. Reidel, Dordrecht, 1983.

Jaakko Hintikka and Jack Kulas, "Different Uses of Definite Descriptions", *Communication and Cognition* (forthcoming, 1985)

The material is here reprinted by the permission of the editors and publishers of the journals in question.

Jayne Moneysmith has read the entire book and has made many valuable suggestions, substantial as well as stylistic.

The production of a camera-ready copy was made possible by the help of the staff of the Editorial Office of the Department of Philosophy, FSU, including Constance Jakubcin, Leigh Campbell (Garrison), and Florene Ball.

We are also grateful to D. Reidel Publishing Company for accepting the volume for publication in Synthese Language Library.

Jaakko Hintikka
Jack Kulas

Note on the Notation

Because of typographical limitations, we are using (Ex) and (Ax) as the existential and the universal quantifier, respectively, instead of the more commonly employed symbols. For the same reason, we are using "→" instead of the horseshoe for a conditional symbol and the symbol ɟ instead of Russell's inverted iota in our symbol for definite descriptions.

PART I

INTRODUCTION TO
GAME-THEORETICAL SEMANTICS

1. General

This introductory part presents enough of the basic ideas of game-theoretical semantics (GTS) to serve as a basis for a new theory of anaphoric pronouns to be presented in Part III, below. Not all of the details will actually be needed for the account we are going to offer of the semantics of anaphoric pronouns, but since the attractiveness of our account is partly due to its being an aspect of a more comprehensive systematic theory, it is in order to sketch the basic ideas of game-theoretical semantics in general.[1]

GTS is a variant of truth-conditional semantics (cf. Hintikka forthcoming b). Games come in as mediators of truth-conditions. GTS can be explained by explaining the truth-conditions it yields for different kinds for sentences. It is also instructive to compare the truth-conditions resulting from GTS with the usual Tarski-type truth-definitions on which, e.g., Montague semantics is based. We shall assume that the reader is familiar with the basic ideas of Tarski-type truth-definitions.

2. Formal First-Order Languages

The basic ideas of GTS are explained most easily in terms of a formal (but applied) first-order language L. Such languages have been the favorite tool of philosophers in the last hundred years for the purposes of formalization, and one of the most frequently used media of semantical representation among linguists. This popularity may or may not be deserved, but it is in any case salutary to note that there is nothing sacred about the way the semantics of first-order quantificational languages is normally developed (see Hintikka 1981, 1984). GTS offers in fact a theoretically motivated alternative to the usual treatments. It offers an explicit semantical representation that does the same things as the usual semantics for first-order logic or for the higher-order modal logics employed in Montague semantics, but that is both more flexible and also much closer to natural languages than logicians' old systems with their Tarski-type semantics – over and above admitting of a much deeper philosophical motivation.

Since the given first-order language L is assumed to be an applied language, one is given for the purposes of a truth-definition a model M consisting of a domain of individuals do(M) and an interpretation of all the primitive predicates of L on do(M). This interpretation determines the truth-values of all atomic sentences in every language L(I) that is an extension of L obtained by adding to it a finite set I of names of members of do(M). As an actual definition of truth for such atomic sentences we can use the clause for atomic formulas in any one of the usual Tarski-type truth-definitions.

For instance, an atomic sentence of the form "Pa" is defined to be true if and only if the interpretation v(a) of "a" in do(M) is a member of the class v(P), which is the interpretation of "P" in do(M). For other atomic sentences, the definition is similar.

The game-theoretical truth-definition serves the same purpose as the other (recursive) clauses in a usual (Tarski-type) truth-definition. The main difference is that, whereas the recursive clauses in a usual Tarski-type truth-definition work their way from the inside out, start-ing from the simplest formulas, a game-theoretical truth-definition works its way from the outside in, defining in effect a semantical analysis of the sentence in question. This makes a difference, for it means that GTS is indepen-dent of the assumption of compositionality (semantical context-independence), and works even when composition-ality fails (see Hintikka and Kulas 1983, chap. 10).

The semantical analysis effected by GTS is obtained by associating with each sentence S of L a two-person zero-sum game G(S). Its two players will be called Myself and Nature. It can be thought of as an attempt on the part of Myself to verify S. Conversely, Nature can be thought of as trying to falsify S. The sentence S is true if Myself can verify it no matter what Nature does. That means that there exists in G(S) a winning strategy for My-self, i.e., a strategy that wins against any strategy of Na-ture's. A strategy is a rule that tells a player what to do (which move to make) in every conceivable situation that may come up in the course of the game. Clearly, when the strategies of all players in a game are fixed, the course of the game, and hence also its outcome, is completely determined.

Myself wins and Nature loses a play of the game G(S) if it ends with a true atomic sentence in some extension L(I) of L, obtained by adjoining to L a finite set I of names of individuals from the domain of the model on which the game is played. If G(S) ends up with a false sentence, Nature wins and Myself loses.

The sentence S is false if there exists a winning strategy in G(S) for Nature. The basic rules of the games G(S) are as follows:

(G. v) The game $G((S_1 \vee S_2)$ begins with a choice by Myself of a disjunct S_i (i = 1 or 2). The rest of the game is as in $G(S_i)$.

(G. &) The game $G((S_1 \text{ & } S_2))$ begins with a choice by Nature of a conjunct S_i (i = 1 or 2). The rest of the game is as in $G(S_i)$.

(G. E) The game $G((Ex)S[x]$ begins with a choice by Myself of an individual from do(M). Let the name of this individual (either in L or in an extension L(*l*) of L) be "b". Then the game is continued as in $G(S[b])$.

Here S[b] is the outcome of replacing every free occurrence of "x" in S[x] by "b".

(G. U) $G((Ax)S[x])$ begins likewise, except that the individual is chosen by Nature, and is continued likewise.

(G. ∿) The game G(∿S) begins by a switch of roles by the two players as defined by these game rules and the rules for winning and losing. Then the game is continued as in G(S).

The game G(S) will be called a semantical game. Their rules are obvious in the light of the basic idea of semantical games as games of verification and falsification. For instance, in order to verify $(S_1 \vee S_2)$, one obviously has to verify S_1 or to verify S_2; hence the rule (G. v). Similarly for the other rules.

It is seen that each application of our rules for semantical games reduces the number of logical symbols in the sentence that is going to be considered in the next move (if any) by one. Hence each semantical game G(S) will come to an end after a finite number of moves. This number is no greater than the number of logical symbols in S. Hence

our rules for winning and losing are applicable to every
semantical game.

Instead of "Myself" and "Nature", the two players are
sometimes called "Verifier" and "Falsifer". Rule (G. ∿)
shows that this is misleading because either player may in
the course of the same game try to verify a sentence and at
another time try to falsify a sentence that has come up as
the output of an earlier application of one of our game
rules.

3. Equivalence with Tarski-Type
Truth-Definitions

It is also fairly obvious on the basis of the general nature
of our semantical games that in a usual applied first-order
language L our game-theoretical truth-definition is equivalent to the usual Tarski-type one. This can be proved
very simply as follows: Let us call our notion of truth,
true(GTS), and the usual one, true(Tarski). [Likewise for
false(GTS) and false(Tarski).] These two notions agree by
definition on atomic sentences. Therefore it suffices to
prove the following:

Lemma 1. If the input sentence of a move in a semantical game rule is true(Tarski) and Myself is trying to verify it, then Myself can choose the move in such a way that
the output is also true(Tarski). If the input sentence of a
move in a semantical game is false(Tarski) and if Myself is
trying to falsify it, then Myself can choose the move in
such a way that the output is also false(Tarski).

This is ascertained by inspecting all the different cases. It follows from Lemma 1 that if S is true(Tarski), Myself can choose the successive moves in such a way that he
or she ends up winning. In other words, if S is
true(Tarski), Myself has a winning strategy in G(S), i.e.,
S is true(GTS).

Lemma 2. If there is a winning strategy for Myself in
G(S), then S is true(Tarski).

Proof: By induction on the number of logical symbols
in S. If there are none, S is atomic and true(GTS), which

by definition means that it is also true(Tarski). This
yields a basis for induction.

The inductive step is proved by reviewing all the different cases. For instance, if the sentence in question is
of the form (Ex)S[x], then Myself must be able to choose
from do(M) an individual, say the one named by "b", such
that Myself has a winning strategy in G(S[b]). But S[b]
contains fewer logical symbols than (Ex)S[x]. By the inductive hypothesis, we can therefore conclude that S[b] is
true(Tarski). But, in virtue of the usual truth-definition,
then (Ex)S[x] clearly is also true(Tarski).

Again, in the game G((Ax)S[x]) Myself has a winning
strategy if and only if there is a winning strategy for Myself in each S[b], where "b" is the name of some one member of do(M). But, in virtue of the inductive hypothesis,
each such S[b] is then true(Tarski). Consequently so is
(Ax)S[x].

The other cases can be dealt with equally easily,
which completes our sketch of a proof.

4. Translation to Higher-Order Languages

If the usual logical principles are modified, however, GTS
enables us to formulate easily and naturally the semantics
for languages for which Tarski-type truth-definitions don't
work or don't work equally easily. In order to indicate
what these extensions are, it is helpful to note first a way
of spelling out the mechanism of GTS.

The truth of S is defined in GTS as the existence of a
winning strategy in G(S) for Myself (the initial verifier).
Now Myself's strategy is a function that tells what do depending on Nature's earlier moves. The part of such a
strategy that pertains to (unnegated) existential quantifiers
(quantificational moves by Myself) is codified in what are
known as Skolem functions. The existence of a winning
strategy for Myself can therefore be expressed by a
higher-order sentence that asserts the existence of such
Skolem functions as codify partly a strategy that wins
against any moves by Nature. Thus, the implications of
GTS can be studied by means of a translation of first-order
languages into higher-order ones ensuing from GTS. This
translation, in fact, illuminates the nature of GTS. Here
are some examples of the translation:

(1) $(Ax)(Ey)\ S[x,y]$ translates as
(2) $(Ef)(Ax)\ S[x,f(x)]$.

(3) $(Ex)(Ay)\ S[x,y]$ is its own translation.

(4) $(Ax)(Ey)(Az)(Eu)\ S[x,y,z,u]$ translates as
(5) $(Ef)(Eg)\ (Ax)(Az)\ S[x,f(x),z,g(x,z)]$.

(6) $(Ax)(Az)(Ey)(Eu)\ S[x,y,z,u]$ translates as
(7) $(Ef)(Eg)(Ax)(Az)\ S[x,f(x,z),z,g(x,z)]$.

It is especially interesting here to see how the (linear) order of quantifiers is reflected by the choice of arguments that different Skolem functions have.

In general, the higher-order translation will have a quantifier prefix of the form

(8) $(Ef_1)\ (Ef_2).\ .\ .\ (Ag_1)(Ag_2).\ .\ .$

where f_1, $f_2,...$ range over the Skolem functions representing (partial) strategies for Myself and $g_1, g_2, ...$ range over functions representing the quantificational part of Nature's strategies.

5. Partially Ordered Quantifiers

This higher-order translation helps us to describe certain extensions of the usual first-order languages for which GTS automatically yields a semantics. One of them is obtained by allowing informational independence between different quantifier moves. This can be formally reflected by allowing quantifier prefixes to be partially ordered instead of linear (see Hintikka and Kulas 1983, bibliography). The impact of GTS on such partially ordered quantifier sentences is shown by the same higher-order translation as was explained above for the linear case. This is best seen from sample translations:

(9) (Ex)
                        $\diagdown$
                             $>$ $S[x,y]$ translates as
             (Ay) $\diagup$

(10) $(Ex)(Ay)\ S[x,y]$.

(11) $(Ax)(Ey)$

(Az) ⟶ $S[x,y,z]$ translates as

(12) $(Ef)(Ax)(Az)\ S[x,f(x),z]$

which is equivalent to

(13) $(Ax)(Ey)(Az)\ S[x,y,z].$

(14) $(Ax)(Ey)$

$(Az)(Eu)$ ⟶ $S[x,y,z,u]$

translates as

(15) $(Ef)(Eg)(Ax)(Az)\ S[x,f(x),z,g(z)].$

These examples show that sometimes a sentence with a partially ordered quantifier prefix is equivalent to a linear first-order quantifier sentence. This is not always the case, however. It can be shown, e.g., that quantifier prefixes of the form (14) don't always (i.e., for all choices of S[x,y,z,u]) reduce to linear first-order sentences.

In fact, the logical theory of branching first-order sentences with a branching-quantifier structure is an extremely strong logic, almost equivalent to the entire second-order logic (with the standard interpretation). In fact, it has a decision problem with the same degree of difficulty as second-order logic.

6. Subgames and Functional Interpretations

In this work, branching (more generally, partially ordered) quantifiers will not play a major role. However, another extension (or modification) of the usual first-order languages and their accustomed logic will be important to us. It is explained most concisely by the very means of our game-theoretical approach. It consists in allowing a semantical game to be divided into several subgames (see Hintikka and Kulas 1983, chap. 3). Such a subgame is sometimes played with the usual roles of the two players reversed. Whether or not such an exchange takes place is specified by the relevant game rule, which also specifies which of the strategies used by the two players are available to which of the players in later subgames.

Once again, the easiest way to explain the relevant rules is by means of a higher-order translation. For instance, one possible game rule for conditionals is the following:

(G. cond)   Let

(16) $(S_1 \rightarrow S_2)$

be a conditional, and let the higher-order translations of S_1 and S_2, respectively, be

(17) $(Ef)(Ag) \, S_1'[f,g]$

and

(18) $(Eh)(An) \, S_2'[h,n]$

where the lower-case letters stand for sequences of variables of any type.

Then the translation of the conditional is

(19) $(EG)(EH)(Af)(An)(S_1'[f,G(f)] \rightarrow S_2'[H(f),n])$.

The import of (19) is not hard to fathom. First, a subgame is played with the antecedent of (16), with the roles of the two players interchanged. If Myself wins this subgame, Myself wins the entire game. If Nature wins, even though Myself knows Nature's strategy f, the game goes on to the second subgame, played with the consequent of the conditional, with the usual roles. In this second subgame, Myself has access to the strategy Nature used in the first subgame, while Nature does not have any such inside information. This is one way of implementing the natural idea that the consequent of a conditional comes into play only if the antecedent turns out to be true, and comes into play depending on how it turned out to be true. This "how" (a verifactory strategy) is what f codifies.

Other, variant subgame rules for conditionals are also possible. Instead of (19) we can have, for instance,

(20) $(EG)(EH)(Af)(An) \, (S_1'f,G(n)] \rightarrow (S_2'[H(f),n])$

or

(21) $(EG)(EH)(Af)(An)(S_1'[f,G(f,n)] \rightarrow S_2'[H(f),n])$.

Other subgame rules are likewise easily formulated. One of them is for negation. If the translation of S is

(22) $(Eg)(Ah)$ $S'[g,h]$,

the translation of $\sim S$ is

(23) $(EH)(Ag)$ $\sim S'[g,H(g)]$.

Subgame rules can be complemented by a restriction on the ranges of higher-order functions, for instance, by restricting them to recursive values. If this is also done to the strategy functions that govern Myself's choices in propositional moves, and if suitable rules are chosen for conditionals and negation, we can obtain Gödel's interpretation of first-order logic (Gödel 1980). (In fact, the rules expressed by (21) and (23) for conditionals and negation, respectively, will serve this purpose.) More generally, the higher-order translations yielded by GTS are among what are known in the foundational literature as "functional interpretations". The relevance of such interpretations to linguistic semantics has not been fully appreciated in the literature.

7. Extension to Natural Languages

GTS can be extended to natural languages like English. One kind of extension is obtained as soon as the natural language in question can be translated into the first-order logical notation (possibly amplified by intensional operators), which is what many philosophers and some linguists are trying to do. However, we distrust such translations as long as they do not have the benefit of a prior semantical theory. Hence, we shall develop game-theoretical semantics directly for an unspecified fragment of English, without assuming a prior translation of English into first-order notation (or similar). We shall maintain the same general framework, associating to each sentence of our fragment of English a two-person zero-sum game G(S) between Myself and Nature. The definitions of winning and

of truth (the truth of S in some model in which the basic
vocabulary of our fragment of English has been defined)
are the same as in the case of formal languages. Even the
game rules are in many cases obvious. For instance, the
game rules (G. and) and (G. or) for clausal conjunctions
and disjunctions, respectively, are but mild variants of the
corresponding formal rules (G. &) and (G. v). (These
rules can also be extended to uses of "and" and "or" to
connect phrases rather than clauses.) Likewise, negation
can be handled, for our purposes in this work, in the same
way as in the case of formal languages.

Quantifier rules have to be different, for there are in
natural languages no formal variables for which the players
could substitute names of chosen individuals. What can be
done, however, is to substitute such names for entire
quantifier phrases, such as the following:

(24)   some X   who Y
            every X   which Y
            an X   where Y
            each X   whose Y
            an X   where Y

Of course, the force of the quantifier phrase itself will
then have to be taken into account by means of added conjunctions or antecedents. This leads us to game rules illustrated by the following:

(G. some) (special case) If the game has reached a
sentence of the form

(25)   X - some Y who Z - W

then Myself chooses a person from the domain of the
model with respect to which the game is being played.
If the name of the individual is "b", then the game is
contained with respect to

(26)   X - b - W, b is a Y, and b Z.

This special case of a game rule requires a number of
comments in order to serve as a paradigm case for the general situation.

(a) The choice of an individual is not made from a uniform domain of the model in question, but from a subset of the domain. This subset is indicated sometimes by the relative pronoun occurring in the quantifier phrase. If it is "who", the choice is between persons; if "where", between locations in space; if "when", between times; and so on. We shall not discuss this phenomenon, for the details do not matter for our purposes here.

(b) It is assumed in the special case above that "who" occupies the subject position in "who Z". If not, "b" enters into the output sentence (26), not to the beginning of the third clause, but instead (in the appropriate case and with the appropriate prepositional construction) in the location where the wh-movement moved the relative pronoun from in the first place.

For instance, a less restricted application of (G. some) might take the players from

(27)   Some man to whom he had spoken saw Tom.

to

(28)   Reginald saw Tom, Reginald is a man, and he had spoken to Reginald.

There are no problems in formulating this aspect of (G.some) explicitly – at least no problems that are not shared by every theorist who is trying to deal with relative clauses and wh-movement.

(c) In the game rules, the sentences that the players face are assumed to be given in the usual labelled-tree form (or in the equivalent bracket notation). For instance, the input sentence (25) of the rule (G. some) should strictly speaking have been written

(29) $[X \ [[\text{some } Y]_{NP} \ [\text{who } Z]_S]_{NP} \ W]_S.$

We shall nevertheless try to keep our presuppositions concerning the syntactic structure at a minimum.

(d) It is assumed that "some" is singular in (25). The plural case has to be dealt with separately.

(e) In the output sentence (26) of the special case of (G. some) above, the order of the three conjunctions is free, i.e., can be chosen by Myself. This is a characteristic feature of the rule (G. some). There is not a similar option in all the other rules.

The rule (G. a(n)) for the indefinite article "a" or "an" is formulated likewise, except that "a(n)" replaces "some". The rule (G. every) for "every", in the special case analogous to the special case of (G. some) formulated above, is analogous, the differences being the following:

(i) The input sentence is

(30)   X - every Y who Z - W.

(ii) The choice of b is made by Nature.

(iii) The output sentence is

(31)   X - b - W if b is a Y and b Z.

The order of the antecedent and consequent as well as the order of the two conjuncts in (31) is again free.

Game rules for "each" and for the singular "any" are formulated in an analogous way.

8. Similarities and Differences between Formal and Natural Languages

Several of the general theoretical insights that were registered above in connection with formal languages can be extended immediately to natural languages. They include the possibility of informationally independent quantifiers and, more importantly for our present purposes, the division of semantical games into subgames.

The latter idea is especially important in that it enables GTS to extend many of its insights to discourse theory by treating the successive sentences uttered in discourse as giving rise to subgames that are parts of a wider "supergame". The relation of different subgames is in the simplest case of asserted utterances by the same speaker conjunctive. In more complicated cases, it is regulated by special rules characteristic of discourse theory, such as the rules governing question–answer relations. In this way, many of the observations that can be made about semantical games connected with individual sentences can be extended to discourse.

In moving from sentence semantics to discourse semantics, the notions of winning and losing have to be redefined. The reason is that discourse games are no longer purely verificatory ones; sundry other purposes are also involved. This is also the reason why the precise definitions of winning and losing will depend on the kind of discourse we are dealing with, such as questioning, commanding, negotiating, etc. We cannot discuss the details of the different definitions here.

There are nevertheless also relevant differences between formal and natural languages. Perhaps the most important one is the following: in formal first-order languages, the syntactical form of the sentence reached at each stage of the game determines completely which rule is to be applied next. In contrast to this determinacy, in many cases more than one game rule can be applied to a given sentence, other things being equal. For instance, there may be rules that apply to an ingredient in X, Z, or W in the input sentence (25) of (G. some). Which rule is to be applied first?

It is clear that our game rules have to be complemented by a set of ordering principles that govern the order of application of the rules. There are two different kinds of ordering principles, general principles and special ones. The former depend only on the syntactic structure of the sentence in question; the latter govern the relative order of particular rules and hence depend also on the particular lexical elements occurring in a sentence. General ordering principles are the weaker ones; they can be overruled by the special ones.

The most important ordering principles are the following:

(O. LR) In one and the same clause, game rules are applied from left to right.

(O. comm) A game rule must not be applied to an ingredient of a lower clause if a game rule applies to an ingredient of a higher one.

Here a node N_1 is said to be in a higher clause than N_2 if the S-node most immediately dominating N_1 also dominates N_2, but not vice versa.

Normally, (O. LR) also šeems to apply to expression in conjoint (correlated) clauses, provided that they do not give rise to different subgames.

Of a slightly different nature is the principle governing the order of subgames:

Progression Principle: Subgames are played in the left-to-right order.

It remains to be studied to what extent the order of subgames depends on the subordination (commanding) relations in a sentence, in the same way as the order of rule applications does. (Cf. (O. comm) above.) It seems that the Progression Principle applies much more strictly to subgames connected with successive sentences in discourse than to different clauses (S-nodes) in one and the same sentence.

Another ordering principle governs nested prepositional phrases:

Nested prepositional phrases are unpacked from the end (in the right-to-left order).

The effects of this ordering principle can be seen from examples like the following:

(32)   Harold talked to some student from every college.

This ordering principle does not seem to be exceptionless, however, but subject to lexical variation. (For observations concerning this matter, see Van Lehn's unpublished dissertation, Department of Computer Science, MIT.) An example of exceptions is the following:

(33)   Every ape near a tree ran for it.

We shall return to this matter in Part III, sec. 23.

We shall return to these ordering principles later (see especially Part III, chap. 5). Here it is especially relevant to note how naturally they ensue from the basic ideas of GTS.

To take some examples of the application of the order-ing principles, we can note that (O. LR) is what assigns the right meaning to such sentences as the following:

(34)   Some boy loves every girl.
(35)   Every girl is loved by some boy.

The effects of (O. comm) can be seen from the following example:

(36)   That someone will some day beat him never occurs to any real champion.

Here "any" and "never" are treated before "someone" and "some day" because of (O. comm), lending (36) its normal intended force.

The analogy with formal first-order languages shows that the earlier a quantifier or a propositional connective is treated in a semantical game, the wider its scope is. This observation will in practice enable us to determine the "log-ical form" of a natural-language sentence in the usual sense of its logical representation in first-order notation. We can, for instance, see that our ordering principles have the effect of assigning the following "logical forms" to (34)-(36):

(37)   (Ex) ((x is a boy) & (Ay)((y is a girl) →
          (x loves y)))
(38)   (Ay) ((y is a girl) → (Ex)((x is a boy) &
          (x loves y)))
(39)   (Ax) ((x is a real champion) → ∼(Et)(it occurs to
          x at time t that (Ez)(Eu)((u is a future day) &
          (z beats x on day u))))

Now we can also see one reason why the ordering principles of GTS are so important: they determine (to use the usual jargon) the "scopes" of different quantifiers and other operator-like ingredients of natural-language sentenc-es. We cannot always reach a first-order representation, however, as a consequence of the possibility of branching quantifiers.

Furthermore, the very notion of scope is a treacherous one. In fact, we are here dealing with another relevant difference between formal and natural languages. In formal languages, a quantifier always comes with its scope indicated, either by brackets or by some other syntactical device. Such a scope indicates two different things: (i) The logical order of the different quantifiers: the wider the scope, the earlier a quantifier has to be treated game-theoretically. (ii) The part of the sentence in which variables are bound to the quantifier in question.

In natural languages, there are no scope indicators. Moreover, there is, at least prima facie, no counterpart to (ii). However, the logical order of different quantifiers (i) must still be indicated. The most important way in which this happens is precisely by means of ordering principles. However, they do not indicate "quantifier scopes" in the sense (ii).

The special ordering principles govern the priorities in applying particular game rules. Examples of such principles are (O. any), which among other things says that (G. any) has priority over (G. not), (G. or), modal (nonepistemic) rules, and the rule (G. cond) for conditionals; and (O. each), which says that (G. each) has priority over propositional rules and over other quantificational rules.

These principles explain, among other things, the force of the following sentences:

(40)   Richard doesn't date any girl.
(41)   John cannot beat Jim or anyone else.
(42)   If anyone comes, I'll be surprised.
(43)   You may pick any apple, but you must not pick
          every apple.
(44)   Some man or boy loves each girl.

9. Competing Ordering Principles

In view of their importance as systematic explanatory tools, our ordering principle deserve a few more comments. In spite of their simplicity and plausibility, (O. comm) and (O. LR) are not the only candidates for the role of ordering principles. In much of recent linguistic discussion, it is in effect assumed that a different ordering principle is the correct one. In order to compare it with our principle, we can first define a couple of syntactical notions. In them, we shall assume that a sentence S is represented in the usual way in the tree form.

A node N_1 is said to s-dominate another node N_2 iff the closest s-node dominating N_1 also dominates N_2.

A node N_1 is said to c-dominate another node N_2 iff the closest branching node dominating N_1 also dominates N_2.

A node N_1 is said to s-command another node N_2 iff N_1 s-dominates N_2 but not vice versa.

A node N_1 is said to c-command another node N_2 iff N_1 c-dominates N_2 but not vice versa.

With these definitions, (O. comm) can be expressed as follows:

> If a node N_1 s-commands another node N_2, no game rule must be applied to N_2 if some rule applies to N_1.

In recent literature, it has been assumed in effect that the following ordering principle should be used instead of (O. comm) and (O. LR) (see Reinhart 1976, 1978, 1981, 1983a, 1983b):

> (O. CR) If a node N_1 c-commands another node N_2, then no game rule must be applied to N_2 if some rule applies to N_1.

It seems to us, however, that (O. CR) is not correct. Direct comparisons between different ordering principles are not easy, for all comparisons depend on what the syntactical (labelled tree) structure of the sentences in question is assumed to be. We do not want to get involved in syntactical controversies. Some comparisons are nevertheless possible without controversial syntactical assumptions. Here are some examples that are relevant here:

(45)   Near some spectator, everybody saw a snake.
(46)   On the top of every single hill, someone has built a house.

In (45), the intended scope of "some spectator" is obviously wider than that of "everybody". Hence a rule must be applied to "some spectator" before any rule is applied to "everybody". However, on apparently plausible assumptions concerning syntactic structure, "everybody" c-commands "some", and hence ought to be dealt with first, if (O. CR) is correct. This presupposes only that there is no branching node between the one for "everybody" and

the top node of (45).   The need of this assumption seems
to be confirmed by the fact, to be established in Part III
chap. 5, that in the structurally similar sentence

(47)   Near him, John saw a snake

a rule has to be applied to "John" before one is applied to
"him".   Hence, whatever the syntactical structure is which
is shared by (45) and (47), if (O. CR) yields the right
prediction concerning one of them, it yields the wrong one
concerning the other.
        This line of thought might be objected to by claiming
that "everybody" does not really c-dominate "some" in (45).
This presumably would mean the postulation of a node immediately dominating "everybody" and being dominated by the
top node of (45).   Then we would obtain the right order of
quantifiers in (45).   However, now the order of rule applications would be wrong in (47), as we indicated.   Moreover, there are other examples, admittedly elliptical ones,
to which this objection cannot apply.   For instance, the
following:

(48)   Who do I owe money to?   At some time in the near
            future, everybody.

It is hard to say what the syntactical structure is of elliptical sentences like the second sentence in (48).   But the order of quantifiers in such sentences as in (48) seems to be
determined in general in the same way as in nonelliptical
sentences, that is to say, on the basis of their elliptical
rather than filled-in structure.   If so, since "some time" in
(48) has a wider scope than "everybody", we obtain at
least prima facie evidence against (O. CR).
        Somewhat similar things can be said about (46).   In
order to defend (O. CR), one would have to assign to (46)
a syntactical structure that results, when combined with
(O. CR), in giving the wider scope to "every" in (46) but
narrower in

(49)   Someone has built a house on the top of every
            single hill.

Again, the syntactical assumptions which would enable (O.
CR) to assign the right scopes to the quantifiers in (46) do
not seem to do so in other cases, e.g., in the following:

(50)   What should I give to the children for Christmas?
        To some boy, nothing.

And even apart from such examples, it seems to us somewhat unnatural to postulate a structure in that the nearest
branching node dominating "every" in (46) would dominate
"someone", as it would have to do if (O. CR) were to explain the logical order of quantifiers in (46). Hence we
cannot find solid evidence for (O. CR).

Focusing on particular examples is somewhat misleading
here, however. The real argument against (O. CR) is that
all the phenomena that (O. CR) was in effect introduced to
explain can be explained by means of the less demanding
principles (O. comm) and (O. LR). This argument can only be given later, however (see Part III, chaps. 5-6,
below).

10.   Atomic Sentences

A further general difference between formal and natural
languages is the following: in the usual formal languages,
the atomic sentences that serve as end-points of semantical
games are easily characterized syntactically (formally), and
the truth-conditions for such atomic sentences are easily
formulated for all cases at once. In natural languages, the
sentences to which our game rules cannot any longer be applied can be fairly complex, depending of course on the set
of rules that are being used. For instance, end-point sentences may contain various prepositional constructions.
Furthermore, the admissibility of such a prepositional construction in connection with a given verb depends on the
verb in question, and has to be specified by a lexical rule
characteristic of that verb. Likewise, the meaning of a
prepositional construction with a noun may depend on the
noun in question. For instance, the mother of a man, the
wife of a man, the car of a man, the face of a man, the age
of a man, etc., are each "his" in a different way. Hence
no single structural truth-condition for "atomic" (i.e.,
end-point) sentences will suffice. Thus GTS inevitably
needs, as an indispensable complement to its game rules and
ordering principles, a lexical theory, both syntactical and
semantical. In this direction, GTS fits in well with the
lexicalist-functionalist approach to grammar.[2] It is not our
purpose in this work to develop the lexical component of an

overall semantical theory, however, even though we shall
later make a few remarks on the treatment of prepositions.

It is not clear, sight unseen, that the semantical game
G(S) connected with a natural-language sentence S inevitably comes to an end with an "atomic" sentence, i.e., a sentence whose treatment can safely be relegated to the lexical
component of the overall semantical theory. However, even
if no such termination should take place, the game-
theoretical framework still applies, provided that we can
define winning and losing (and tying) also for the resulting
infinite plays of a game. There is in principle no problem
about such definitions, as every game theorist knows.
Such infinitary games might even be helpful in treating
some of the semantical paradoxes. Indeed, there are formal
languages (including game-quantifier languages and
infinitely deep languages) that also allow for infinitely long
plays of semantical games (see Hintikka and Kulas 1983,
bibliography, for references).

In the cases dealt with in this work, simple supplementary rules nevertheless can be given which guarantee
termination of a semantical game in a finite number of
steps.

11. Further Rules for Natural Languages

So far, we have discussed only those aspects of natural-
language semantics that have analogies in formal first-order
languages. GTS when applied to natural languages can be
extended to enable us to treat a large number of phenomena
other than quantifiers and propositional connectives.
Among the other types of expressions for which one can
easily develop a game-theoretical semantics there are the
following:

(i) Modal and intensional concepts can be handled by
combining GTS with a suitable version of possible-worlds
semantics. At each stage of a semantical game, the players
are then facing not only a sentence but also a world, which
can be changed in a move. For instance, necessity marks
Nature's move: Nature chooses an alternative world that
faces the players at the next move, after the necessity
operator has been dropped. This motivates, e.g., the
following game rule:

(G. necessarily)　If the game has reached the sentence

(51)　　　　Necessarily X

and a world w_1, then Nature chooses a modal alternative, say w_2, to w_1. The game is then continued with respect to X and w_2.

(ii)　One of the intensional notions which can be dealt with in this way is *knowing that*. The resulting game-theoretical treatment of epistemic logic can be extended to allow a treatment of the semantics of questions.

Among the relevant game rules for knowing are the following:

(G. knows that)　If the game has reached a sentence of the form

(52)　　　　b knows that X,

and a world w_1, then Nature may choose an epistemic b-alternative w_2 to w_1. The game is then continued with respect to X and w_2.

(G. knows who)　If the game has reached a sentence of the form

(53)　　　　b knows who X

and a world w_1, then a well-defined individual (defined by a world line) may be chosen either by Myself or by Nature, say, one named by "d". If the choice is made by Myself, the game is continued with respect to w_1 and

(54)　　　　b knows that d X and b knows who d is.

If the choice is made by Nature, the game is continued with respect to w_1 and

(55)　　　　b knows that d X if b knows who d is.

For simplicity, we have assumed here that "who" occupies the subject position in "who X".

Strictly speaking, in the output of (G. knows that) and (G. knows who) X should be replaced by an expression that is like X except that third-person masculine singular pronouns are replaced by "b" (if "b" is masculine and singular) or that third-person feminine singular pronouns are replaced by "b" (if "b" is feminine and singular), etc..

These epistemic rules illustrate another difference between formal and natural languages. As (G. knows who) shows, the "who" in (50) is in effect an ambidextrous quantifier: it can be either an existential or a universal quantifier. This is an instance of a much more general phenomenon. In many rules for semantical games, the move can be made either by Myself or by Nature, with no other essential differences between the two kinds of applications. Thus GTS helps to spell out what is common to the different uses of such ambidextrous expressions.

(iii)   Tenses and temporal particles can be dealt with by assuming a suitable time structure, e.g., a forward-branching structure (Hintikka and Kulas 1983, chap. 5). At each stage, the players are considering some time point in that structure. Tenses can be interpreted through game rules that involve a choice of an earlier or a later moment of time.

None of the extensions (i)-(iii) will play a major role in this book. However, certain other extensions will be attempted in the following. They include:

(iv)   The definite article, especially in its anaphoric uses.

(v)   Anaphoric pronouns.

These will be discussed in Part II and Part III, respectively, of this work. Certain other extensions will also be introduced in the course of our book. They include the following:

(vi)   It is part of the spirit of semantical games that even proper names have to be "interpreted" (assigned a reference) in the course of a semantical game (see Part III, sec. 4, below). For the course of a semantical game can be described by saying that all underdetermined expressions, such as quantifier phrases, which the players are dealing with, are "interpreted" for the purposes of that play of the

game.   But if so, it lies close at hand to think that the
players in the course of a semantical game have to ascertain
of each proper name who or what it stands for.   Equally
clearly, this game rule (G. name) will have priority over
several other rules.

Sometimes the unmistakable need of ascertaining, as a
part of the semantical analysis of a sentence or a segment
of discourse, who or what a certain proper name refers to
surfaces in actual discourse.   Here is an example from Pa-
tricia Moyes, *Murder Fantastical*, Holt, Rinehart and
Winston, New York, 1984, p. 8, where Sir John Adamson is
with some difficulty trying to elicit from George Manciple
over the phone a coherent account of what happened to
George's late guest:

(56)   "Just tell me exactly what happened, George," he
            said.
            "But I've told you.   The fellow was visiting us at
            the time, which is why I feel under an obligation.
            . . . Thompson is talking about getting on to
            Duckett, but I wouldn't have that, not at any
            price.   'I'll ring Sir John,' I said.   Least I could
            do."
            "I presume," said Sir John with commendable re-
            straint, "that by Thompson you mean Dr. Thomp-
            son, and that the Doctor has advised you to get
            in touch with Sergeant Duckett at the police sta-
            tion in Cregwell Village.   Am I right?"
            "Of course you're right.   It's perfectly simple,
            isn't it? . . ."

Simple or not, Sir John's question was amply called for,
and the same goes for the moves connected with proper
names made by the players of our semantical games.

(vii)   A game rule is needed for genitives.   It has
certain similarities with the rules for quantifier phrases.   It
can be tentatively formulated as follows:

(G. genitive)   If the game has reached a sentence of
the form

(57)   X - Y's Z - W,

an individual may be selected by Myself.   If its (his,
hers) name is "b", then the game is continued with
respect to

(58)   X – b – W and b is a(n)/the Z of Y.

Here the choice between "a(n)" and "the" is left dependent
on further factors (see Carlson forthcoming).   Small exceptions in the formulation of the output sentence may also be
needed in some cases.
The set (category) of entities from which b is chosen
is subject to the same (or similar) comments as the choice
of an individual prescribed by the quantifier rules (see
Hintikka and Kulas 1983, chap. 9).

(viii)   An interesting observation is that many prepositional constructions have to be dealt with in the way
similar   to   genitives.   In   a   sense,   there   is   thus   a
quantifier–like element to prepositions.   For instance,   a
game rule for "near" could be formulated as follows:

(G. near)   If the game has reached a sentence of the
form

(59)   X – near Y – Z

one of the players may choose a location, say one
named by "b".   The game is then continued with respect to

(60)   X – prep + b – Z and b is near Y.

Here prep + b is "b" with an appropriate prepostion, such
as "in b", "on b", etc.
Similar rules can be formulated for other prepositions.
They deserve a few explanatory comments.
In the output sentences of such rules, the order of
the clauses is not free, as it was in the rules formulated
earlier.   Even though there probably is no "transcendental
deduction" of this asymmetry among our game rules, this
difference between different rules is entirely natural.   The
second clause in (60) (and in similar output sentences of
prepositional rules) is much more of an explanatory after-
thought to the first clause than in the rules formulated earlier.   For this reason, the order of the two clauses in (60)

is naturally the one that it is there stipulated to be. We shall return to this matter in Part III, sec. 23, below.

A possible generalization of these observations is the following: The order of clauses or sentences is fixed in the output of a game rule that helps to define the semantics of some nonlogical lexical item (e.g., of a preposition), whereas the order is freer in rules connected with logical or other "syncategorematic" notions. More work is nevertheless needed to test this putative generalization.

It is also to be noted that in many of their occurrences prepositional phrases have to be dealt with as parts of "atomic" sentences. That is, they will have to be handled by means of the lexical rule for the main verb of the clause in which the preposition occurs. In some cases, there is a choice of the way a prepositional phrase is to be dealt with. We have found good evidence that there actually is this kind of option for the treatment of certain prepositional phrases (see Part III, sec. 23, below).

12. Explanatory Strategies

A few comments on the way GTS serves as tool of linguistic explanation may be in order.

(i) First, GTS facilitates semantical explanations in the same sense as any theory that attempts a translation of natural languages into a logical notation. In the simplest cases, we can obtain translation into the usual quantifier notation, as indicated in sec. 8 above. In general, we obtain a translation into a higher-order language, as indicated in secs. 4-6 above. (The ideas expounded there for formal languages can of course be extended to natural languages.) Then a special inquiry is perhaps needed to show whether the higher-order translation can be reduced to a linear first-order equivalent.

By means of these translations, we can explain many things about natural-language sentences: which ones are synonymous; which ones are ambiguous and what their several readings are; what the relative scopes of quantifiers and other operators are and why; and so on.

With respect to this kind of explanatory strategy, GTS is in a better position than some competing approaches. Our semantical rules are geared to natural-language expressions, and do not presuppose any prior translation into

logical notation.   Furthermore, GTS offers in some respects
a richer repertoire of representations than comparable approaches,   which   typically   do   not   use   branching
(informationally independent) quantifiers (and other operators)   or   the   subgame   idea   (functional   interpretations).

(ii)   One particular mode of explanation is worth separate mention.   It   sometimes turns out that an otherwise
normal-looking sentence S is in reality logically false: Nature can always win in the associated game G(S).   Then an
assertion of S would be pointless, for it cannot convey any
honest information, and it cannot be used for the purposes
of lying, either, because its falsity can be seen from its
linguistic form alone.   Such a sentence S is felt to be deviant, and our treatment can supply an explanation of this
deviance.

It is important to realize, however, that a deviant sentence of this kind can be both syntactical and semantically
unexceptionable; syntactically unexceptionable, in the sense
of being formed by the right generative rules, and semantically unexceptionable, in the sense of being interpretable.
Indeed such an S can only be shown to be logically false
and hence deviant by means of its semantical interpretation.

We shall encounter such sentences in Part III of this
book.   In fact, this is the kind of explanation we shall offer for the deviance of many sentences with anaphoric pronouns that are sometimes thought of as being syntactically
anomalous.   The following turns out to be a case in point:

(61)   Two men were walking on the road.   Suddenly he
            stopped.

(We disregard here the possibility that the reference of
"he" might be supplied contextually.)

(iii)   This indicates the variety of explanatory strategies that GTS makes possible.   There are still others.   For
instance, the impossibility of certain readings of sentences
may be explained by pointing out that the applications of
game rules that would produce these readings would give
rise to syntactically ill-formed expressions.   (Jaakko
Hintikka employed this explanatory strategy in Hintikka
1976.)

(iv)   The basic ideas of GTS lead to a contrast between   two   different   kinds   of   meaning   (cf.   Hintikka
forthcoming a).   This contrast will be exploited in Part III
below. Here we shall indicate only the basic idea on which
the distinction is based.

In GTS, the truth of a sentence S means that there
exists a winning strategy for Myself in the correlated game
G(S).   Hence to assert S is to assert the existence of such
a strategy.   It is not to assert that the speaker knows
such a strategy, or a part thereof.   This is an imporant
respect   in   which   GTS   differs   from   oversimplified
verificationist and operationalist theories of meaning.

The kind of meaning that our game rules thus help to
define will be called "abstract meaning". Often, a speaker
who utters a sentence S nevertheless conveys more information than just the existence of a winning strategy for Myself in G(S).   Often, there is something in S that also
indicates what one particular winning strategy might look
like.   Such clues will be said to contribute to the "strategic
meaning" of S.

This contrast will be discussed briefly in Part III,
sec. 17, of this study.   Here it is mentioned mainly as an
example of what a many-splendored thing meaning is shown
to be by GTS.

(v)   Last, it is important to realize that our game
rules have a great deal of psycholinguistic plausibility.   In
fact, the situations the players may encounter in G(S) are
precisely the situations one may have to face in investigat-
ing a world in which S is true, of course with the proviso
that the values of (unnegated) universal quantifiers are individuals one perhaps chances upon, whereas the values of
(unnegated) existential quantifiers are individuals one can
find through one's own efforts.   Now the basic idea of all
truth-conditional semantics is that the truth-conditions of a
sentence S specify what the world is like when S is true.
Usual truth-conditions for a quantified sentence S in effect
utilize quantification over the same domain as the quantifiers in S.   Hence they do not really offer a direct explanation of what the world is like when S is true.   They are
directly applicable only by an agent who can survey the
entire   universe   of   discourse   do(M)   in   a   glance.
Game-theoretical semantics offers a noncircular and much
more concrete account, by telling us what might happen if
one were transported to a world in which S is true and

launched a "game of exploring the world" in it.   It is thus
not unnatural to assume that a competent speaker's knowledge of the truth-conditions of a sentence S is best interpreted as his or her knowledge of what might happen in the
course of exploring a world in which S is true, i.e., what
might happen in G(S).

Another aspect of the same psycholinguistic plausibility
of our approach is that each particular game rule that we
need is virtually obvious as soon as the leading ideas of
GTS are adopted.

NOTES

[1] For more information about GTS and its applications, see Jaakko Hintikka and Jack Kulas, *The Game of Language*, D. Reidel, Dordrecht, 1983.

[2] For this approach, see Joan Bresnan, editor, *The Mental Representation of Grammatical Relations*, The MIT Press, Cambridge Mass., 1982. Another link between GTS and the lexicalist-functionalist approach is our reliance on lexically triggered rules and on ordering principles governing them (special ordering principles). For instance, in GTS we do not have a single rule for subordinate questions, but separate rules for the different verbs (or other lexical eleménts) which take a construction with a subordinate question.

PART II

DEFINITE DESCRIPTIONS

1. Russell on Definite Descriptions

Is there really a problem about the logic and semantics of definite descriptions, or *the*-phrases, as we shall also call them? There is in fact a perspective in which the last word on the subject was very nearly said by Bertrand Russell in his theory of descriptions (Russell 1905 (reprinted in Lackey 1973); Klemke 1970). Even though Russell's theory is currently unfashionable, and even though Russell's theory needs further development in any case, this perspective deserves serious attention.

Russell's treatment of definite descriptions was part of his much more general campaign for first-order logic. He was trying to reduce as many different kinds of sentences as possible to what these days would be called a language of (extensional) first-order logic or a quantificational language. This campaign, launched before Russell by Frege, has since been quite successful by the standards of popular acceptance.[1] Many features of Frege's and Russell's ideas have been commonplaces through much of the twentieth century. A case in point is their claim that words like "is" are multiply ambiguous, a claim which is embodied in the very notation of first-order logic. Quantificational idiom remains the favorite framework of many philosophers of language (Quine, Davidson, et al.), many linguists (Chomsky, George Lakoff, et al.) and many logicians. It is this success that prompted Ramsey to call Russell's theory "the paradigm of philosophy".

Even though Russell's treatment has encountered vigorous criticism, it still remains a natural starting point for any discussion of the logic and semantics of definite descriptions. Even in the face of the admitted shortcomings of Russell's original theory, its conceptual economy prompts one to wonder if its basic insights could somehow be saved. David Hilbert once characterized his foundational work as an effort to regain the paradise of Cantorian set theory from which paradoxes had banished mathematicians. Perhaps we can, at least initially, see our efforts as an an attempt to revise and extend Russell's theory in order to reinstate the paradise - or perhaps rather the paradigm -

that Russell's 1905 theory truly was for philosophical and linguistic semanticists. In other words, it seems to us that time is ripe to turn the tables on Russell's critics. This part of our work can be seen as a first step towards a general theory of definite descriptions that borrows its inspiration from Russell's theory, even though the conceptual tools it uses go beyond Russell's methods. Because of this spiritual affinity, whatever success our theory may enjoy serves also as a partial vindication of Russell's original theory.

We shall assume that the reader is familiar with the main ideas of Russell's theory. Nevertheless, we recall here what it is all about. Russell's theory is directly applicable to expressions that are couched in the familiar logical notation. In this notation, which is not unproblematical, the definite description "the individual (call it x) such that D[x]" is expressed by "($\jmath$x)D[x]".

What Russell's "theory" (better, treatment) of definite descriptions does is to analyze away each occurrence of a definite description "($\jmath$x)D[x]" in a given context (say, in the context C[ ]) by interpreting the overall sentence to assert the existence of a unique individual x of which it is true that D[x] and of which it is also true that C[x]. In brief,

(1)   C[($\jmath$x)D[x]]

is taken to be equivalent to

(2)   (Ex)[D[x] & (Ay)(D[y] → y=x) & C[x]].

In this way, the rules governing definite descriptions can all be thought of as being consequences of the general logical rules governing quantifiers and other such logical notions, and they turn out not to incur any ontological commitments or model-theoretical problems over and above those already involved in the use of these basic logical notions. This is an important part of the Russellian strategy mentioned earlier.

Russell clearly thought of his treatment as being applicable also to English and perhaps also to other natural languages. As will be explained later, there are some uses of *the*-phrases in English to which Russell's theory is obviously inapplicable but which we shall try to deal with. However, there are other uses of *the*-phrases that Russell seems to have had primarily in mind. They give rise to those occurrences of *the*-phrases in English which are, in some obvious sense, context-independent and in which the speaker is in some (perhaps slightly less obvious) sense attributing or presupposing uniqueness. We shall call such occurrences of *the*-phrases *Russellian*. They are the uses of *the*-phrases to which the philosophers' term "definite description" applies most happily.

Among the uses of *the*-phrases to which Russell's theory does not even begin to do justice there are the uses that we shall call the *anaphoric* use and the *generic* use. These are illustrated by the following examples:

ANAPHORIC:
(3)   If you are accosted by a stranger, don't talk to the man.
(4)   A man was seen walking down a path, but soon the man turned back.
(5)   If Bill owns a donkey, he beats the donkey.

GENERIC:
(6)   The beaver builds dams.
(7)   The tiger is a dangerous animal.
(8)   The modern girl wore trousers. The modern woman wore trousers. Miss Cragg herself wore trousers (V.C. Clinton-Baddely, *My Foe Outstretched Beneath the Tree*, Dell, New York, 1981, p. 123).

In cases of anaphoric uses of *the*-phrases, uniqueness of reference is not required in the sense of there being a unique individual of which the *the*-phrase is true. Instead, such a use of a *the*-phrase typically picks up the reference made by the use of an earlier occurring noun phrase, rather as a pronoun would do. Indeed, in many sentences, an anaphorically used *the*-phrase can be replaced by a pronoun, or vice versa, without any change of meaning. For instance, in (4) we could thus replace "the man" by "he", and in (5) we could replace "the donkey" by "it", without changing the meaning. This affinity between anaphorically used *the*-phrases and other anaphorically used expressions (e.g., pronouns) puts our enterprise in an interesting light. It suggests that if we can successfully deal with anaphorically used *the*-phrases, we can perhaps better understand anaphora in general.

But even when the applications of Russell's theory are restricted to Russellian uses of *the*-phrases, they are controversial and not without problems. We shall here mention three different prima facie difficulties.

The first difficulty is a limitation of Russell's logical language as a canonical notation for natural-language *the*-phrases. There are natural-language uses of *the*-phrases where even Russell's notation proves inadequate. Cases in point are so-called Bach-Peters sentences, i.e., sentences with crossing anaphoric relations,[2] such as the following:

(9)   The boy who was fooling her kissed the girl who loved him.

This sentence cannot be translated into Russell's iota-notation, for reasons closely related to those that have made it hard for syntacticians to generate it by means of a natural pronominalization rule.

The reason for this difficulty is clear: If you try to find a formal translation of the *the*-phrase "the boy who was fooling her", the formal definite description (say $(\jmath x)A[x]$) serving as a translation will have to contain as a part the translation of "the girl who loved him", because of the presence of the pronoun "her" in the former *the*-phrase. But, by the same token, the second formal definite description (say $(\jmath x)B[x]$) should contain the former (i.e., $(\jmath x)A[x]$) as a part, because of the presence of the anaphoric pronoun "him". These two requirements are incompatible, however. This problem is closely related to the difficulties that have arisen in connection with attempts to give an account of sentences like (9) in terms of generative grammars, e.g., in transformational grammar. Indeed, the two problems can be seen as reflections of one and the same basic difficulty.

This difficulty is easily disposed of by means of the main conceptual tool of this study, game theoretical semantics. Part I of this volume contains a brief introduction to game-theoretical semantics; hence we are here assuming some familiarity with its basic ideas. The forte of game-theoretical semantics is the treatment of quantification in natural languages like English. Hence it may be expected that Russell's theory, which relies essentially on quantifiers, should be easy to capture in game-theoretical semantics. This expectation turns out to be well founded.

It is easy to formulate a game rule for definite descriptions. For formal first-order languages, the rule might be formulated as follows:

(G. ⱼ) If a game has reached a sentence of the form

(10)   C[(ⱼx)D[x]]

then an individual, say b, is chosen by Myself from the domain D, whereupon Nature chooses a different individual, say d, from D. The game is then continued with respect to

(11)   D[b] & C[b] & ∿D[d].

If b and d do not already have proper names, such names, say "b" and "d", are given to them and added to the underlying language.

If the domain D = {b}, Nature's choice is impossible and the game is continued with respect to

(12)   D[b] & C[b].

Since Myself's choices correspond to existential quantifiers and Nature's choices to universal quantifiers, this rule makes (10) equivalent to

(13)   (Ex) (D[x] & C[x] & (Ay)(y≠x → ∿D[y]))

which is equivalent to (2). Hence our treatment does not yield much that is new in its application to formal languages.

It can be extended to natural languages like English, however. Moreover, the way to do so is quite obvious. Parallel with the rule (G. ⱼ) we can have the

(G. Russellian the) When a game has reached a sentence of the form

(14)   X - the Y who Z - W,

an individual, say b, is chosen by Myself, whereupon a different individual, say d, is chosen by Nature. If these individuals do not already have names, the

players give them names, which are assumed to be "b"
and "d".   The game is then continued with respect to

(15)   X – b – W, b is a Y, b Z, but d is not a Y
            who Z.

The choices are made from the appropriate "category",
which in the case of "who" is the set of persons.
        This rule is really a special case, for its formulation is
predicated on the same limitations as our other rules (cf.
Part I above).
        The output sentence of this rule is clearly parallel to
(11).   Hence (G. Russellian the) is essentially the
game-theoretical codification of Russell's treatment of definite descriptions applied to English.

                2. Prima Facie Difficulties with Russell's Theory

There are nevertheless advantages in dealing with Russell's
theory by means of a game-theoretical formulation, instead
of the usual strategy of first translating English sentences
into the formal quantificational idiom.   For instance, there
is   now   no   problem   about   the   Bach–Peters   (crossing
pronominalization) sentences (see Hintikka and Saarinen,
1975).   In fact, applying the rule (G. Russellian the) to
(9) yields a sentence of the following form:

(16)   Harry kissed the girl who loved him, Harry is a
            boy, Harry was fooling her, but Dick is not a
            boy who was fooling her.

A second application of (G. Russellian the), this time to
(16), yields – with a modicum of obvious rewriting – something like

(17)   Harry kissed Harriet, Harry is a boy, Harry was
            fooling her, Dick is not a boy who was fooling
            her, Harriet is a girl, Harriet loved him, but
            Margaret is not a girl who loved him.

Although there are further questions to be raised about the
semantics of (17), they no longer raise the kinds of difficulties that prompted linguists' worries about (9) and that
can be used as arguments against a Russellian treatment of

definite descriptions. In brief, the limitations of Russell's notation are automatically overcome in game-theoretical semantics.

It is of some interest to note what the success of game-theoretical semantics in dealing with Bach-Peters sentences ("crossing pronominalization sentences") is based on. The problem with (9) was the semantical context-dependence of its different constituents. The interpretation of the first *the*-phrase depends on the interpretation of the second, because of the pronoun "her", and, conversely, the interpretation of the second depends on that of the first, because of the pronoun "him". Such interdependencies are hard to deal with in any approach, syntactical or semantical, that works its way from inside out, that is to say, from the simplest constituents of a sentence to more and more complicated expressions. Generative syntax and generative semantics based on the principle of compositionality are cases in point.

In contrast to such approaches, game-theoretical semantics proceeds from outside in, and hence can perfectly well take into account semantical context-dependencies of the kind illustrated by (9). For this reason, there is no problem about the treatment of Bach-Peters sentences in game-theoretical semantics.

Another feature of Russell's treatment that our game-theoretical approach can clarify is his distinction between primary and secondary occurrences of definite descriptions (Russell, 1973, pp. 114-15). Once again, this is an interesting problem which our game-theoretical analysis immediately leads us to.

Indeed, it is seen at once that the game rule (G. $_j$) leaves things at large that are normally quite determinate in formal languages. This rule can be applied, as it stands, to any sentence containing a (formal) definite description $(_jx)D[x]$. But this sentence can contain other definite descriptions, and other rules may apply to it. Which rule is applied first? To what definite description is (G. $_j$) applied before others? It is clear that we have here either a source of multiple ambiguities or else a need to introduce further principles that govern the order of different game rules in relation to (G. $_j$). By analogy, the same applies obviously, mutatis mutandis, to Russell's own treatment (cf. (1)-(2)) and to the treatment of definite descriptions in game-theoretical semantics.

What Russell does, in effect, is to consider solely the case in which only one other rule besides (G. $_J$) applies to (10). Then Russell calls those occurrences of ($_J$x)D[x] *primary* in which the other rule is applied after (G. $_J$), and those *secondary* in which it is applied before (G. $_J$). The same contrast applies of course to natural-language sentences like (14).

For instance, if (14) is

(18)   George knew that the author of *Waverly* is Scott

the two readings will be, in a semiformal formulation,

(19)   (Ex)(x authored *Waverley* & (Ay)(y authored *Waverley* → y=x) & George knew that (x = Scott))

and

(20)   George knew that (Ex)(x authored *Waverley* & (Ay) (y authored *Waverley* → y=x) & x = Scott).

Here (19) results from taking the definite description to have a primary occurrence and (20) from taking it to have a secondary occurrence.

What (19) says is that there exists a unique author of *Waverley* and that George knew him (or her) to be identical with Scott. What (20) says is that George knew that there exists a unique author of *Waverley* who is Scott.

There is nothing wrong with making a distinction like Russell's. However, what Russell says is only a beginning. It has to be supplemented in two different directions.

First, Russell offers no account of how it is that definite descriptions can occur in sentences in two different ways. In contrast, game-theoretical semantics shows at once what is involved, viz., two different orders in which the rules of semantical games can be applied.

Second, Russell offers no account of when, in a natural language like English, a definite description can be taken to have a primary or a secondary occurrence. In game-theoretical semantics, this would mean specifying the order in which (G. Russellian the) is applied in relation to other game rules. Far from being overlooked by game-theoretical semanticists, the question of the relative order of different game rules is one of the most central topics in that approach.   Regularities of rule order are one of the most powerful ways of explaining semantical phenomena characteristic of game-theoretical semantics. Even though we are not going to discuss the ordering principles that govern (G. Russellian the) in any detail, what has been said suffices to show how game-theoretical semantics has refined and deepened Russell's insights.

An example of the effects of rule-ordering may nevertheless be in order.   At first sight, it may seem that a Russellian "the" and "the only" must behave in the same way.   Indeed, most of what has been said so far applies to both.   We could - and should - set up a game rule (G. the only) that is parallel to (G. Russellian the).   But if so, why do the following pairs of examples exhibit a distinct difference in meaning?

(21)   Dick is not the person who altered the tape.
(22)   Dick is not the only person who altered the tape.
(23)   George forgot that the author of *Waverley* is Scott.
(24)   George forgot that the only author of *Waverley* is Scott.

An answer is easy.   The rules (G. Russellian the) and (G. the only) are governed by different ordering principles. In fact, it is easily seen that this explains the differences between (21)-(22) and between (23)-(24).   In fact, the preferred reading of (21) and one possible reading of (23) is obtained by applying (G. Russellian the) first, and the other rule only after that.   In contrast, the normal reading of (22) is obtained by applying (G. neg) first and (G. the only) after that; and likewise for (24).

It is of some interest to note that (21) and (23) receive the same force when "the" is given emphatic stress. Such stress apparently often indicates narrow "scope", i.e., in our approach, later rule application.   Even though we don't know how widely this generalization holds, it lends further credibility to the game-theoretical diagnosis of the phenomena we are dealing with.

Furthermore, there may be more than one other rule competing with (G. Russellian the).   If so, there could be more that two possible readings of the sentence in question. Then Russell's dichotomy will be incapable of doing justice to the situation.   As an example, consider the following:

(25)   George does not know that the author of *Waverley*
            is Scott.

Applying our game rules, including (G. Russellian the), in
three different orders and expressing the results in a self-
explanatory semiformal notation we obtain the following
three readings:

(26)   (Ex) (x is a unique author of *Waverley* & ∿George
            knows that (x is Scott))
(27)   ∿(Ex) (x is a unique author of *Waverley* & George
            knows that (x is Scott))
(28)   ∿George knows (Ex) (x is the unique author of
            Waverley) & (x is Scott))

In (26), George does not know of the individual who as a
matter of fact is a unique author of *Waverley* that he is
Scott.   In contrast, (27) is the negation of (19) and (28)
the negation of (20).   All these three are different in
meaning.   For instance, (27) would be true if there were
no unique author of *Waverley*, whereas there must be one
in order for (26) to be true.   In contrast to (26)-(27), the
last reading (28) does not deal with good old George's
knowledge (or lack thereof) about some particular person,
but with his knowledge of facts.   Hence the three are obviously quite different.   Hence Russell's dichotomy is insuffi-
cient.   Moreover, our treatment explains ipso facto how
such a multiplicity of readings is possible, and what the
peculiar force of each reading is.
        Thus we can straighten out the shortcomings of Rus-
sell's treatment that manifest themselves in connection with
Bach-Peters sentences and Russell's own distinction between
primary and secondary occurrences of definite descriptions.
There have been other criticisms, however, of Russell's
theory of descriptions.   One kind of criticism is exemplified
by Strawson, who has among other things criticized Russell's treatment of the existential force of definite descriptions (Strawson 1950, 1964).   This force is built into the
existential quantifier in (2) and into the choice by Myself of
the individual b in (G. Russellian the).   Strawson has argued that in using a definite description one is not asserting the existence of a unique entity so described, but
rather presupposing it.   There is in fact something true
about Strawson's claims.   Unfortunately, his own treatment
has not been very illuminating, either.

The reason is not hard to find. Concepts like presupposition are primarily discourse concepts. They deal with the relation of an utterance of a sentence in an extended discourse to other utterances, earlier and later, in the same discourse. Strawson's interest is in fact unmistakably focused on discourse phenomena rather than sentence-centered phenomena.[3] However, in his actual treatment Strawson in effect uses concepts like presupposition as attributes of utterances of a single sentence. In general, in spite of his insightful emphasis on the discourse character of several interesting logical and semantical phenomena, Strawson fails almost totally to build any systematic theory of the subject.

These remarks also provide a key to handling the problems with Russell's theory to which Strawson calls our attention. They will be a part of the logic and semantics of discourse, as distinguished from the logic and semantics of isolated propositions (sentences). It is not our purpose in this work to develop such a discourse semantics. Hence we are not going to discuss the discourse-dependent behavior of definite descriptions in full detail, either. It is nevertheless easy to see what the main character of a game-theoretical treatment of definite descriptions in discourse is going to look like (see Hintikka forthcoming; Carlson, forthcoming).

The crucial idea is that the rules and especially the ordering principles of discourse semantics will be such that if the uniqueness and existence components of a definite description are not satisfied, that failure will normally have stopped the semantical game (played on a segment of discourse) before the rule (G. Russellian the) is applied. For instance, if the sentence

(29)   The present king of France is blond

is uttered as an answer to the question

(30)   What is the hair color of the present king of France?

then this question may be posed only if its presupposition (in a technical sense introduced by Jaakko Hintikka in his theory of questions, Hintikka 1976) is satisfied, i.e., only if the hair of the present king of France has some one color, which in turn can be the case only if there exists a unique present king of France.   Hence the question of unique existence arises in this case, not in connection with (20), but in connection with the earlier uttered question (30).   Moreover, the presuppositions of questions can be dealt with without any problems.

Thus, even without an explicit discussion it is fairly obvious how the phenomena Strawson was concerned with can be dealt with in a satisfactory discourse semantics without modifying the basic game rule (G. Russellian the), i.e., without giving up the fundamental ideas of Russell's theory of definite descriptions.

Another development that is calculated to go beyond Russell's theory and to complement it is Keith Donnellan's distinction between what he calls referential and attributive uses of definite descriptions (Donnellan 1966, 1970).   The distinction can be illustrated by a familiar example.   If I say at a party,

(31)   The man standing next to the hostess is a famous
            economist

and it turns out that the gentleman I have in sight and in mind is standing next to the hostess's identical twin, I may still be able to express a meaning and convey some true information to my audience, even though according to Russell's theory, (31) ought to refer to whomever (maybe in the next room) is actually standing next to the real hostess.   If (31) is taken to refer to the intended gentleman, however misdescribed, we have what Donnellan calls a referential use of the definite description in (31).   Whereas the reading to which Russell theory apparently forces us results from what Donnellan calls an attributive use.   Russell's theory of definite descriptions thus seems to concern their attributive uses only, and exclude their referential uses.

However, there is no difficulty in capturing Donnellan's referential use in the general framework of a suitable possible-worlds or possible-situations semantics.   All we have to do is to assume the following:

(i)   The intended force of the "referential use" of (31) is captured more faithfully by

(32)   The man who - I believe - stands next to the
            hostess is a famous economist.

(ii)   The "Russellian" quantifiers needed to deal with (32) are to be taken to range over perceptual (perceptually cross-identified) individuals rather than descriptively identified ones.

(iii)   The rule (G. Russellian the) is to be applied first in (32).

All three of these assumptions are very natural. Clearly (31) deals with how the situation seems to be to me, as far as the referred-to person is concerned. Hence (i) is eminently natural. Moreover, (31) obviously deals with a perceptual situation. Indeed, uttering (31) can most naturally be accompanied by the gesture of pointing to the man in question. This virtually forces us to assume (ii). And what (iii) says is that I am dealing with the man who as a matter of fact satisfies the descriptions, not with the way by which he satisfies it.

Now it is our thesis that once assumptions paralleling (i)-(iii) are made in each case of what Donnellan calls the referential use of definite descriptions, Donnellan's entire theory of the "referential use" then becomes simply a special case of any reasonable theory of definite descriptions in intensional contexts developed ad hoc rather than as a part of such a general theory. This is not the occasion to argue extensively for this thesis, but what has been said suffices to make it plausible.

Thus neither Strawson's nor Donnellan's views occasion any changes in the basic ideas of Russell's theory.

3. Can We Localize Russell's Theory?

The many attractive features of Russell's treatment of definite descriptions or, as we shall also call them, *the*-phrases, make its failure as an overall theory ever more so poignant. This failure needs few comments. Even if, pace Strawson, Russell's theory works perfectly when applied to definite descriptions like "the present King of France", we have noted that it fails to account for the uses of *the*-phrases that pick up an earlier reference. These we have called the anaphoric uses of *the*-phrases. Examples of such uses were given as (3)-(5) above in sec. 1. Likewise, Russell's theory does not enable us to deal with the

so-called generic uses of the definite article.   They were
illustrated by (6)-(8) in sec. 1.

But is it perhaps possible to modify Russell's treatment
to overcome its limitations and failures?   This is what we
shall be striving to do in this section and its successors.
For reasons that will be spelled out more fully later, we
shall consider the anaphoric use of *the*-phrases as their semantically basic use (see Hintikka and Kulas 1982, 1983,
forthcoming).   The main reason for proceeding in this way
is that by so doing we hope to be able to account for the
other uses as being somehow derived from the anaphoric
use, and hence explicable by reference to it.

Hence our task here is to modify Russell's treatment of
definite descriptions to enable us to handle anaphoric uses,
while keeping its attractive features intact.   How can we do
this?   One's first idea here is likely to be to try to "localize" Russell's theory in the sense of letting the quantifiers
that he relied on range, not over the whole universe of
discourse (or some category of entities in the universe),
but rather over some contextually determined part of it.
This plausible idea works in some cases.   For instance, the
usage that Hawkins calls "the larger-situation use based on
general knowledge" can be accounted for in this way
(Hawkins 1978).

However, in spite of its plausibility, the idea of simply
contextually restricting the ranges of Russell's quantifiers
does not work.   Sometimes the existence requirement that is
integral to Russell's treatment cannot be satisfied by any
restriction; sometimes Russell's uniqueness requirement cannot be so satisfied.   Examples of the former are the
following:

(33)   Don't wait for the change; vote for it.
(34)   Nobody stole your diamonds, unless the thief
          scaled a slippery 50-foot wall.

Here (33) is adapted from a political commercial.   For
the sake of the argument, we may assume that no change of
the intended kind will ever take place.   Likewise, in (34)
there clearly is no actual thief for the definite description
to pick out.

(35)   Dan will never pet a lion, for he knows that the
          beast will bite his hand off.

Examples of the second kind of failure are the following:

(36)   Some man is capable of falling into love with any woman, at least if the woman is a blonde.
(37)   Even if you send a personalized invitation to each of your friends, at least one of your friends will not read the invitation.

If in order to obtain uniqueness the relevant range of individuals is restricted so that only one woman is included in (36) or one invitation in (35), the whole force of their universal quantifiers is lost. (The whole point of using a universal quantifier is to speak of several different individuals.)

Furthermore, the attempted restriction cannot always stay constant throughout a discourse or even throughout a single (complex) sentence. Intuitively speaking, the individual picked out by one and the same *the*-phrase can change from one part of a discourse to another and even from one part of one and the same sentence to another. The following are cases in point:

(38)   In the first inning the first batter struck out, but in the fourth inning the first batter hit a home run.
(39)   In the United States the president now has far greater powers than were enjoyed by the president in the nineteenth century.

4. Game-Theoretical Solution to the Localization Problem

Hence a simple restriction of the ranges of Russellian quantifiers does not vindicate his theory. This might suggest that nothing like Russell's treatment of *the*-phrases will work for their anaphoric uses. The suggestion is wrong. Indeed, it is here that our game-theoretical semantics comes to our assistance. One way of putting the main point is to say that GTS gives us a different and more dynamic way of restricting the ranges of quantifiers involved in Russell's treatment of definite descriptions. We have seen that it will not do to try to restrict the ranges of Russellian quantifiers to some contextually given (but otherwise fixed) part of the universe of discourse. What GTS enables us to do is to restrict those ranges relative to the stage a semantical game has reached at the time when a given *the*-phrase is treated in the game. This restriction is different in kind from the one envisaged earlier, and more dynamic.

It is now obvious what the simplest restriction of the new kind is. It confines the quantifiers that we rely on in a Russell-style treatment to the set of individuals chosen by either player in the game up to the move in which a definite description is assigned a reference. Likewise it is clear how this idea can be implemented by means of explicit game rules. What we have to do is to start from the game rule that codifies the generally accepted Russellian treatment. This game rule was formulated above in sec. 1. The question we are facing is, What can we do to adapt this treatment to the behavior of anaphoric *the*-phrases? What can be done is to restrict the two players' choices that are connected with the different Russellian quantifiers to a set *I*. This is, roughly speaking, the set of all individuals chosen by the two players up to that point. In brief, our tentative game rule for *the*-phrases in their anaphoric use is the following:

(G. anaphoric the) When a semantical game has reached a sentence of the form

(40)   X - the Y who Z - W

then an individual, say b, may be chosen from a set *I* of individuals by Myself, whereupon Nature chooses a different individual, say d, from the same set *I*. The game is then continued with respect to

(41)   X - b - W, b is a(n) Y, and b Z, but d is not a(n) Y who Z.

Here *I* is the set of all individuals chosen by either player earlier in the game. If *I* is a unit set, *I* = {b}, then the game is continued with respect to X - b - W, b is a(n) Y, and b Z.

The motivation of the rule is clear. The only individuals that can considered by the two players (at the time they are supposed to apply the rule (G. anaphoric the) to (40)) are the members of *I*. If you believe in the spirit of Russell's theory of descriptions, you therefore keep his theory, but let the Russellian quantifiers range over I. This is precisely what (G. anaphoric the) says.

The rule, (G. anaphoric the) is subject to the same comments and qualifications as the usual quantifier rules used in GTS. They were discussed briefly above in Part I sec. 7, of this work. The main points are worth repeating here with some additions:

(i) Y and Z are assumed to be in the singular. A different rule is required to cover the case in which they are plural. We shall not try to formulate it here, however.

(ii) Instead of "who", in (40) we might of course have "that", "which", "where", "when", etc. They are treated analogously, except for small variations that will not be taken up here. Likewise in (40) we could have a prepositional phrase containing one of the words just listed. There are no major theoretical problems in extending the rule.

(iii) The next question is how the realm of the choice of b in (41) is affected by the difference between the different words and phrases mentioned in (ii). This problem will not be taken up here (see Hintikka 1983).

(iv) Such game rules as (G. anaphoric the) will have to be supplemented by provisions for making sure that anaphoric relations that obtain in (40) are preserved in (41). Once again, this problem is not discussed here. It pertains to all game rules for quantifiers and most rules for quantifier-like expressions, not just to (G. anaphoric the).

(v) What we have said of the way the set I is determined applies primarily to games played with respect to one sentence S_0, whether or not it is split into subgames or not. When our treatment is extended to discourse, by treating games connected with successive sentences S_1, S_2, ... , uttered by the speakers as interrelated subgames of some larger semantical game, the definition of I will have to be supplemented by rules governing the way in which "too old" individuals are dropped from I. The way this happens requires a separate investigation. It is reasonably clear, in any case, that there are no hard-and-fast syntactical rules mandating the omission of members from I when the players move from $G(S_i)$ to $G(S_{i+1})$. The regularities that apparently hold here belong either to pragmatics (they are partially due simply to limitations of human memory) or, more interestingly, to discourse semantics. This semantics is still being developed, however (see Carlson 1983).

5. Anaphoric "The" in Formal Languages

In spite of these qualifications, the basic idea on which our game rule (G. anaphoric the) is based is crystal clear. This clarity is illustrated by the fact that a similar rule can be set up for formal first-order languages that contain a symbol analogous to Russell's $(\jmath x)$ for anaphorically used "the". We shall use "(νx)" as such a symbol. The rule that corresponds to (G. anaphoric the) can then be formulated as follows:

(G. anaphoric νx) When a semantical game has reached a sentence of the form

(42) $S[(\nu x)F[x]]$,

an individual, say b, from the set I of individuals chosen by the two players up to that time in the game, may be selected by Myself, whereupon Nature selects a different individual, say d, from the same set I. The game is then continued with respect to

(43) $(S[b]$ & $F[b]$ & $\sim F[d])$.

Here S is the relevant context of $(\nu x)F[x]$ in (42). $S[b]$ is like (42) except that some occurrences of "$(\nu x)F[x]$" have been replaced by occurrences of "b" and F[b] (and F[d]) are like F[x] except that all the free occurrences of "x" have been replaced by "b" (and "d", respectively). If $I = \{b\}$ the game is continued with respect to $(S[b]$ & $F[b])$.

This game rule gives rise to a semantics in which sentences can be shown to be valid, invalid, or neither. Examples of valid sentences include the following:

(44) $(Ax) (F[x] \rightarrow (G[x] \rightarrow G[(\nu x)F[x]]))$.

(45) $(Ax)(Ay) (F[x] \rightarrow (G[(\nu x)F[x]] \rightarrow (G[x]$ & $\sim F[y])))$.

(46) $(Ay)(Au)$ $[(Ex)$ $(x = (\nu z)F[z]$ $\rightarrow$
             $((F[y]$ & $\sim F[u])$ v $(\sim F[y]$ & $F[u]))].$

6. Applications

It turns out that our game rule (G. anaphoric the) needs several further refinements. Before discussing them, however, we have to see how the rule just formulated works. Also, the problems into which the first simple-minded-restriction suggestion ran present challenges to our treatment. We have to show that our treatment succeeds where the other suggestion failed.

First, let us take an example to see how (G. anaphoric the) works. In selecting such an example, it is useful to remember that GTS is calculated to apply to discourse and not only to sentences one by one. In the simplest cases of such a treatment, successive declarative sentences by the same speaker or writer are treated as if they were conjuncts. Hence the following is a legitimate example:

(47)   A stockbroker and his mother live in a village close to Sturbridge castle. Every morning the stockbroker takes a train to London from the village, while the old lady goes for a walk.

This is easily treated by means of GTS. The subgame associated with the first sentence has to be dealt with first by the players. Two applications of (G. a(n)) and one application of (G. genitive)[4] yield something like

(48)   Kenneth Widmerpool and Ethel Widmerpool live in Sturbridge Greens close to Sturbridge castle. Kenneth Widmerpool is a stockbroker. Sturbridge Greens is a village. Ethel Widmerpool is the mother of Kenneth Widmerpool.

The players move on to deal with later sentences only if all the clauses of (48) are true. Then the set I open for the next application of (G. anaphoric the) is {Kenneth Widmerpool, Ethel Widmerpool}. Hence the second sentence of (47) is true, i.e., there is a winning strategy for Myself, if and only if a choice of two individuals, x and y, by Myself from I is possible such that x is the only stockbroker in I, y the only old lady in I, and it is true that

(49)   Every morning x takes a train to London from the
            village while y goes for a walk.

Clearly the only viable candidates are (x = Kenneth
Widmerpool) and (y = Ethel Widmerpool). In other words,
the force of the second half of (47) is, given players'
choices displayed in (48), to assert that Kenneth
Widmerpool takes a train to London every morning while
Ethel Widmerpool goes for a walk. This is of course precisely the intuitive force of (47).

       Our theory also enables us to deal with the problem
cases mentioned in sec. 3 that the "restricted range" idea
was unable to handle. For instance, (34) can be dealt with
by means of the subgame idea first expounded by Hintikka
and Carlson (Hintikka and Carlson 1979). The first
subgame is played on "Nobody stole your diamonds". In it,
Nature chooses an individual, say Gregory. Myself wins if
the following is true:

(50)   Gregory didn't steal your diamonds.

If (50) is false, players go on to play another subgame on

(51)   The thief scaled a slippery 50-foot wall.

In this second subgame, the players "remember" Nature's
strategy in the first one, i.e., have Gregory in *I*, as we
shall explain in Part III below. Hence an application of (G.
anaphoric the) will yield

(52)   Gregory scaled a slippery 50-foot wall, and Greg-
            ory is a thief.

This is true (in view of the falsity of (50)) if and only if
Gregory scaled a slippery 50-foot wall. This obviously
yields the right meaning to (34).

       This shows how one game rule yields the right seman-
tics for sentences of the first problem kind.

       Likewise, our rule enables us to handle the second
group of problem cases. They will nevertheless be discussed in detail only later (see sec. 11 below).

       The third class of problem cases is also amenable to
our approach. An explicit treatment would require rules
for tenses, which we will not try to formulate here. Even
without such rules, we can see that different individuals

are picked out by one and the same *the*-phrase in its different occurrences.   If these occurrences are handled at different stages of the game, the set *I* mentioned in (G. anaphoric the) may be different on the two different occasions, which in turn can lead to the selection of different individuals for the role of b (see (G. anaphoric the)) for the two different occurrences.

7. Epithetic and Counterepithetic *The*-Phrases

Over and above the problem cases so far treated, our treatment handles several other problems. They include, prominently, the treatment of epithetic *the*-phrases, which are illustrated by the following examples:

(53)   Harry borrowed ten dollars from me, but the bastard never paid me back.

(54)   I challenged a kibitzer to a chess game, but the disguised grand master mated me in ten moves.

For instance, in the game associated with (54) an application of (G. a(n)) yields a sentence of the form

(55)   I challenged Boris to a chess game, but the disguised grand master mated me in ten moves, and Boris is a kibitzer.

An application of (G. anaphoric the) to (55) yields

(56)   I challenged Boris to a chess game, but Boris mated me in ten moves, Boris is a kibitzer, and Boris is a disguised grand master.

Hence (56) is true only if Boris is a grand master. Thus part the force of the use of an epithetic *the*-phrase in (54) on our theory is to let it be known that the kibitzer in question was a disguised grand master. Of course this is precisely the point of using the epithetic *the*-phrase.

The other example, (53), can be dealt with after we have made a small change in the rule (G. anaphoric the). (See sec. 10 of this part, below.)

All the other epithetic uses of *the*-phrases are likewise easily accounted for.

The success of our theory in dealing with epithetic uses of *the*-phrases encourages us to continue further the exploration of the semantical behavior of these phrases. In its epithetic use a definite description is employed to attribute properties to the entity described that are not attributed to it by the head of the anaphoric definite description. Conversely, an anaphoric *the*-phrase need not mention all the properties specified by its head, as illustrated by the following examples:

(57)   An old fisherman walked toward the beach. The fisherman was thinking of the day ahead.

(58)   When Nancy Reagan went to a Sears mall store, she was disappointed to find that the store had no designer room.

We might call such *the*-phrases counterepithetic.

8. Vagaries of the Alleged Head-Anaphor Relation

Furthermore, the head of an anaphorically used *the*-phrase need not specify a unique individual, but may specify several, or perhaps a whole set of, individuals:

(59)   A couple was sitting on a bench. The man stood up.

(60)   Two men walked along the road. The taller man carried a rucksack.

(61)   In a committee the chair cannot second any motion.

It is clear that our treatment can handle these cases. For instance, the initial sentence in (60) prompts the choice of two individuals by Myself. If the subgame associated with that sentence of (60) is to be followed by the subgame associated with the other sentence, the former subgame must be won by Myself. For this purpose, the individuals chosen must be men walking along a road. Then there exists a winning strategy for Myself in the latter subgame, viz., one of choosing the taller of the two men as the b mentioned in (41) of (G. anaphoric the), if and only if this man carried a rucksack. This obviously yields precisely the right semantics for (60).

But there is more involved here than this. Instead of a sharply defined syntactic head for an anaphoric *the*-phrase, there need only be some antecedently handled expressions to introduce the members of the set *I*, so that there is some structure on it that enables the players to pick out suitable individuals from it (if the sentence in question can be used to make a true statement). The following are cases in point:

(62)   In every group, the unit element commutes with any other element.

(63)   A freight train went by. The caboose was painted green.

(64)   When a plain virgin of forty-five falls in love for the first time and gets her first taste of sex, God help the man (P.D. James, *The Skull Beneath the Skin*, Warner Books, New York, 1983, p. 179).

This mechanism enables us to make statements about the subject matter of the antecedent expressions by using a definite description. The idea is that the use of such a description can yield a true statement only if the intended conditions are satisfied. This is illustrated by the following examples:

(65)   Surely there is night life in Tallahassee. Unfortunately, this weekend the lady is in Tampa.

(66)   Of course they have a graduate program in philosophy. They even managed to find a job for the student.

For instance, the two sentences of (65) can both be true only if the night life in Tallahassee consists of one lady only. This is of course part of what (65) serves to express.

This phenomenon is, in a sense, a generalization of the epithetic uses of *the*-phrases. In these uses, a *the*-phrase is used to attribute further properties to a previously introduced individual. In the examples just discussed, a *the*-phrase is employed to put other conditions on the state of affairs outlined in the earlier part of the semantical game, viz., conditions that serve to guarantee the truth of what is being expressed by means of the definite description and thereby guarantee the existence and uniqueness that figure in the output sentence (41) of (G. anaphoric the).

This observation is interesting in that it shows that at least occasionally the requisite existence and uniqueness are not simply presupposed in a use of a definite description, but asserted thereby. This provides evidence against Strawson's thesis concerning definite descriptions.

9. The Anaphoric Use of Definite Descriptions as a Semantical Phenomenon

Our series of examples has led us further and further away from cases in which we can find a clearly defined head for the apparently anaphoric *the*-phrase. At the same time, the relation between the head and the *the*-phrase becomes increasingly less syntactical and less clear-cut. For instance, in (64) the relation of "the lady" to the only possible candidate for its head, "night life", is clearly not characterizable in any normal syntactical terms. Yet our game rule (G. anaphoric the) – which was originally formulated by focusing on the relation of clearly anaphoric expressions to their heads – handles (64) without any problems and without any qualifications.

These observations serve to call our attention to certain important features of our game rule (G. anaphoric the) and through it to the nature of our approach to *the*-phrases. First and foremost, what is called the anaphoric relation, i.e., the relation of an anaphoric expression to its so-called head, plays no role in (G. anaphoric the) and hence no relevant role in our approach. What determines the individual referred to by an anaphoric definite description (i.e., the individual playing the role of the b in (G. anaphoric the) in an optimal strategy for Myself is the whole set *I*. This set is not specified by any one phrase, but typically by several different phrases. Of course, one and only one of them will normally refer to b. That phrase will be the counterpart to the head of an anaphoric expression in the conventional treatments. However, we shall see later that it is not even clear that such a phrase can always be found. And even when it can be found, it is not determined by its syntactical relations to the anaphoric *the*-phrase in question. Rather, it is determined semantically via the determination of an optimal strategy for Myself. Hence, what in the traditional treatments was the cornerstone of the treatment of an anaphoric *the*-phrase, i.e., its relation to a head, is in our treatment a derivative relation of a somewhat dubious status, without any direct explanatory value.

Moreover, the set *I* is not determined in any straight-forward way by the syntactical relations of the *the*-phrase in question to other ingredients of (40). The relation of the *the*-phrase to *I* is thus also semantical rather than syntactical.

This implies that in our view the notion of head has lost most of its role in the treatment of what we have been calling anaphoric *the*-phrases. This fact can be illustrated by means of further examples. For instance, we may con-sider the following pair of examples (adapted from examples by Lauri Karttunen):

(67)   If Stewart buys a car or a motorcycle, he will take good care of the vehicle.
(68)   If Stewart buys a car and a motorcycle, he will take good care of the vehicle.

Here our rule (G. anaphoric the) assigns the right meaning (right truth conditions) to (67) (after the changes to be made in sec. 11 below). Applied to (68) it leads to the result that (68) is always false. Since this can be read off from the form (68), this sentence is useless for the purposes of discourse. Most linguists would probably mark it with an asterisk, i.e., would classify it as an unaccept-able string. We can now see, however, that the acceptabil-ity of (68) is a pragmatic matter, which has to be dealt with in discourse theory. There need not be anything syn-tactically or semantically anomalous about (68). In particu-lar, the fact that the head of "the vehicle" is not determined in (68) is no reason for disqualifying it, for its "head" is similarly indeterminate in (67).

In general, the difference between (67) and (68) is virtually impossible to explain in terms of any syntactical head relation. For syntactically (67) and (81) are on a par, the only difference being the exchange in one place of "and" and "or". Hence any syntactical head relation would have to be sensitive to this lexical difference. It seems im-possible to give such a syntactical relation a reasonable theoretical motivation.

We can argue as follows: What is the head of "the ve-hicle" supposed to be in (67)? It cannot be either "a car" or "a motorcycle", for they are in the same boat: one can-not be the head more or less than the other. Hence it

must be the disjunctive phrase "a car or a motorcycle".
But if so, why isn't the corresponding conjunctive phrase
"a car and a motorcycle" a bona fide head for the same
the-phrase "the vehicle" in (67)?   And what is its head in
the following?

(68)   If Stewart buys a car or even if he buys a mo-
            torcycle, he will take good care of the vehicle.

    In fact, the relation of an anaphoric *the*-phrase to its
putative "head" can go wrong in almost any imaginable way.
Here is a brief taxonomy of them:

    (i) Sometimes there is no syntactically privileged
head at all (cf. (64) above).

    (ii) When there is a plausible candidate, it may be of
the wrong semantical category (cf., e.g., (62)-(63) above).

    (iii) In other (acceptable) cases, there are two or
three potential heads (cf. (66) above).

    (iv) In other cases syntactically analogous to (iii), the
duality of heads seems to make the sentence unacceptable
(cf. (67) above).

    (v) In some cases, the head gives more information
about its referent than the anaphoric *the*-phrase; in other
cases, less.

    At this point, our terminology might seem inappropri-
ate.   Anaphora is normally conceptualized in terms of some
head (antecedence) relation.   Pronouns offer to us the pur-
est cases of anaphora, and the very term "pro-noun" be-
trays this antecedence idea.   Since the head relation plays
no major role in our treatment, it might seem misleading to
call its objects anaphoric *the*-phrases in the first place.
    This claim nevertheless prejudices an answer to an im-
portant question.   Maybe anaphoric *the*-phrases don't behave "anaphorically".   But do other so-called anaphoric
expressions, including pronouns, behave in the expected
"anaphoric" way?   In Part III of this book we shall argue
that they do not, thus vindicating our terminology.

10. The Quantifier-Exclusion Phenomenon
in Natural Languages

In order to reach a fully satisfactory theory of definite descriptions, we nevertheless have to make a few changes in the crucial game rule (G. anaphoric the). The first change is due to the presence of individuals referred to by proper names occurring in S. One's first impulse is to require that they all be included in *I*. It turns out, however, that each one of them has to be thought of as being introduced by a special rule (G. name).[5]

The second change is a special case of a widespread phenomenon that does not seem to have been discussed in the literature in the terms employed here. The case that concerns us here is seen from examples of the following sort:

(69)   John saw the man.
(70)   Harry Truman was an early riser. Newsmen frequently talked to the peppery politician during his early morning constitutional.
(71)   Every company commander received the battle order. The order was acknowledged by the officer.
(72)   Every company commander received the battle order from the officer.
(73)   Jane remembered her misfortunes. The poor girl was in tears.
(74)   Jane remembered the poor girl's misfortunes. She was in tears.
(75)   The poor girl remembered her misfortunes. Jane was in tears.
(76)   Jimmy doubted the president.
(77)   Jimmy doubted that the president could do that.

In (69) "the man" cannot refer to John, while in (70) "the peppery politician" obviously refers to Harry Truman.

In (71), "the officer" could refer to a company commander, whereas in (72) it cannot. In (73), "the poor girl" can refer to Jane, while it cannot in (74). In (76), Jimmy is not the president, whereas in (77) "the president" can refer to Jimmy.

The generalization that is illustrated by these examples is that an anaphoric *the*-phrase cannot refer to an individual introduced by a word or phrase occurring in the same clause as it. In terms of our approach, this means that the set *I* must not contain individuals introduced by expressions that in the input sentence of the introduction step occur in the same clause (are commanded by the same sentence markers) as the *the*-phrase "the Y who Z". "Being introduced by" means here either being referred to as by names) or being introduced by applications of game rules as a value (reference of a substitution-value) for.

We shall call the phenomenon codified by this change in *I* the "exclusion phenomenon" and the principle governing it the "Exclusion Principle".

This modification deserves several further comments. First, its force is somewhat hidden by another, altogether different principle that seems to be largely conversational and that says, roughly, that whenever an anaphoric pronoun serves the same purpose as an anaphoric *the*-phrase, the former is to be preferred to the latter. For this reason, there is a shade of awkwardness in having "the poor girl" in (73) to refer to Jane. However, this principle seems to be merely conversational, and merely preferential.

Secondly, the Exclusion Principle, codified by the second change in *I*, is much more general, and seems to characterize all anaphoric expressions, e.g., pronouns. This case has been discussed by Bach and Partee (see Bach and Partee 1980). Indeed, one can find parallel examples employing pronouns instead of *the*-phrases that illustrate an analogous phenomenon.

This exclusion phenomenon (in the case of the semantical behavior of pronouns) is described by Bach and Partee as constituting a "striking contrast" to the way variables of quantification behave in formal languages. There is indeed a sharp difference between the two cases, but there is also a partial but striking counterpart to the exclusion phenomenon in formal quantification theory (predicate calculus). There is a natural but rarely discussed variant of the usual formalisms of quantification theory that is closely related to the exclusion phenomenon (see Hintikka 1956; 1973, chap. 1). It is what Wittgenstein preferred in the *Tractatus*. He put his point as follows:

> Thus I do not write 'f(a,b).a=b' but 'f(a,a)' (or 'f(b,b)'); and not 'f(a,b).∿a=b', but f(a,b)'.
> And analogously I do not write
> '(Ex,y).f(x,y). x=y', but '(Ex).f(x,x)'; and not
> '(Ex,y).f(x,y). ∿x=y', but '(Ex,y).f(x,y)'.

(So   Russell's   '(Ex,y).f(x,y)'   becomes
'(Ex,y).f(x,y). v .(Ex).f(x,x)'.)   (5.531-2.)

This way of treating quantifiers and free singular terms nevertheless amounts to a relatively small change in the use of quantifiers. It can be captured in semantical games connected with formal languages by means of the following rules:

(G. E$_{ex}$)   When the game has reached the sentence (Ex)F[x], an individual, call it   "b", may be selected by Myself, different from all the individuals introduced as values of quantifiers in whose scope (Ex)F[x] occurs in the game and different from the individuals referred to by the individual constants in the initial sentence. The game is then continued with respect to F[b].

(G. U$_{ex}$)   The same for the sentence (Ax)F[x], except that b is chosen by Nature.

We shall call these the exclusion rules for quantifiers. The difference between them and the usual (inclusion) rules can be explained intuitively by thinking (as we all do in elementary probability theory) of the choices of individuals connected with quantifiers (in semantical games) as draws of certain "balls" (individuals) from an "urn" (the model with respect to which our formal language is interpreted). Then the inclusion rules codify a quantification theory with replacement, as probability theorists say, whereas the exclusion rules formalize a logic of quantification without replacement.

Thus the Exclusion Principle marks only an insignificant departure from the usual treatments of quantification theory. It does not constitute a striking contrast between formal and natural languages.

All told, the exclusion phenomenon merely means that in natural languages a partially exclusive interpretation of quantifiers is presupposed. The only thing that prevents us from formulating a precise counterpart to the modified rule (G. anaphoric the) for formal languages is that in these languages the requisite notion of clause (syntacticians' s-node) is not defined in a way that would give rise to interesting results.

There are certain apparent exceptions to what has been said above about the exclusion phenomenon and also certain asymmetries between pronouns and *the*-phrases that might seem to belie what we have said. In reality, however, these exceptions prove to be merely apparent. Hence they serve to illustrate forcefully the advantages of a game-theoretical approach.

These phenomena are illustrated by the following examples:

(78)   Jane saw her sister.
(79)   Jane remembered her misfortune.
(80)   Jane remembered the poor girl's misfortune.

Contrary to what we perhaps have led the reader to expect, "her" can mean the same as "Jane's" in (78)-(79), while "the poor girl's" in (80) can't.

An explanation is easily obtained, however. In Part I above, we have formulated an approximation to a game rule for genitives in English.[6] That rule will take the players from (78) to a sentence of the form

(81)   Jane saw Jill, and Jill is a/the sister of hers.

Likewise, the same rule will have the effect to replacing (79) by an expression similar to the following:

(82)   Jane remembered the Great Crash of 1929,[7] and
              the Great Crash of 1929 is a/the misfortune of
              hers.

Now in (81)-(82) "hers" occurs in a clause different from that which contains "Jane". Hence, it can pick out Jane.

In contrast, in (81) (G. anaphoric the) presumably is to be applied before (G. genitive), and such an order of rule application has the effect of excluding Jane from being the poor girl mentioned in (81).

Thus an explanation of the apparent discrepancies is easily obtained. Notice that this explanation does not make any use of the relation of coreference as a primitive explanatory concept.

We shall return to the Exclusion Principle in Part III below, especially in chap. 3.

11. Inductive Choice Sets (and Other Forms of Dependence)

Now we are also in a position to deal with Mates-type uses of definite descriptions (Mates 1973). What is involved in examples of this type is that, in our terms, the choice of b in (G. anaphoric the) might depend on earlier choices of individuals by the players, including Nature, and this possibility is built into our treatment.

Relevant examples include the following:

(83)　　Every marriage has its problems. Sometimes the husband is the source of the problems, sometimes the wife.

(84)　　The best advisor of every young mother is her own mother.

This idea can be pushed further. Indeed, a change in our treatment is needed in cases where several subgames are involved in a semantical game. The game rule (G. anaphoric the) is predicated on the idea that the members of I are intuitively speaking the individuals available to the players at the time (G. anaphoric the) is applied. If such an application takes place in one of the later subgames, say G, the players have available to them more than those individuals chosen by the players at the earlier stages of the ongoing subgame. They may also have access to certain strategies used by one of the players in earlier subgames. (This is the gist of the subgame idea. Cf. Part I above and see Hintikka and Carlson 1977.) What are these strategies? They are functions whose arguments and values are members of our domain of individuals, or functionals whose arguments can be such functions, etc. Hence the definition of I in (G. anaphoric the) has to be extended further. The new definition will be the following:

Definition of I: I is the smallest set that contains J and is closed with respect to the totality of functions and functionals available to Myself at the time when the application of (G. anaphoric the) is made, where J is the set of individuals chosen by the players up to that point in the subgame in question plus the individuals introduced by (G. name) in earlier subgames.

Following the terminology of logicians, we shall call this definition of I an inductive one.

An example where this new definition of *I* comes into play is the following:

(85)   If John gives each child a present for Christmas, some child will open the present he or she was given today.

Here the strategy of the player who is trying to verify the antecedent of (85) in the subgame associated with this antecedent is "remembered" by Myself when (G. anaphoric the) is applied in the second subgame, which is connected with the consequent of (85). This strategy is codified in a function f that maps children into their presents, if the overall game is to go into as much as the second subgame. Hence, *I* does not only contain the individual (say c) chosen by Myself in the second subgame to instantiate "some child". It also contains the f(c) that is, the gift given to that child. With that proviso, (G. anaphoric the) assigns the right meaning to (85). In the second subgame, there exists a winning strategy for Myself if there exists a child c who opens the present f(c) today. This is precisely when we would, intuitively, consider the consequent as true in circumstances in which the antecedent is true, i.e., in circumstances in which there is a function f that assigns to each child a gift given to him or her by John. In the same way we can now deal with examples like (37) (above, sec. 3).

12. Other Uses of "The"

We indicated earlier that we propose to treat the anaphoric use of *the*-phrases as the fundamental one and try to understand other uses of the definite article by means of it. The time has come to show what we mean. What we shall do is consider (G. anaphoric the) as the fundamental rule, and we shall try to explain the other subcases of (G. the) as pragmatically determined variants of (G. anaphoric the). In this explanation, important use will be made of the so-called principle of charity.

This procedure is also supported by the following observation. It seems to us that when the anaphoric interpretation of *the*-phrases is possible (i.e., when the set *I* is not empty), the anaphoric reading excludes the Russellian one. The following might perhaps be examples:

(86)   All fifteen of Bob's schoolmates were interested in chess. They all admired the best chess player.

(87)   You want to see Mr. Lowell? Well, today the president is in Washington, conferring with Mr. Roosevelt. (Reputedly said by a Harvard secretary in the early thirties to a visitor who wanted to see Abbott Lawrence Lowell.)

Let us first point out two deviations from (G. anaphoric the) that are easily explainable pragmatically. First, we must normally admit into *I* more individuals than it has so far been allowed to contain. Over and above the individuals referred to by the proper names occurring in the initial sentence, we must also admit certain individuals given contextually. If an animal trainer is in trouble and I shout:

(88)   Look out for the tiger!

the intended reference of the *the*-phrase is specified neither by an earlier proper name nor by the selection from individuals chosen earlier in a semantical game. What is involved in such uses? At first sight, it might look as if we had to deal with a simple relativization to a contextually restricted domain of entities. There are some uses of *the*-phrases where this is the right diagnosis, e.g., the following:

(89)   When driving through the town of Stone Mountain, John wanted to mail a postcard but he could not find the post office.

However, mere relativization is not all that can happen. If we recall the treatment of Donnellan-type examples proposed above in sec. 2, we can see that in many cases apparent relativization really means letting one's quantifiers range over perceptually identified objects.

This procedure might seem to be motivated more epistemologically than linguistically. It has a striking etymological precedent, however, in that *the* is a descendant of the Old English demonstrative *se*, *seo*, another form of which has come down to us as the demonstrative *that*. As Russell already recognized, demonstratives are the archetypal ways of referring to an object of acquaintance. As we may put it, one can refer demonstratively in an utterance to an object and be understood if and only if the object referred to belongs to the perceptual objects of both the speaker and the hearer.

Our formulation of (G. anaphoric the) opens the door for another extension. Above it was noted that by using certain anaphoric *the*-phrases we can attribute various properties to individuals chosen by players earlier in the game or referred to by proper names in relevant preceding sentences. This was what the epithetic use of *the*-phrases amounted to. It was likewise seen that by using anaphoric *the*-phrases we can impose conditions on the individuals that are introduced by expressions dealt with earlier in the semantical game. The so-called epithetic use of *the*-phrases is a case in point.

Now it is equally natural for a speaker to use *the*-phrases to indicate which individuals he or she is including in the background set *I'* that we just introduced. When a cabinet minister in answering a parliamentary question addresses an M.P. as "the right honorable member", he is not thereby branding all other members as "right dishonorable". He is indicating that at the time of utterance his selected set *I'* contains only one member, that is, that he is temporarily restricting his attention to the one member he is addressing.

13. The Russellian Use

So far, we have not attempted a treatment of the Russellian use of *the*-phrases. Such a treatment – a pragmatic one – is nevertheless very easy. Suppose, as we propose, that the anaphoric use is the normative one and that it is governed by our rule (G. anaphoric the). All we have to do is to ask, How would one naturally interpret a *the*-phrase in circumstances (in a context) in which the anaphoric reading does not make any sense or in which it is clearly not what the speaker means? Russellian uses of *the*-phrases are typically cases in point. Suppose someone says to us,

(90)   The author of *Waverley* is a Scot.

How am I to understand this utterance? Here we can profitably borrow a leaf from Donald Davidson's book and resort to the crucial principle of charity (Davidson 1973). It

seems to us that linguists and philosophers have not realized to what an extraordinary extent Davidson is right
about the use of the principle of charity in the semantical
interpretation of various utterances.

But how is the principle of charity supposed to guide
us in understanding (90)? The understanding of (90) by
means of (G. anaphoric the) depends on the possibility of
the two players of our semantical games making certain
choices from a contextually given set I of individuals. But
in the example (unless there is more to the context than we
have mentioned) there is no such set available to the players. Yet the speaker is obviously trying to convey something to us.

What, in such circumstances, is more natural – more in
keeping with the principle of charity – than to assume that
the domain of choice I that the speaker intends is the domain of individuals that is given to us and to him and to
all speakers of the language together with the normal interpretation of the English language? Surely the natural thing
is to take I to be the domain over which standard quantifiers of the same kind as are normally used in (90), e.g.,
"someone" and "everyone", range.

But, as was pointed out above, this results precisely
in the Russellian treatment of the-phrases. Russell's "theory of descriptions" thus assumes a relatively modest niche
as a special case of our treatment of "the", which assigns
the pride of place to anaphoric uses of the definite article.
Russell's theory is, as it were, a special case of ours dis-
torted by contextual, pragmatic pressures. From another
perspective, however, the honors nevertheless belong to
Russell, for our "anaphoric" theory was originally inspired
by him.

It is thus possible to see in pragmatic terms how the
Russellian use of the-phrases can be considered as a variant of the anaphoric use. Briefly, since there is no
nonempty set I in the sense of (G. anaphoric the) available, the hearer interprets the the-phrase by making the
next most obvious choice, that is, setting I equal to the
whole domain of discourse (strictly speaking, to the relevant category). It is important to realize that such a reading is very much a reading by default. It is the best one
can do in the absence of further relevant background information. When such information is available, other things
may happen that, for instance, can lead us to the so-called
generic uses of the-phrases.

It would be very interesting to ask whether the absolutistic character of Russell's theory of definite descriptions, reflected by the fact that Russell, as it were, sets *I* equal to the whole fixed domain of discourse, is based on Russell's belief in "language as the universal medium" in Hintikka's sense (Hintikka 1981). After all, one of the main corollaries to that belief is that the ranges of our quantifiers cannot be varied, that our universe of discourse is fixed once and for all. It is fairly clear that this in fact was the background of Russell's theory. However, the historical details are hard to pinpoint, and the question whether the corollary is really an inevitable one remains to be answered.

14. The Generic Use Motivated

Our pragmatic account of the generic use of *the*-phrases will assume that the anaphoric use of *the*-phrases is the normal (and even normative) one. It can be dramatized in the form of an imaginary internal monologue that I carry out when someone addresses the following sentence to me:

(91)   The tiger is a dangerous animal.

"Is the speaker trying to warn me?" I turn quickly and look around to see whether there is a situationally given big cat that the speaker might be referring to. (Or, for that matter, any other animal around that the speaker might have mistaken for a tiger). This usage of *the*-phrases is what that set *I'* discussed above was supposed to enable us to handle.) Seeing and hearing none, I continue: "The speaker is obviously serious, and is obviously trying to make a nontrivial remark." There's also no indication that he he might be intending his words in a nonliteral sense. "Now what can he possibly mean? There is no non-empty set *I* given in the sense of (G. anaphoric the); hence the speaker cannot be using the *the*-phrase anaphorically to make a non-trivial point. Moreover, he knows and he knows that I know that there is more than one tiger in existence. Hence, he cannot, by the same token, be using the *the*-phrase in a Russellian way either, for then the falsity of what he is saying would be patent. What, then, can, he possibly mean by speaking of the tiger? He is obviously presuming that the statement he made is true - or

at least not obviously and trivially false.   Now the use of
the definite article presupposes uniqueness for the truth of
(87).   Hence the utterer must be envisaging an imaginary
situation in which there is precisely one tiger in the set *I*
of invidiuals that is to be considered.   More generally,
there presumably is (by parity of cases) one representative
individual´ from one of a range of species in which the *I*
that is being presupposed - something like a pragmatic
'axiom of choice' - is being invoked here."

"How is this tiger to be selectred then?   The context
gives me no infomation that would guide the choice.
Moreover, 'tiger' is a word for a biological species, and we
know that such a species is fairly uniform.   Therefore, the
only requisite for the role of the single tiger to be
considered is its representativeness.   Hence the force of
(91) will have to be an assertion of what is true of a
species-typical tiger."

This, of course, is precisely what the force of (91) is.
The line of thought just sketched can be generalized, and
through this generalization we get a "transcendental deduction" (more accurately, "pragmatic deduction") of the force
of generic *the*-phrases in ordinary discourse.   A number of
comments on this "pragmatic deduction" are in order, including further conclusions we can draw from it.

15. Conclusions from the "Pragmatic Deduction"

(a) First and foremost, the deduction shows that generic
the-phrases serve to express species-characteristic properties.   This seems to be the case.   Notice that the precise
force of "species-characteristic" is important here.   For instance,   notwithstanding   contrary   claims,   generic
the-phrases do not express per se lawlike characteristics.
This can be shown by means of a variety of examples.
Even if some of the instances of this usage can perhaps be
taken to express nomic connections, the following is a clear
counterexample to the lawlikeness claim:

(92)   The kangaroo lives in Australia.

No nomic connection is required for the truth of (92).   It
is a geographical and geological accident that kangaroos are
confined to Australia.   If a herd of kangaroos should es-
cape from a zoo, multiply, and fill South America, no

natural laws would be violated.   Yet (92) would become
false.

(b) Generically used definite articles have a meaning
closely related to comparable uses of the indefinite article.
For instance, (91) says almost the same as

(93)   A tiger is a dangerous animal.

However, the mechanism through which this meaning
comes about is quite different in the two cases.   The indefinite article functions much more like the usual universal
quantifier.   This difference will sometimes show up in differences of meaning.   The following examples illustrate a
case in point:

(94)   The mammoth lived in Siberia during the ice age.
(95)   A mammoth lived in Siberia during the ice age.

Here (95), but not (94), easily prompts one to ask: Which
mammoth are you talking about?   Or do you mean "A species of mammoths ..."?

(c)   Should our "museum scenario" (our postulated situation in which precisely one representative from each of a
number of kinds of individuals is present), which was used
in the "deduction" of the semantical force of generic
the-phrases, strike the reader as being unrealistic,
Jespersen reminds us that a class of generic uses of the
definite article are, historically speaking, based on precisely this type of situation (Jespersen 1933):

> "The article in to play *the* fool, act *the* lover, etc.,
> originates from the old character-plays. ... Similarly
> with look:
>
> I made shift look the happy lover.
>
> This leads to the use of the definite article to denote
> 'the typical', whatever it is, chiefly in the predicative:
>
> He is quite the gentleman.
> She was the perfect girl, the perfect companion.
> Mr. Lecky is always the historian, never the
> partisan (MacCarthy)."

The role of our "museum scenario" is here played by character plays, in which each of the players represents one character or type.

(d)   Our "deduction" shows the different assumptions that the generic sense of the definite article depends on. Not only must the context rule out both the anaphoric and the Russellian uses of the definite article.   More importantly, the range of entities from which the one representative is thought of as being chosen (say, all the Xs) must be uniform as far as typical speakers of the language are concerned.   If that range is not as uniform as a biological species is, there may be a naturally designated individual which serves as *the* X.   For instance, if, instead of the species tiger, we were considering a Highland clan, we would not find uniformity.   Instead, there would be a natural candidate for the role of a distinguished individual, to wit, the head of the clan.   Thus,

(96)   The MacDonald

is to be expected to be, not a typical member of the clan, but *the* MacDonald, the head of the MacDonald clan.   This expectation turns out to be correct.   For instance, the sentence

(97)   The Macleod is very frugal.

does not claim that frugality is a characteristic mark of the Macleods.   It is a statement about himself (another Highland locution for the head of a clan), one particular man, the chief of the Macleods.   (We are here grateful to Eve Clark for highly useful information.)
   Hence we have reached, as a by-product of our general line of thought, an explanation of a rare but interesting use of *the*.   This use of *the* may appear not only rare but exceedingly far-fetched.   There is nevertheless a similar use that is quite common.   Even though it is a plural use of *the* and therefore does not fall within our treatment, it is clearly essentially similar to the Highland usage.   It is illustrated by examples like the following:

(98)   We invited the Smiths over for dinner, but they
          could not find a babysitter.

(99)   The Joneses are getting a divorce, but it has not
            been decided who will have the custody of their
            children.

In this usage, the phrase *the* Xs, where X is a family
name, does not refer to all the members of the family, but
to the two distinguished members of it, viz., the husband
and the wife, rather in the same way as *the* Macmillan picks
out the distinguished member of the clan, viz., its chief.
    A closely related but more general type of usage is the
one acknowledged in the *OED* where the phrase *the* X is
used to refer to the pre-eminent X, the only one worth
speaking of and hence, we can put it, the natural choice
from the set of all Xs. Usually, this kind of *the* is emphasized. An example is

(100)   Caesar was *the* general of Rome.

    (e) Another usage that deserves a discussion is the
Platonic one. It amounts to using the phrase *the* X to refer to the Form of X. This Form is best construed, it
seems to us, as the paradigmatic instance of X-hood, imitat-
ed by the other, less perfect Xs. So conceived, the X is a
particular entity, albeit an abstract one (see Vlastos 1971).
    This Platonic usage has strong overtones of the gener-
ic use. On a purely historical level, it is an open question
how strong an element of the generic usage there was in
Plato's actual thinking. It is nevertheless clear that the
Platonic usage, as we shall label it, differs from the generic
one. The following are examples that are true on a generic
construal of the definite article but false on the Platonic
one:

(101)   The tiger lives in many parts of Asia.
(102)   The tiger can lose its stripes when it gets old.

    How is the Platonic usage to be accounted for? The
following sketch will have to suffice here:
    It has been argued by several linguists and
psycholinguists that systematically the comparative is prior
to the positive (Fillmore 1971, Clark 1976). If this was
Plato's view, we could at once understand his problems with
a thing that is, at the same time, both great and not great
(namely, in relation with different objects of comparison).
If we could also let Plato assume, as it has been argued

that Aristotle did, that any sequence of comparisons will have to come to a unique end in a finite number of steps, then there is going to exist an absolute X for each adjective word X derived from the corresponding comparative (relational) term (Beth 1964, pp. 9-12). Then the phrase *the* X is naturally taken to refer, when used absolutely, to this absolute X.

The difference between the generic and the Platonic uses of the phrase *the* X can be characterized by saying that in the generic use, the phrase *the* X is used to refer to a typical or characteristic X, whereas the phrase *the* X used Platonically refers to the perfect X, the best representative of all X's, instead merely a normal one. The Platonic use is therefore closely related to the Highland use of such phrases as *the Macleod* discussed above. What is characteristic of Plato's usage, on this interpretation, is that the field of a general term is assumed not to be uniform in the way that in our pragmatic deduction above necessitated the choice of a typical X as the reference of the phrase *the* X. Fields of Platonic general terms are no democracies. Each of them has a distinguished member, the pre-eminent X. It is thus no accident that Plato referred to the Form of X as *the* X and identified it with the perfect X. Even though this subject needs a great deal of further discussion, it can already be seen that our observations help to put Plato's views in a highly interesting systematic perspective.

(f) Related to the generic and the Platonic uses, but different from them, there is a use of "the X" to mean "the species X", sometimes "the kind X" or even "the color X", etc. For instance, on this reading, *the* tiger would not be a species-typical tiger or the paradigm tiger, but the biological species, and *the* aquamarine would not be a typical example of the color or even a defining color-sample, but a certain hue of blue. (The fact that the definite article is omitted in the case of the most familiar colors does not vitiate our point.) This usage is exemplified, e.g., by the following:

(103)   The shark is evolutionarily older than the whale.
(104)   The mammoth is extinct.

Ordinary usage of the-phrases is often an amalgam of (d)-(f). It is nevertheless important for the understanding

of the theoretical situation to distinguish them.   It is also
significant that it is often awkward to mix the different uses.   For instance, the following sentence is deservedly
strange:

(105)   *The mammoth has large tusks, is brown, sparse-
             ly haired, and extinct.

      (g) Sometimes in the generic use the context shows
that the intended choice is to be restricted to some subset
of the relevant class, e.g., to male or female members of a
species.   A case in point is the following:

(106)   The lion usually weans its cubs when they are
             four months old.

Of course, only lionesses do this, not lions in general.
This kind of restricted choice does not contradict our diagnosis of the generic use, however.   It can easily be taken
into account in the "pragmatic deduction" above.   The context can show that *the* X is intended to be selected to be a
typical example, not of X's at large, but of some designated
subset of X's.   After all, museums and zoos have usually
typical specimens both of the male and of the female of each
species, not to mention Noah's Ark.

NOTES

[1]   For a discussion of the Frege-Russell paradigm, see Jaakko Hintikka, "Semantics: A Revolt Against Frege", in G. Floistad, editor, *Contemporary Philosophy*, Volume 1: *Philosophy of Language, Philosophical Logic*, Martinus Nijhoff, The Hague, 1981 and "'Is'; Semantical Games, and Semantical Relativity", *Journal of Philosophical Logic* 8 (1979), 433–468.   The main development in Russell's views from the *Principles of Mathematics* to "On Denoting" is that sentences containing what he called "denoting phrases" can now all be paraphrased in the quantificational idiom. Russell's treatment of definite descriptions was, in his eyes, the most difficult part of the reduction, and has hence gained most of the attention.   In the proper historical perspective, however, the other parts of the reduction are undoubtedly much more important.

[2]   For a survey of this problem, see Pauline I. Jacobson, *The Syntax of Crossing Coreference Sentences*, Indiana University Linguistics Club, Bloomington, 1979, with references to the literature.   Lauri Karttunen (1971) demonstrates the untranslatability when considering McCawley's treatment of Bach-Peters sentences (pp. 173–76).   The problem here may have more to do with pronominalization, however, than with *the*-phrases themselves.   Karttunen says, "Pronouns [in natural language] are sometimes used in a way that is not possible with variables in the more restricted syntax of predicate calculus" (n. 12, p. 176).

[3]   This is unmistakable on the basis of Strawson's examples and the problems he raises.   For instance, he repeatedly considers statements as answers to questions. Furthermore, the general principles he considers in the first few pages of "Identifying Reference and Truth-Values" are clearly conversational (discourse) principles, referring among other things to the state of knowledge of different speakers in a communication situation.

[4]   For the rule (G. genitive), see Jaakko Hintikka and Lauri Carlson, "Pronouns of Laziness in Game-Theoretical Semantics", *Theoretical Linguistics* 4 (1977), 1–29.   See especially pp. 7–8.

[5]   For the ordering principles that govern (G. name), see Part III of this work.

[6]   See note 5 above.   In that paper (G. genitive) is formulated to be applicable to sentences of the form

$$X - Y's \ Z - W,$$

where Y is a proper name.   But an extension to pronouns
is mentioned there that is different from what we do here:
"We can nevertheless extend (G. gen) to situations in which
'Y's' is replaced by the genitive of a pronoun.   Then in the
output of (G. gen) 'Y' must be replaced by its antecedent."
In this work we extend the rule to pronouns, for we do not
here rely on any antecedence relation that would enable us
to replace a pronoun by its antecedent.
7 We are treating, for the sake of argument, "The Great
Crash of 1929" as if it were a proper name.

PART III

TOWARDS A SEMANTICAL THEORY OF
PRONOMINAL ANAPHORA

CHAPTER I

DIFFERENT APPROACHES TO ANAPHORA

1. Approaches to Anaphora in Terms of the Head Relation

How do anaphoric pronouns operate? The accounts one is likely to find in philosophically and logically oriented literature run somewhat like the following:

(a) The first idea likely to occur to one here is that an anaphoric pronoun is literally a pro-noun, acting as a "placeholder for its head" (or, grammatical antecedent), and determining its reference in the same way as its head. We might call this the "placeholder account" of anaphoric pronouns.

Alas, an abundance of examples can be produced against this view. Account (a) works reasonably well if the head is a (logically) proper name, but it fails if the head is, e.g., a quantifier phrase, as in the following:

(1)   Every man is happy when he is in love.
(2)   Every man is happy when every man is in love.

These do not mean the same, although on view (a) they ought to.

Only in relatively rare cases, known in the trade as "pronouns of laziness", will the placeholder account tell the true story (see Hintikka and Carlson 1977, and sec. 34, below):

(3)   A man who gives his paycheck to his wife is wiser than a man who gives it to his mistress.

This is (on its most natural reading) equivalent to the result of replacing "it" by its grammatical antecedent "his paycheck", as required by (a).

One of the questions a theory of anaphora should address is whether such "pronouns of laziness" constitute a use of pronouns essentially different from their normal one (whatever that might be).

79

(b) In other, more frequent cases, a pronoun does something apparently different from serving merely as a placeholder for its head. What it does is refer to the same entity as its head. On the placeholder account (a), the pronoun reaches out to its reference in the world in the same way as its head would have done in its stead; in (b), there is no need for it to seek out a reference again, for its head has already done that. All that remains for the pronoun to do is to re-refer to the already established reference. A pronoun does not on this view replace its head; it repeats the reference of the head. We shall call this the "repeated reference account".

(c) Unfortunately, the notion of reference is not applicable in all the contexts where pronouns are used[1]. For instance, if the head of a pronoun is a quantifier phrase, it makes little sense to say that it refers to any particular entity. In such cases, a pronoun's function is often assimilated to the function of formal variables of quantification theory. We shall call this the "bound-variable" account of anaphoric pronouns. The function of anaphoric pronouns will then be to indicate which variables are bound to which quantifiers. The quantifier to which a variable-like pronoun is bound is, on this view, its grammatical head.
We find the assimilation of anaphoric pronouns to variables of quantifications mistaken. Some reasons for our view will be given later. An easy general argument against such an assimilation is the irrelevance of the concept of scope for quantifier phrases in natural languages (see Hintikka 1979, pp. 81-83).
One dimension we shall not investigate in any detail here is the relation of the three ideas (a)-(c) to syntax. Can they, or some of them, be related to a systematic syntactical theory? It seems fair to say that constructive results have not been plentiful in answering this question. The placeholder account (a) lost its best syntactical ally with the demise of the putative rule of pronominalization in transformational grammar a long time ago (see Wasow 1979; Bresnan 1970). Early attempts to use the bound-variable account (c) as a key to the behavior of pronouns got short shrift from transformational grammarians (Wasow 1975, 1979), but recently the idea of assimilating the behavior of anaphoric pronouns to the behavior of the bound variables of quantification theory has again become fashionable both among transformational grammarians (Chomsky, Higgin-

botham) and among Montague semanticists. We shall not discuss directly any syntactical issues here, but if semantics and syntax go together at all, our criticism in this work of the alleged similarity of anaphoric pronouns and bound variables can be expected to tell also against their syntactical parity. We shall argue that the semantical mechanism underlying anaphoric pronouns is radically different from that on which the operation of the bound variables of quantification theory is based (cf. sec. 6 below.)

All three accounts (a)-(c) share a presupposition that is not obvious and that we suggest must be discarded in general, excepting certain special pronominal uses. They all assume that the relation of an anaphoric pronoun to its head can somehow be determined, so that one can utilize it for the purpose of giving an account of the semantics of the pronoun. In short, all these three accounts (a)-(c) presuppose that an anaphoric pronoun operates by means of its special grammatical relation to its head. In reality, however, there seems to be ample cause to challenge this assumption. In the following, we shall give several examples illustrating the dubiousness of all theories that rely essentially on the pronoun-head relation.

2. Recent Approaches to Anaphora in Terms of Coreference Assignments

In recent years, a different approach to anaphora has gained currency. In it, generally speaking, head-anaphor relations are dealt with as special cases of relations of coreference holding between different NPs in a sentence. These relations of coreference are not found in the underlying syntactical structure of the sentence, but come about, as it were, in the course of its semantical interpretation. The crucial question in this approach is how the assignment of possible coreference relations depends on the syntactical structure and, more generally, the syntactical generation of the sentence in question (see Reinhart 1974, 1976, 1978, 1981, 1983a, 1983b).

There is some leeway within this approach concerning the stage of generation at which coreference relations are assigned. Interpretativists like Jackendoff think that the assignment is carried out basically at the level of surface structure (Jackendoff 1972), whereas Chomsky, for instance, assumes that this happens on the level of case-marked S-structure (see Chomsky 1980, 1981, 1982; Higginbotham 1980; and Radford 1981).   Though some lin- guists emphasize the pragmatic element in the coreference assignment (Dougherty 1969; Shopen 1972), most represen- tatives of this approach believe that the system of coref- erence relations is firmly grounded on the syntactic structure of the sentence in question, and that pragmatic factors serve merely to filter out only certain otherwise possible assignments of coreference.   Indeed, certain gen- eral ideas about how the syntactic structure of a sentence S restrains possible relations of coreference between different NPs in S seem to be fairly widely agreed upon in their main features.   They go back mainly to Langacker, and they are utilized in some way or other in much of the recent work on anaphora (Langacker 1969).

This kind of approach uses as its main conceptual tool a system of indexing NPs in a given sentence.   Two NPs can be coreferential only if they can have the same index. This technique is closely related to the idea of binding on which quantification theory is based.   Indeed, when the head of an anaphoric pronoun is a quantifier phrase, the function of the pronoun is usually identified in so many words with that of the bound variables of first-order logic.

This approach provides an interesting object of com- parison with our approach.   It is nevertheless subject to various objections.   Three such objections will be raised and motivated in this work, apart from the specific conse- quences of the different approaches to anaphora.   These objections are the following:

(i) The concept of coreference that is relied on in this approach is unclear, and cannot be interpreted as either actual or intended identity of entities referred to (see sec. 19 below).   Yet without a clear model-theoretical interpretation of the coreference (coindexing) relation, the theoretical basis of the entire enterprise remains shaky. This problem has been recognized by some of the most recent analysts of anaphora, especially by Reinhart.   She suggests that we might need a "three-valued" system of coindexing in order to capture the different phenomena one faces with respect to coreference: obligatory coreference, obligatory noncoreference, and optional coreference.   We shall argue below, however, that these different phenomena have to be dealt with by means of the same set of rules and principles (cf. sec. 28 below).   But even if the difficulty of interpreting the notion of coreference is acknowledged, the objection remains – and is indeed reinforced by what we will find – that the explanatory value of coreference relations in determining the semantical interpretation of a sentence is not as great as has been assumed.

Of course, the notion of coreference has its uses. Indeed, we shall avail ourselves of this term and its cognates in what follows. It is to be kept in mind, however, that for us it is a derivative, sometimes misleading, and occasionally inapplicable concept that cannot function satisfactorily as a semantical primitive and that has to be cashed in for more fundamental notions in problem cases.

(ii) Virtually all work in coreference approaches has been predicated on the assumption that coreference relations are determined by the syntactical structure of the sentence in question. In this work we shall find indications that this assumption is highly dubious. For one thing, the lexical items a sentence contains may have an effect on its coreference relations (see secs. 23 and 27 below). Secondly, it is not clear that the appropriate generalizations can be formulated by means of the usual grammatical categories, such as S, NP, VP, etc. (cf. sec. 30 below). Thirdly, it can be seen that many of the crucial phenomena related to anaphora – for example, the admissibility of reflexive pronouns (or nonreflexives, for that matter) – can depend on the semantics of sentences in which they occur rather than on their syntax alone (see, e.g., secs. 14 and 33 below).

(iii) Even when the coreference analysis yields the right predictions, it does so only at the level of empirical generalizations. No deeper theoretical explanation is usually given in the literature for such generalizations. They are not connected in any systematic fashion – say, as special consequences of more general laws – with an overall semantical theory. This makes the resulting generalizations very hard for one to get an overview on, and consequently very hard to evaluate. For one thing, without an overview it is difficult to see where one is likely to find counterexamples. Hence the unsystematic character of these generalizations makes it hard to test them even as merely empirical generalizations.

This absence of more general characterizations also makes many generalizations found in the literature somewhat unlikely as accounts of how competent hearers of language actually semantically process pronouns. It seems to us that we are here dealing with a frequent flaw in recent linguistic theorizing. Elaborate rules, often of Byzantine complexity, are set up as straightforward generalizations from data, but they lack any unifying general principle or clear intuitive plausibility. These criticisms are elaborated elsewhere in this book (see chaps. 5-6 below and sec. 12 of Part I above).

Objections (i) and (iii) can be partly summed up by saying that coreference studies do not amount to a genuine theory of anaphora as a semantical phenomenon. In contrast, the main aim of this work is to present a sketch of such a theory.

A further aim for such a theory may be worth noting here. It is characteristic of many recent treatments of anaphoric pronouns that different kinds of pronouns are dealt with separately, because it is alleged that the underlying semantical mechanism is different in different cases. For instance, it is sometimes argued that in some cases pronouns can be assimilated to the variables of quantification theory but in other cases not, or that in some cases pronouns must be syntactically controlled – for example, pronouns of laziness – but in other cases not. Such case-by-case treatments strike us as somewhat suspect to begin with, for it is hard to find any intuitively felt differences between the allegedly unlike cases. What is also important here is that the allegedly different kinds of anaphoric pronouns exhibit in their semantical behavior many interesting similarities, as Wasow (1977, chap. 5) has ably spelled out. This uniformity is hard to explain on the basis of a nonuniform treatment. Later in this work we shall offer a general theoretical reason for the uniform behavior of different kinds of pronouns, i.e., anaphoric and deictic (see sec. 7 below).

3. Discourse Anaphora. Anaphora vs. Deixis?

This prompts another critical remark on approaches to anaphora in terms of coreference relations. Whatever grammatical differences may distinguish coreference relations between anaphoric pronouns and their antecedents from the relation of variables of quantification to the antecedent quantifiers to which they are bound, such bound variables offer the closest logical paradigm for coreference relations. Accordingly, as was noted, Chomsky and others are in effect using logicians' quantification theory as a source of semantical representations for English sentences. This does not work in discourse, however, for there anaphoric pronouns and their prima facie antecedents are in different sentences. (For an analysis of the situation this creates, see sec. 10 below.) Accordingly, discourse anaphora has to be dealt with in a way different from intrasentential anaphora in a coreference-based approach. This distinction between intrasentential anaphora and discourse anaphora has been of a characteristic feature of many recent treatments of anaphora.

From the vantage point of game-theoretical semantics, however, this contrast appears as one of the many artificial and theoretically harmful attempted separations of different kinds of anaphora from each other. In contrast to approaches in which such distinctions are made, in our theory practically everything that is said in this work about intrasentential anaphora can be extended to discourse anaphora. The way of doing this is clear. For certain types of intrasentential anaphora, we must think of the semantical game played on a given sentence as being divided in subgames (see Part I, sec. 6, above). Special rules govern the information that is available to the players in later subgames about earlier subgames. This treatment can be extended to discourse by the simple expedient of considering discourse as a long "supergame" consisting of several successive subgames, with essentially the same rules (suitably extended, of course) governing the transfer of information from a subgame to later ones as in the intrasentential case, each played on a separate sentence in the discourse on the left-to-right (earlier to later) order. We shall spell out this idea and examine some of its consequences below, especially in secs. 9-10.

Of course, the step from sentence semantics necessitates several changes in the general setup of our semantical games. These changes affect even the ideas of winning and losing, for parties in a dialogue, however idealized, have other aims besides the verification or falsification of a certain sentence. Furthermore, rules for different kinds of nondeclarative sentences (questions, commands, etc.) are needed. (For an excellent discussion of the resulting "dialogue games", see Lauri Carlson 1983.) It is a remarkable fact that these changes do not affect the mechanism of anaphora, with one exception, to be mentioned below in sec. 5. This is the phenomenon of "forgetting" members of the choice set I.

Meanwhile, another observation is in order. Usually, anaphora is contrasted with deixis. The reference of an anaphoric expression is said to be determinable with the help of only its linguistic environment, whereas the reference of a deictic expression is said to be supplied by the nonlinguistic context of an utterance. The typical case of the reliance of an anaphoric expression on its linguistic context is of course its repeating the reference of its head. Since we have suggested above – and shall argue below – that anaphoric pronouns do not operate by means of a grammatical relation to their supposed head, their relation to deictic expressions has to be reconsidered. Is there perhaps more similarity between the mode of operation of anaphoric and deictic expressions than first meets the eye? We shall return to this question later (see sec. 7 below). It is clear that anaphoric pronouns are not like the most typical deictic expressions, since they don't as a matter of course get their reference from the nonlinguistic context of utterance. However, it should not be excluded that there might be some other kind of nonlinguistic context that can serve the same purpose.

Sometimes the term "deictic" is extended to uses of pronouns in which the reference is supplied by the discourse context, not by the sentence in which the pronoun occurs. This terminology is misleading, however, in that it presupposes that somehow intrasentential anaphora is different in kind from discourse anaphora. As was pointed out earlier in this section, for us there is no difference in principle between the two. There is, admittedly, an important difference between anaphora that does not involved a step from one subgame to another and anaphora that does involve such a step. However, this contrast is different from the distinction between intrasentential anaphora and discourse anaphora.

CHAPTER II

A GAME-THEORETICAL APPROACH TO ANAPHORA

4. Anaphoric *The*-Phrases as a Paradigm Case

Let us return to our main question. How, then, do anaphoric pronouns operate? How can they operate, if the grammatical relation of a pronoun to its antecedent is not relied on? An interesting alternative is suggested by our treatment of anaphoric *the*-phrases expounded in the second part of this book (cf., Hintikka and Kulas 1982, 1983, forthcoming; Kulas 1982). Instead of relying on the grammatical relation between an anaphoric *the*-phrase and its antecedent, that treatment relies on a contextually given set of entities, called *I*. Its members are not grammatical objects, but entities of the kind one's language speaks of. This set is not determined by the definite-article phrase alone, nor is it determined in conjunction with the sentence S in question. It is not constant for all the *the*-phrases occurring in one and the same S. It consists essentially of those individuals (of the appropriate category) that have been picked out in the semantical game G(S) associated with S (or otherwise available to the players) at the time a rule is applied to the *the*-phrase in question in the game. This treatment of anaphorically used *the*-phrases relies essentially on game-theoretical semantics. For the contextual determination of the set *I* is accomplished in this treatment by reference to what the players of a semantical game have done up to a certain stage of the game. This determination seems to be impossible to accomplish satisfactorily in any other way, as we argued in Part II above.

The precise game rule we use for *the*-phrases further specifies the definition of *I*. The rest of the game rule follows Russell's theory of descriptions, except that values for quantified variables are restricted to *I*:

(G. anaphoric the) When a semantical game has reached a sentence of the form

(4)   X - the Y who Z - W,

then an individual, say b, may be chosen from a set *I* of individuals by Myself, whereupon Nature chooses a different individual, say d, from the same set I.

(We shall call I the "choice set".)   The game is then continued with respect to

(5)   X - b - W, b is a(n) Y and b Z, but d is not a(n) Y who Z.

If I is a unit set, the game is continued with respect to a sentence of the form

(6)   X - b - W, b is a(n) Y and b Z.

Here I is restricted to entities of the relevant category, in the sense spelled out in Hintikka 1983. If I equals the whole category in question, we obtain Russell's treatment of definite descriptions. This is, we have argued (Hintikka and Kulas, forthcoming), a special and derivative use of *the*-phrases. In order to capture the anaphoric use, which appears to be the basic one, a different choice of I is needed. We can try to obtain this choice by stipulating that I contains (i) all the individuals (of the relevant category) picked out by the players up to the move in question, (ii) the individuals referred to by proper names in the original sentence (the input sentence of the game) and possibly (iii) individuals prominent in the perceptual situation in question. Furthermore, this set is the smallest set closed with respect to all functions and functionals that have been used by the players as (parts of) their strategies in earlier subgames and "remembered" in the subgame in which (4) is treated.

We have come to realize, however, that this definition of I is unsatisfactory. In order to reach a satisfactory definition, we must say more about the treatment of proper names in semantical games. In earlier books and papers on game-theoretical semantics, it was assumed in effect that the referents of all proper names occurring in a sentence S are given to the players at the onset of the game G(S). This assumption is oversimplified, and has to be given up. (Some interesting arguments for a closely similar conclusion have been given in Grice 1969.) The bearer of each proper name in S has to be thought of as being introduced by an application of a game rule (G. name) to the name in question, as was explained in Part I, sec. 11, para. (vi), above. The appearance that such a rule is dispensable is caused by the fact that (G. name) has priority over many of the other game rules applicable to the constituents of the same clause. However, (G. name) does not normally over-rule the structural principles (O. comm) or (O. LR). (For these principles, see Part I, sec. 8, above, and sec. 20 below.) This fact will be illustrated by several examples offered below.

After this change, the definition of *I* can be formulat-ed by saying that *I* contains the following:

(i)   all individuals introduced by the players earlier in the same subgame;
(ii) all individuals introduced by (G. name) in earlier subgames;
(iii) all individuals that can be obtained from (i)-(ii) by means of functions and functionals "remembered" from earlier subgames.

Moreover, *I* is stipulated to be the smallest set containing (i)-(iii).

An explanation concerning the notion of subgame is needed here. Suppose a part of a semantical game is played before a rule (for instance, the rule (G. cond) for conditionals) forces the players to divide it into subgames. Then this common part is taken to be a part of each of these subgames, in so far as the definition of *I* is concerned.

From the definition of *I* it follows that an individual *i* chosen by one of the players in an earlier subgame is in *I* only if (a) the choice of *i* is the entire strategy of one of the players in the earlier subgame and that strategy is available to the players when our rule is applied or (b) if it is chosen in accordance with (G. name).

Even though the explanation just given concerning *I* is lengthy, its main idea is very simple. The set *I* consists of those individuals of the relevant kind that are available to the players at the time (4) is treated. The explanation simply spells out this intuitive idea, i.e., spells out the different ways in which an individual may be available to the players.

A few further comments are needed here, neverthe-less, to complement this definition of *I*. Not only can func-tions that encode remembered strategies be applied to members of *I* to yield new ones. The entities that have been introduced as values of quantifier phrases are not all of the logical type of individuals. Sometimes they can be of the nature of functions. Then they too can be applied to members of I, which must be closed with respect to such functional applications.

The game rule (G. anaphoric the) of course has to be used in conjunction with other rules for semantical games. The version of it formulated above is a special case of a more general rule that can be generalized in the same way as other comparable quantifier rules. The reader will find a selection of them formulated in the survey of the main ideas and results of game-theoretical semantics that is given in Part I above and in Saarinen 1979 and Hintikka and Kulas 1983.

5. Game Rules for Anaphoric Pronouns

The first guiding principle of our treatment of anaphoric pronouns is that they behave essentially in the same way as anaphoric the-phrases. The parallelism between the semantical behavior of the two is obvious, and will be spelled out in some detail in sec. 8 below. This parallelism motivates the formulation of rules for pronouns analogous to (G. anaphoric the). The following is a case in point:

(G. he)   When a semantical game has reached a sentence of the form

(7)   X – he – Y,

an individual of the appropriate kind (a person or an animal), say b, may be chosen by Myself from I, whereupon Nature chooses another individual, say d, from I. The game is continued with respect to

(8)   X – b – Y, b is male, but d is not male.

Here I determined in the same way as in (G. anaphoric the).

As was indicated above in Part II, sec. 4, further explanation is needed when rules like (G. he), which involve a choice set I are used in discourse. Individuals may have to be omitted from I when they become "too old", i.e., when they have been introduced in a too distant earlier subgame. (It is to be noted, to be precise, that what matters for the question whether a member of *I* may be omitted is not always how long ago it was introduced, but how long ago it was last picked out by one of the players.) The conditions on which individuals may thus be omitted from *I* have to be studied separately.   The omission of a member *i* of *I* from it is obviously connected with the limitations of human short-term memory, and will be referred metaphorically as a player's "forgetting" *i*.   This phenomenon is probably at least in part pragmatic in nature.   Studying it is an enterprise that belongs to discourse semantics; it has no counterpart in sentence semantics.   We shall not undertake such a study in the present work.

A specification of how far down in a discourse a one-time member of *I*, say an individual introduced as a value of a quantifier phrase Q, is allowed to linger there, defines one of the several different ideas that are included under the heading of the "scope" of Q.   We shall return to this observation in sec. 10 below.

Instead of (7), we could of course have X – him – Y, or X – his – Y.   The only change is that in the latter case we must have, instead of (8),

(9)   X – b's – Y, b is a male, but d is not a male.

If *I* is a unit set {b}, the output sentence (8) reduces to

(10)   X – b – Y and b is male.

Here, and likewise in (8) and (9) above, we may have, instead of a conjunction, simply a list of sentences:

(11)   X – b – Y. b is a male.

Moreover, it is to be noted that in this rule (unlike some other rules) the order of conjuncts in the output sentence (9) or (10) (and, by the same token, the order of the sentences in the output list like (11)) can vary.   For instance, instead of (8) we may have (or, rather, Myself can choose to have)

(8)'   b is a male and X – b – Y, but d is not a male.

However, the order of clauses or sentences in the output of (G. he) need not be completely free. We shall not inquire into the precise limits of possible order variation here, however.

Similar general rules (G. she) and (G. it) can easily be formulated. These rules amount in their present form essentially to treating "he" as if it were "the male" or "the man", and to treating "she" as if it were "the female" or "the woman". This parity is an eminently natural idea as a first step. Nevertheless, it is important to see where it begins to break down.

The limits of applicability of these rules are best examined after we have studied some of their consequences. Rules for reflexive pronouns will have to be formulated separately. They will be discussed in sec. 13 below.

The leading idea of our treatment of pronouns as being closely related semantically to anaphoric the-phrases is virtually the same as Paul M. Postal's old suggestion "that the so-called pronouns *I*, *our*, *they*, etc., are really articles, in fact types of definite articles" (Postal 1969, p. 203). What GTS does for us here is to offer a way of implementing this idea in explicit detail.

We do not propose to deal with plural pronouns explicitly in this work. The reason is that their peculiarities, over and above those aspects of their semantical behavior that they share with singular pronouns, are connected with the general problem of the plural, and would hence take us beyond the scope of this book. Many of the differences between singular and plural pronouns can nevertheless seen to ensue from the fact that plural pronouns involve (in game-theoretical terms) the choice of a "class" of individuals rather than of a single one (see Hintikka and Carlson 1979; Hintikka and Kulas 1983, chap. 3; Carlson 1982).

As illustrations of our rules, let us consider some examples. Take, first, the sentence

(12)   A former basketball player entered politics, and
            eventually he became a U.S. Senator.

It turns out that we can here disregard, for our present purposes, all questions of tense and temporal particles, such as "eventually". If we do so, the first rule applicable is obviously (G. a(n)). It yields a sentence of the following form

(13)   Bill entered politics, and eventually he became a
         U.S. Senator. Bill is a former basketball player.

In applying (G. he) to the first sentence of (13), we have
/ = {Bill}.   The next sentences to be considered in the
game are therefore

(14)   Bill entered politics, and eventually Bill became a
         U.S. Senator. Bill is a male.

This indicates how our rules work. A case in which they
don't is the following:

(15)   Three men were walking down the street. Sud-
         denly he stopped.

Here an application of a game rule may yield the following:

(16)   Tom, Dick, and Harry were walking down the
         street. Tom, Dick, and Harry are men. Sud-
         denly he stopped.

Here it is blatant that Nature can win no matter what is
done by Myself in applying (G. he). For I = {Tom, Dick,
Harry}, and whichever of them is chosen, Nature can
choose a different member of / of whom Myself cannot show
that he is not a male. Because the resulting falsity of (16)
can be seen plainly from its form, there is no point for using it for any serious purpose.   Hence it is normally
deemed unacceptable (cf. here Part I, sec. 12, above).
     In contrast to (16), notice that the pair of sentences

(17)   Gail and Billie were walking down the street.
         Suddenly he stopped.

is acceptable, and carries the implication that one and only
one member of the pair {Gail, Billie} is male.   This is
clearly predicted by our treatment of "he".   For Myself has
a winning strategy in the game connected with (17) only if
precisely one of the two is male.
     It is perhaps worth pointing out also that for us there
is no problem in our approach about crossing anaphora.
For consider the sentence

(18)   A boy who was fooling her kissed a girl who
            loved him.

A pair of applications of (G. a(n)) can yield a sentence of
the following form:

(19)   Thomas kissed Thomasina, Thomas is a boy,
            Thomas was fooling her, Thomasina loved him,
            and Thomasina is a girl.

Here I = {Thomas, Thomasina}, and the rules (G. he) and
(G. she) apply without further ado in the expected way.

6. What is the Logic of Anaphoric Pronouns?

One way of describing our line of thought in this work is
to consider the question, What is the right logical model for
anaphoric pronouns? Among other things, we consider it a
serious mistake to try to assimilate the semantical modus
operandi of anaphoric pronouns to that of bound variables
of quantification theory. This assimilation should appear to
an unbiased observer extremely unlikely a priori because of
the absence of explicit syntactical ties between quantifier
phrases and the "variables" allegedly bound to them, and
because of the absence of scope indicators in natural languages. Indeed, the assimilation appears to be due almost
completely to the historical accident that quantification
theory happens to be a popular and easily accessible source
of models for explicit semantics.
        If a model is sought for anaphoric pronouns from log-
ic, our diagnosis is that their behavior is essentially like
that of independent choice terms such as Hilbert's
epsilon-terms. Like epsilon-terms, the reference of each
anaphoric pronoun has to be determined independently,
perhaps not always independently of the evaluation of other
anaphoric pronouns, but certainly by an operation different
from the determination of the reference of any syntatically
determined "head" or "antecedent". Unlike epsilon-terms,
their values are not selected from the universe of discourse
at large, but from a choice set I, which is determined mainly by what has happened earlier in a semantical game. Potential syntactical antecedents come into play only as
contributing their references to the set I.

It is not hard to convince the reader that anaphoric *the*-phrases behave in this way. After all, Russellian definite descriptions behave very much like epsilon-terms, and anaphoric descriptions differ from Russellian ones only in that the choices are made from a set that is determined by the past history of the semantical game in question – at least, this is what our theory maintains. And, in the case of anaphoric *the*-phrases, this analysis is at least in its main features so natural as to seem almost trivial. Hence, one indirect way in which we can support our diagnosis of the semantics of anaphoric pronouns is to show that they behave in essentially the same way as anaphoric *the*-phrases. Such will be our strategy in the next few sections of this work. Even though the evidence obtainable in this way is indirect, it seems to be quite telling. We shall argue, moreover, that the differences between anaphoric pronouns and anaphoric *the*-phrases are explicable in terms of the differences between the semantical game rules for the two.

7. Different Kinds of Pronouns

One particular way in which we can use the analogy between anaphoric *the*-phrases and pronouns is the following. Somewhat in the same way as nonanaphoric uses of descriptions can be obtained by changing the definition of the choice set I in the rule (G. anaphoric the), as was shown above in Part II of this work, we can obtain rules for different kinds of pronouns. Even though we are not in this work interested primarily in nonanaphoric uses of pronouns, it is important to place them into a more general perspective.

For the purposes of generalization, let us note first that a generalization to discourse is already present in the rule (G. he) and in related rules presented above. For the earlier subgames mentioned in (G. he) need not be connected with another clause in the very sentence that contains the pronoun, but can be introduced by earlier sentences in the same discourse.

Furthermore, just as we allow contextually prominent individuals (individuals identified by acquaintance) into I when we semantically evaluate *the*-phrases, we can extend the game rules for pronouns to allow us to deal with deictic and not just anaphoric pronouns. The remarkable thing about this extension is that it does not involve any other changes in our game rules. The only difference between the two kinds of pronouns is the way their values happened to enter into the choice set I.

Thus it can be seen already at this stage of our discussion how the different uses of pronouns can have as much in common as they in fact have. If the game rules for pronouns have roughly the form we have given them, then the only influence of other parts of the sentence in question on the interpretation of an anaphoric pronoun takes place through a contribution of a member to the choice set I. Now other members of I can be contributed by the discourse environment of the sentence in question and even by the nonlinguistic environment in which the sentence is uttered. It is seen that, in a sense, that will not make any difference to the operation of a pronoun (if it can be handled by means of suitably extended forms of our game rules). For the only thing that matters when a pronoun is treated in game-theoretical semantics is the choice set I, not the way it comes about. Even though we shall not systematically study nonanaphoric pronouns (e.g., deictic ones) in this work, the basic ideas of our theory of anaphoric pronouns are obviously not only extendible to such other pronouns, but extendible without major changes.

Here we can also see in its main features what constitutes the difference between anaphoric and deictic pronouns. In the case of anaphoric pronouns, the member of the set I whose choice is required by the winning strategy is contributed by an application of a game rule to an expression in the same sentence. In the case of a deictic pronoun, the critical member of I is contributed by the nonlinguistic context. As an intermediate case, we have a situation in which the operative member of I is contributed by the discourse context of the sentence in which the pronoun occurs. (It is instructive to see that there is a considerable confusion in the literature whether these should be classified as instances of anaphoric or deictic pronouns.) The similarity in the semantical behavior of the three is due to the fact that the semantical mechanism is the same in all three cases in that all that a pronoun involves is a pair of correlated choices from the set I, independently of how I is determined.

This is illustrated by parallel examples involving, on the one hand, *the*-phrases and, on the other hand, pronouns. If I want to warn an animal trainer in a circus, I can shout to her, either

(20)   Watch out for the tiger!

or

(21)   Watch out for him!

The same basic identity of different uses of pronouns is further illustrated by the fact that in most cases it is impossible to tell from the syntactical form of a sentence alone where the members of the relevant set *I* came from. (For this point, see secs. 18 and 28 below.)   These re- marks help to explain the fundamental unity of the semanti- cal behavior of pronouns.

The basic similarity between anaphoric and deictic pro- nouns is seen from examples where the same expression functions deictically for one speaker in discourse and anaphorically for another.   The following example involves definite descriptions rather than pronouns, but that does not make any essential difference to the phenomenon in question.   Mr. George Manciple is telephoning Sir John Adamson, Chief Constable of Fenshire:

(22)   "Sorry to bother you at this hour, John," said
           Manciple.   "It's about this fellow Mason.   I'm
           afraid there's nothing for it this time.   You'll
           have to call in Scotland Yard."
           Sir John made a great effort to remain calm. . .
           "I don't know what he has done to annoy you this
           time, but it's after six on Friday evening. . . .
           Monday will be quite soon enough to. . . "
           Manciple sounded bewildered.   "You're surely not
           suggesting that I do nothing until Monday?"
           "I'm suggesting precisely that."
           "But my dear John, what am I to do with the
           body?   I can't keep it here until Monday.   Violet
           wouldn't like it. . . . "
           "*The* body?   What are you talking about?   Whose
           body?"
           "Mason's of course.   Haven't you been listening,
           John? . . . "

> (Patricia Moyes, *Murder Fantastical*, Rinehart,
> Holt and Winston, New York, 1984, p. 8;
> emphasis added.)

Here "the body" is given deictically to Mr. Manciple and
but not even anaphorically to Sir John, even though George
mistakenly thinks so.

A different kind of difference between different pronouns nevertheless necessitates a restriction on the choice
set *I* involved in a rule like (G. he). It is that individuals
used earlier in the game as values of personal pronouns in
other persons, i.e., in the first place "I" and "you", are
excluded from the set *I* presupposed in (G. he); and similarly for other cases. This restriction is of course entirely
natural. It is illustrated by examples like the following:

(23)   I lent your book to John, but he failed to return
            it.

Without the restriction, there would be three members available in *I*: I, you, and John. But of course "he" in (23)
can only refer to John.

8. Consequences of the Rules

The rules formulated in sec. 5 enable us to handle a number of phenomena of different kinds. In accordance with
the strategy explained in sec. 6, our exploration of these
phenomena will largely be guided by the analogous phenomena in the field of anaphoric *the*-phrases. Indeed, a large
number of observations can simply be extended from
anaphoric definite descriptions to anaphoric pronouns (cf.
Part II above). The following is a list of some of the relevant phenomena, with examples parallelling the corresponding examples in terms of *the*-phrases:

(i) The apparent head of an anaphoric pronoun may
specify a set of individuals instead of a single one. Then
the gender clause in (8) and its analogues will have to enforce the uniqueness requirement tacit in (G. he).
Examples:

(24)   A couple was sitting on a bench. He stood up
            and she followed his example.

(25)   A couple was sitting on a bench. The man stood
              up and the woman followed his example.

     (ii) Personal pronouns can be used to make attribu-
tions of gender (where the head does not make them).

(26)   The teacher addressed he girls. He was stern.

This, too, is analogous with what anaphoric definite descriptions can do:

(27)   The teacher addressed the girls. The man was
              stern.

     (iii) Pronouns whose head is a quantifier phrase can
be handled as in Hintikka and Carlson 1979). Examples:

(28)   If Bill owns a donkey, he beats it.
(29)   If Bill owns a donkey, he beats the donkey.
(30)   *If Bill owns every donkey, he beats it.
(31)   *If Bill owns every donkey, he beats the donkey.

How such examples can be handled by means of the
subgame idea was indicated in Part I above. Combined with
the Hintikka–Carlson treatment, we obtain the right semantics for (28)–(31). This is remarkable, for it fills completely the gap that was left in the original paper by
Hintikka and Carlson. (They did not give any precise
rules for how pronouns were to be handled semantically.)
By removing this flaw from their old paper, we can now
vindicate their approach. For instance, their treatment
shows why (30)–(31) are unacceptable.

     (iv) On the reading dealt with in Hintikka and
Carlson, in (28) the indefinite article "a" has the surface
force of a universal quantifier. In other words, (28) is
construed as being equivalent to

(32) $(Ax)[(x$ is a donkey $\&$ Bill owns $x)$ $\rightarrow$ Bill
              beats $x]$.

     The Carlson–Hintikka explanation of how this surface
force comes about is analogous to the treatment of related
sentences that have a *the*-phrase instead of a pronoun. An

explicit argument to this effect will depend on the division of semantical games into subgames. (For this notion, see Part I, sec. 6.) In outline, it might run as follows:

In the subgame connected with the antecedent of (28), players switch roles. The play goes on only if the verifier, who after the switch is Nature, wins the first subgame (even if Myself knows her strategy). In the second subgame, the verifier's (here: Nature's) strategy is "remembered" from the first subgame. This is an instance of clause (iii) in the definition of the choice set I given in sec. 4 above. In the particular game in question, the strategy consists of a choice of an individual whose name is to be substituted for "a donkey". Suppose that this individual is Jenny. Then the second sentence to be considered in the first subgame is

(33)   Bill owns Jenny, and Jenny is a donkey.

The play moves on to the second subgame only if Nature wins the game connected with (33), i.e., only if Jenny is a donkey owned by Bill.

Then this individual (Jenny) is available to Myself in the second subgame, i.e., it is a member of the set I when (G. it) is applied to "it" in the second subgame. This is because the choice of Jenny is the verificatory strategy that is "remembered" by Myself from the earlier subgame. Hence, Jenny is in I because of the clause (iii) of the definition of I. (Not because of (i)-(ii)!) Indeed, I = {Jenny}. Hence the "value" of "it" is Jenny by (G. it). (Furthermore, the "value", i.e., the individual chosen in the game rule applied to it, of "he" is Bill, according to clause (ii) of the definition of I.) Thus Myself wins the second subgame and hence the overall game only if it is true that

(34)   Bill beats Jenny.

Myself has a winning strategy in the overall game connected with (28) if and only if the analogue to (34) is true for all the donkeys owned by Bill that Nature might have chosen in the first subgame. Since the existence of such a strategy is what the truth (28) amounts to, the indefinite article in (28) functions as if it were a universal quantifier. This lends (28) the force it is in fact has on its preferred reading.

The Hintikka-Carlson treatment of sentences like (28) is also easily supplemented to show why sentences like (28) can have another reading on which it has the force of

(35)   (Ex)(x is a donkey & Bill owns x) →
            (Ex)(x is a donkey & Bill owns x & Bill beats x).

All we have to do is to understand "if" as an Austinian "if" of polite uncertainty ("My name is John Doe, if you remember") rather than as a genuinely conditional "if".
        This kind of reading is perhaps more natural for other sentences. For instance, consider the following:

(36)   If a dart was fired, it ought to have been found. It wasn't.   (V. C. Clinton-Baddeley, *Death's Bright Dart*, Dell Books, N.Y., 1982, p. 107.)

This obviously speaks of one (possible) dart, not of what is true of each and every dart.
        (v) The same treatment can be extended to those more complex cases in which strategies in earlier subgames are represented by functions and not just by (selections of) individuals. Examples: [2]

(37)   If you extend an invitation to every friend of yours, someone will disregard it.
(38)   If you extend an invitation to every friend of yours, someone will disregard the invitation.

In other words, the strategy that is carried over from the first subgame to the second does not consist simply of the choice of a single individual, as in the game connected with (28).   After Myself has chosen in the second subgame a value for "someone," say Tom, the invitation extended to Tom is available to the players (in accordance with clause (iii) of the definition of *I* above in sec. 4) as a value of the "remembered" function applied to Tom.   The function has to yield such an invitation as a value, because otherwise it would not codify a winning strategy in the first subgame for the verifier of "you extend an invitation to every friend of yours", which is a necessary condition for the players to have moved on to play the second subgame in the first place.   This illustrates the way in which the closure condition (iii) of the definition of the choice set *I* (sec. 4 above) operates.

(vi) The same treatment extends to cases where the choice by Myself in the antecedent is governed by a disjunction and not by an existential quantifier. Examples:

(39.)   If Stewart buys a car or a motorcycle, he will take good care of it.
(40)   If Stewart buys a car or a motorcycle, he will take good care of the vehicle.
(41)   *If Stewart buys a car and a motorcycle, he will take good care of it.
(42)   *If Stewart buys a car and a motorcycle, he will take good care of the vehicle.

The behavior of anaphora in (39)-(40) illustrates the vagaries of the alleged head-pronoun relation. What is the head of "it" supposed to be in (39)? Why doesn't the same expression serve as a perfectly respectable head in (41) and hence make it an acceptable sentence?

(vii) This uselessnes of the usual concept of head is confirmed further by examples where the use of a pronoun serves to convey information about the subject matter at hand via the uniqueness requirement included in (G. he) and (G. she). Examples:

(43)   Yes, there certainly is night life in Jerusalem. Unfortunately, this weekend she is in Tel-Aviv.
(44)   Yes, there certainly is night life in Jerusalem. Unfortunately, this weekend the lady is in Tel-Aviv.

Here the uniqueness requirement that is built into (G. she) (as well as into (G. anaphoric the)) brings it about that (43)-(44) cannot be true unless the night life in Jerusalem consists in the activities of one lady. Of course, this just what (43)-(44) serve to convey.

(viii) As is already illustrated by several of the examples above, to be dealt with by means of the subgame idea, our suggested treatment of anaphoric pronouns is automatically extended to discourse beyond the boundaries of individual sentences.

This need of resorting to examples involving several sentences is sometimes very real indeed, for pronouns occurring in the same sentence as their "heads" are subject to additional restrictions.

(ix) An additional parallelism between the-phrases and pronouns can be observed in the case of the deictic (demonstrative) uses of definite descriptions (see Part II above, sec. 12). Not only is there an etymological connection between the definite article "the" and demonstratives. There is a similar etymological connection between pronouns and demonstratives. In fact, the definite article in Old English could be used as a pronoun. Consider this quote from a fairly recent grammar of Old English:

> The definite article, of which the masculine nominative form is "se", has two uses; it is either a definite article or a demonstrative. For example, "se stan" means either "the stone" or "that stone". When, as is usually the case, it modifies a noun, it agrees with that noun in gender, number, and case. It may also, however, be used as a pronoun, and when so used it agrees with its antecedent in gender and number, but has the case which is demanded by its construction in the sentence. For example, Ic seah done monn in dam delde; se is god beow; I saw the man in the field: he (or that man) is a good servant (Moore and Knott 1965, pp. 19-20).

Furthermore, the differences between the semantical behavior of anaphoric pronouns and anaphoric *the*-phrases can be explained by reference to the differences between our game rules for the two. By and large, they are due to the fact that anaphoric definite descriptions rely more on the properties of the individuals in questions, whereas pronouns only, as it were, locate their references within a much wider class of entities, sometimes merely an entire category. Thus we can say, e.g.,

(45)   A tinker and a tailor were sitting in a pub. The tinker ordered a lager and the tailor a pint of dark.

However, it is harder to make the same distinction between the two individuals by means of pronouns, so as to say, e.g.,

(46)   A tinker and a tailor were sitting in a pub. He
            ordered a lager and he a pint of dark.

Even though sentences of the syntactical form exemplified in
(46) are in principle interpretable and hence acceptable,
this fact is to some extent clouded by certain subordinate
phenomena, including the possible coordination of applications of (G. he) to be discussed in sec. 12 and the strategic meaning to be discussed in sec. 17 below. We shall
return to these issues later. Notice, interestingly, that an
utterance of (46) makes perfect sense if each "he" is accompanied by a pointing gesture.
        Conversely, when the "head" of an anaphoric expres-
sion (in the secondary sense in which we can speak of
heads of pronouns, cf. sec. 20 below) has little descriptive
content, anaphoric pronouns tend for the same reason to be
more natural. This may be the case when the "head" is a
quantifier word ranging over an entire category (or
equivalent):

(47)   Tom is in love with someone. She is blond.
(48)   Tom is in love with someone. The heiress is
            blond.

This regularity is only a preferential one, however, not
black-and-white. It is explained by the differences in the
game rules for the two kinds of expressions.

9. Subgames and Discourse Anaphora

The way in which our observations can be extended to discourse deserves a few remarks and examples. The basic
idea is simplicity itself. The subsequent sentences in a
segment of discourse are thought of as giving rise to
subgames that are then combined into an overall
"supergame". Hence the whole analysis that we have carried out in terms of subgames can be extended mutatis
mutandis to discourse.
        In doing so, however, we must specify when strategies
from earlier subgames are in fact "remembered" in later
ones. Clause (iii) of the definition of *I* in sec. 4 above assumes that such a determination has already been made,
and relies on it.

This is not much of a difficulty, however, in most
cases.   In the simplest case, subsequent sentences in a
discourse can be thought of as being related to each other
conjunctively.   Then the conditions of transfer are obvious.
In the game $G(S_1$ and $S_2)$ connected with the conjunction
"S_1 and S_2", clearly the subgame $G(S_1)$ is first played
(with the normal roles of the two players).   Only if Myself
wins, i.e., only if sentence S_1 is verified, do the players
go on to play the second subgame $G(S_2)$.   In that second
subgame, the strategy of the verifier (Myself) used in
$G(S_1)$ is "remembered".   The same goes then for two
adjacent sentences in a discourse when they can be thought
of as being conjunctively combined.
    Here is an example of the resulting anaphora:

(49)   Every tourist was offered a free souvenir.   One
              young man refused it.

Here Myself's strategy correlates an object with each tourist.   The strategy is a winning one and hence enables the
players to move to the second subgame only if that object is
in each case a free souvenir offered to that tourist.   That
strategy is available to the players in the second subgame
$G($One young man refused it$)$.   Applied to Myself's choice
of a young man, that strategy function yields the souvenir
he was offered as a value.   Myself can win the second
subgame only if there is a young man who did refuse his
souvenir.   This lends the right force to (49).
    Notice that this line of thought can be carried out only
if the young man in question was one of the tourists.   For
only then does the remembered strategy function assign to
him a sovenir as a value.   This is in fact as things ought
to be: If the gentleman in question were not one of the
tourists, (49) would not make sense, which is why we
spontaneously make this assumption in interpreting (49).
(This phenomenon was first pointed out to us by Lauri
Carlson.)
    Notice the difference between the transfer of strategies
in conditionals and in conjunctions.   If we are dealing with
the conditional "If S_1, S_2", then the strategies Nature used
in $G(S_1)$ are "remembered" in $G(S_2)$.   If we are dealing
with the conjunction $(S_1$ and $S_2)$, it is Myself's strategies
in $G(S_1)$ that are "remembered" in $G(S_2)$.
    Thus Nature's strategies in the first subgame of a
conjunctive game are not remembered in the second one.

This is why expressions like the following are not interpretable, unless the value of "it" is given to us by the
context:

(50)   Some tourist was offered every souvenir in the
            shop. One young man refused it.

     From these observations a number of results follow for
the conditions on which anaphora is or is not possible in
discourse. For instance, it follows that if a conditional occurs in discourse, the strategy used to verify its antecedent is not "remembred" in later sentences of the
discourse. For instance the following is uninterpretable
(except in a suitable wider context):

(51)   If Bill owns a donkey, he beats it. It has to be
            taken to the vet.

This is the case because the two sentences in (51) are conjunctively related to each other. Therefore only the strategies Myself used in the game on the conditional can be
carried over to the last subgame G(It has to be taken to
the vet). But the strategy that gave us a particular donkey to be pronominalized was Nature's strategy. Hence no
particular donkey is available as a member of I in the last
subgame of (51). Hence (51) is not acceptable.
     The vagaries of the conditions on which earlier choices
of individuals are "remembered" (i.e., included in the
choice set I) in our semantical games are illustrated by the
fact that sometimes Nature's choice is "remembered" in the
second sentantial game in a pair of sentences like (51).
Then the example becomes interpretable independently of
the context, and predictably assumes a kind of "generic"
character. (The antecedent of the first sentence so to
speak logically governs both sentences.) The following is a
case in point:

(52)   Whenever Bill buys a donkey, he soon has to sell
            it again.   It never fetches the same price,
            however.

     It can also be seen why the following kinds of sen-
tences are acceptable, even though the possibility of
anaphora in them does not reduce to the kind of anaphora
in conditionals illustrated by (16):

(53)   Some farmer who owns a donkey beats it.

This may be compared with

(54)   Every farmer who owns a donkey beats it.

An application of (G. every) to (54) (with an appropriate order of clauses in the output) yields a sentence of the form of

(55)   If Bill is a farmer and Bill owns a donkey, Bill beats it.

Thus we are back in a situation very much like (28).

In contrast, an application of (G. some) to (53) yields something like

(56)   Bill beats it, Bill is a farmer and Bill owns a donkey.

If the order of clauses is reversed, as the players are allowed to do, we have

(57)   Bill is a farmer, Bill owns a donkey, and Bill beats it.

The possibility of anaphora here is not explainable by reference to the subgame structure generated by a conditional sentence. It is explainable, however, by reference to the subgame structure associated by a conjunction or by two conjunctively connected sentence in discourse. Such an explanation also shows why the indefinite article "a" acts as an existential quantifier in (53) whereas it apparently has the force of a universal quantifier in (54).

It is not the case that all sentences in discourse can be thought of as being conjunctively connected. Studying when this is not possible and what the other alternatives are belongs to the task of discourse semantics.

As an example, let us consider here one case. That is constituted by wh-questions containing an indefinite article, e.g.,

(58)   Whose advice should a young mother trust?

This can prompt the reply:

(59)   She should trust her mother's advice.

What makes anaphora possible in (59)? And why should the indefinite article "a" in (58) have the force of a universal quantifier? Clearly, we are not dealing here with conjunctively connected utterances. Without delving too deeply into the theory of questions and answers, it is reasonably clear that the utterer of the question (58) and the answerer who provides the reply are in some sense opponents. Hence, for the defender of the answer (59), the value of "a young mother" in the question (58) is selected by his or her opponent, whose strategy is remembered in the game connected with the answer (59). The availability of this strategy, which here reduces to the choice of a young mother, provides a value for the pronouns "she" and "her" in the answer (59). The verifier of the answer wins if he or she can win the game connected with the answer against every such opposing strategy. This explains why the indefinite article "a" in (58) has the surface force of a universal quantifier. Indeed, if we replace the question (58) by

(60)   Whose advice should every young mother trust?

the expected answers are likely to be of the form

(61)   Every young mother should trust Dr. Spock's
              advice.

This is because the strategy that governs the treatment of "every" will not be carried over to the subgame connected with the answer if "every" is assumed to have the widest scope in (60). Hence it must be interpreted as having narrow scope, which yields the right reading of the question.
     Thus our theory helps to explain a large number of phenomena in connection with discourse anaphora and other aspects of discourse. These applications also illustrate what effects the different clauses in the definition of *I* (sec. 4 above) have.

10. The Nature of Anaphoric Pronouns and the Concepts of Sentence and Scope

Our theory does not only illuminate particular phenomena; it also throws light on many general theoretical issues and concepts.   Here we shall consider two of them, viz., the concepts of "sentence" and "scope".

Our starting point is the following observation: Especially in the case of discourse anaphora, construing anaphoric pronouns as free terms (see sec. 6 above) is virtually necessitated by certain general facts about language and about discourse. Discourse can be divided in sentences.   What does this division mean logically and semantically? The intuitive answer is clear, but its implementation in explicit formal semantics is much less obvious.   Each sentence is supposed to be an independent unit of discourse, and this idea can scarcely be interpreted otherwise than as a requirement that each sentence must in some sense be capable of being interpreted in its own right.   Since the basis of the semantical interpretation of a sentence is the semantical game connected with it, it follows that each sentence of a discourse must have a self-contained subgame associated with it.   The main exception to this sentence-by-sentence interpretability is obviously discourse anaphora. Hence the question concerning the nature of sentences as units of discourse depends on the treatment of anaphoric pronouns. If anaphoric pronouns were, logically speaking, like quantified variables, sentences could not be independent units.   For, as we have mentioned before, the "scope" of a quantifier phrase Q could then comprise the whole subsequent discourse. If Q occurs in a sentence S, then the force of S depends on the entire discourse, if pronouns behave like variables.   The result is that a logician must construe the entire discourse as one big "sentence" containing Q.   For, for a logician, a sentence containing a quantifier must also contain the entire scope of the quantifier. In order for a sentence to be interpretable independently of the later parts of the discourse where it occurs, anaphoric pronouns therefore cannot behave like bound variables.

The same goes to some extent also for different clauses in the same overall sentence. There, too, different clauses are relatively self-contained semantically.   This implies, among other things, that the semantical interpretation of a sentence (or a clause) should depend on earlier ones only through the values of anaphoric pronouns. As a consequence, rules of semantical interpretation for pronouns must not turn them into bound variables but must treat them as independently interpretable terms.

A completely self-contained semantics for each sentence and for each clause is nevertheless a chimera. However, one of the virtues of game-theoretical semantics is that it can show what the inevitable residual interplay must be like. It is not the kind of interplay that binds pronouns to their "heads", but of the kind that enables the players to "remember" some of their earlier strategies. This is a different kind of interdependence from the one created by "binding" a pronoun to its antecedent. Occasionally, the two kinds of dependence yield the same result. This is the case when the "remembered" strategy consists of the choice of a single individual. Then the carryover of a strategy has the same effect as binding. This special case has undoubtedly encouraged semanticists to think that what is involved in all cases of anaphoric pronouns is quantificational binding. It is, nevertheless, from a general theoretical perspective, only a very special and not particularly representative case.

One consequence of this way of treating discourse anaphora (as well as anaphora between different clauses in the same sentence) is that there is after all a fundamental difference between different kinds of anaphora. Even though there is not the kind of difference between intrasentential anaphora and discourse anaphora as has been generally assumed recently, there is a difference between the way anaphora works within a sentence where no subgames are involved and the way it works from one clause or sentence to another when they give rise to different subgames. This difference is that, while what is "remembered" within one and the same subgame are the individuals chosen, what is "remembered" from other subgames are strictly speaking only strategies of choice, not individuals chosen, subject to an exception for proper names. The cases where these two come down to the same thing are, as was just noted, of the nature of special cases unrepresentative of the general theoretical situation.

This is illustrated by some familiar examples:

(62)   If Bill dates a girl, he sends her flowers.

(63)   If Bill dates a girl, he is pleased with himself.
(64)   If you offer a job to every boy, some boy will re-
              fuse it.

In (63) "a" is clearly just an existential quantifier. However, in (62) we cannot take "her" to be a quantificational
variable bound to "a girl", according to what has been
said. Instead, it is the "remembered" strategy that enables
a player to pick out the girl in question. But this has the
effect (as we have seen) of turning the surface force of the
quantifier in (62) into that of a universal one.

 Likewise, in (64) "it" is not like a variable "bound" to
some earlier quantifier. Its value is obtained by applying a
"remembered" function to the value of "some boy", i.e., to
the value of an expression in the same clause.

 Our treatment of anaphoric pronouns is thus tied
closely to the linguistic concept of sentence, and throws
some light on this concept. In particular, we can now see
more clearly in what sense (and to what extent) sentences
are independent semantical units.

 A partial codification of this idea of sentences and
clauses as independent units is the concept of a subgame
(cf. Part I, sec. 6). Since the rules of the semantical
game G(S) connected with a sentence S are the basis of its
semantical evaluation, one's being able to play a (sub)game
on an expression E means that it can be evaluated semantically as an independent unit. Then the stipulations concerning what has to be known of earlier subgames define
the limits of the independence. In this sense, the concepts
of sentence (or clause) and subgame are very closely related to each other.

 With respect to the treatment of anaphoric pronouns as
independent terms, our theory differs essentially from that
of Hans Kamp (1981), with which it otherwise has points of
contact. Kamp is in effect reduced to the highly unnatural
procedure of considering segments of discourse as long
sentences. Apart from the unnaturalness of Kamp's procedure, it cannot even be applied to all types of discourse,
e.g., to question-answer dialogues. Here we have a clear
instance of the superiority of our theory over a closely related competitor.

 Here we can see a source of confusion in recent discussion. There are two entirely different ideas assimilated
to each other in the notion of scope, especially as it has
been used in connection with anaphoric pronouns. The

first one is the relative logical priority of different operators like quantifiers. If they are Q_1 and Q_2, then the
logical priority is reflected in GTS by the order in which
game rules are applied to Q_1 and Q_2.

The second idea that is in effect dealt with under the
heading of "scope" is the question of how long individuals
introduced into I by Q_1 and Q_2, can stay there – and must
stay there.

It is a presupposition of the usual quantificational notation that these two different senses of "scope" can both
be captured by the same notational device of bracketing.
What we have found shows that this assumption is unjusti-
fied. The two kinds of scope have to be dealt with separately, questions of logical priority by means of ordering
principles, and questions of membership in I by principles
governing the transfer of information available to players
from a subgame to later ones.

In a way, sentences like the "donkey sentence" (28)
serve to show the need of a distinction between the two
senses of "scope". For in (28), logically speaking, the
conditional is prior to the existential quantifier "a".
Hence, it has a wider "scope" in the first sense of the
term. Yet the value of "a donkey" is available to Myself in
the subgame played with the consequent of (28). Hence
the scope of "a" in the second sense of the word (availability as a value of a pronoun) is wider than the antecedent
of the conditional, and can even extend beyond the entire
conditional. This phenomenon cannot be captured by means
of the conventional logical notation.

CHAPTER III

THE EXCLUSION PRINCIPLE

11. Partially Exclusive Interpretation Needed

As was noted in the second part of this book, both anaphorically used the-phrases and anaphoric pronouns are subject to an additional restriction. The tacit quantifiers governing the choice of b in (G. he) and (G. anaphoric the) have to be understood as being partially exclusive (cf. Hintikka 1973, chap. 1). More precisely, the choice of b in (G. he) (and in (G. anaphoric the)) must be restricted by excluding all individuals whose proper names, interpreted by having had (G. name) applied to them, occur in the same clause as (i.e., are, syntactically speaking, dominated by precisely the same S-nodes as) the pronoun (or the definite description) to which a game rule is being applied, at the stage of the game when a rule is applied to it. This general principle – we shall call it the "Exclusion Principle" – can be generalized to cover expressions other than pronouns that are evaluated by applying some game rule to them. It is illustrated in the case of pronouns by the following examples:

(65)   Jimmy doubted him.
(66)   Jimmy doubted that he could do that.
(67)   Every company commander received the battle order from him.
(68)   Every company commander received the battle order.
         He acknowledged it immediately.
(69)   Some girl pitied her.
(70)   Some girl pitied Susan, who was thankful to her.
(71)   Some girl pitied Susan, who was sorry for herself.

In (65), unlike (66), Jimmy cannot be referred to by the pronoun. In (67), in contrast to (68), the pronoun cannot pick out a company commander. In (70), but not in (69), "her" can be the pitier. In (70) Susan cannot be "her". If the speaker wants to allow the identity, a sentence like (71) must be used instead.

One phenomenon that the Exclusion Principle can explain is crossing anaphora in sentences where the same pronoun occurs in both relative clauses, as in

(72)   A boy who knew him watched a man who approached him.

Two applications of (G. a(n)) yield something like the following:

(73)   Peter watched Paul, Peter is a boy, Peter knew him, Paul is a man, and Paul approached him.

Because of the Exclusion Principle, "him" can refer only to Paul in the third clause and only to Peter in the last one. This clearly assigns to (72) the meaning it actually has.

It is worth emphasizing how natural the Exclusion Principle is, if it is viewed semantically. For what is more natural – and easier for language users to enforce – than a principle that says that in the same clause (when dominated by the same S-nodes) different NPs should refer to different entities? Some kind of "one expression – one reference" idea fairly clearly seems to be incorporated in our intuitive semantics. What game-theoretical semantics does here is to spell out the sense of "reference" needed to carry out this idea explicitly.

Even though exclusion phenomena of the kind just discussed are often dealt with in the literature in connection with anaphora, the Exclusion Principle is a much more general phenomenon than mere anaphora. It governs, among other things, the selection of values of quantifier phrases. As was pointed out by Jaakko Hintikka as early as in 1956 (Hintikka 1956), in natural languages quantifiers normally take what he has called an exclusive interpretation. For instance, a sentence like

(74)   Clemenceau despises everyone

is naturally taken not to entail that Clemenceau despises himself. As Lauri Carlson has noted (private communication), this is also the reason why Quine's example

(75)   Everyone loves my baby, but my baby loves only me.

is ordinarily not taken to imply that I am identical with my baby.

Hence our game rules for quantifier phrases will have to be modified in a way similar to the way in which the Exclusion Principle leads as to modify rules like (G. he). It is easily seen how this modification can be carried out. What needs to be done is merely to omit from the range of choice of the player who is making the move all individuals serving as values of phrases that occur in the same clause (i.e., are dominated by the same S-nodes) as the quantifier phrase that prompts the move.

Since the exclusive interpretation of quantifiers can be formalized as easily as the inclusive one, the phenomena covered by it cannot be taken to illustrate differences between natural and formal languages, as some linguists have done (Bach and Partee 1980). This generality of the Exclusion Principle is illustrated by the fact that there are analogues for (65)-(68) for definite descriptions:

(76)   Jimmy doubted the president.
(77)   Jimmy doubted that the president could do that.
(78)   Every company commander received the battle order from the officer.
(79)   Every company commander received the battle order. The officer acknowledged it immediately.

This generality and independence of the Exclusion Principle from the specific principles that govern anaphora justify our treating it as a separate ingredient in the interpretation of anaphoric pronouns, independent of the particular rules that govern such pronouns. We shall return to the Exclusion Principle repeatedly in later sections.

What we are here calling the Exclusion Principle has sometimes been taken to be a special case of more widely applicable regularities concerning disjoint reference. This idea differs from our treatment, which is strictly restricted to occurrences of phrases in the same clause, for it is supposed to cover occurrences of phrases in different clauses. (For an example of ideas in this direction, see Chomsky 1981, p. 144, note 79.) We shall argue, however, that the Exclusion Principle is restricted to intraclausal occurrences and that the examples Chomsky and others have proposed of extraclausal exclusion can be explained by means of other factors (see sec. 32 below).

It is important to appreciate the precise import of the Exclusion Principle.   The individuals that are excluded by it from *I* are the references of (interpreted) proper names occurring in the same clause as the expression E to which a rule involving *I* is applied "at the time of this application". Values of expressions that at earlier stages of the game, including its input sentence, occur in the same clause as E are not necessarily excluded, provided that intervening rule applications have moved them to other clauses by the time a rule is applied to E.   We shall return to this fact in sec. 22 below.

12. Pecularities of Pronouns

So far anaphoric pronouns have been operating in analogy with anaphorically used *the*-phrases.   There are, neverthe-less, apparent differences between the two.   The exclusion phenomenon we noted above in sec. 11 is closely related to another one, which seems to be peculiar to pronouns.   It is the following: When (G. he) is applied, it may be applied to all the pronouns "he" ("him", "his", etc.) occurring in the same clause at the same time.   A different individual may be chosen by Myself from the relevant set *I* to serve as a value of each of them.   (In making these choices, the players must of course obey the Exclusion Principle.) Their names are plugged in for the respective pronouns. Thereupon Nature must try to choose yet another member of *I*, say d, and "but d is not male" is conjoined to the output sentence with respect to which the game is to be continued. Other rules, e.g., (G. she), are to be reformulated in the same way.

A separate investigation would be required to deter-mine how widely the possibility of a joint application of game rules to different pronouns is applicable.   Is it re-stricted to a single clause?   To a single sentence?   If it is applicable to larger segments of text than to a sentence, how long can admissible segments be?   We shall not discuss the details of these problems here, however.   (These are, in a sense, also scope problems, illustrating further the complexities of the customary notion of scope.)   The unproblematic cases already yield enough explanatory power for the purposes of our discussion.

For instance, consider the following sentence:

(80)   Susan met Mrs. Carstairs when bringing up the
              tea, whereupon she had some words with her.[3]

In dealing with the pronouns "she" and "her" the relevant
set *I* consists of Susan and Mrs. Carstairs, and no one
else.   If the players should try to deal with either pronoun
alone, the necessary uniqueness could not be satisfied, and
the sentence would be trivially false.   Obviously, the two
pronouns have to be dealt with together.   Since there are
no other females in *I*, the requisite uniqueness is now
obvious.

What happens then is that there are two ways in which
Myself can deal with (80).   They yield as output sentences

(81)   Susan met Mrs. Carstairs when bringing up the
              tea, whereupon Susan had some words with Mrs.
              Carstairs

or else,

(82)   Susan met Mrs. Carstairs when bringing up the
              tea, whereupon Mrs. Carstairs had some words
              with Susan.

The truth of (80) means that there exists a winning strategy in the correlated game for Myself.   In terms of the example, this works out as saying that either (81) or (82) is
true.   This is clearly the semantical force of (80).   On the
basis of grammatical facts alone there is no way of telling
which of the two is true, even if one knows that (80) is.
Factual considerations and conversational clues have to be
resorted to.   (Would the daughter of a mere butler dare to
have words with one of his lordship's invited guests?   Yes,
if she had been married in secret to his son, the heir of
Warbeck Hall.)

In sec. 17 below it will be shown how phenomena of
the kind we are dealing with here (e.g., the "ambiguity" of
(80)) can be accommodated more generally under the concept of strategic meaning.

Here it is seen especially clearly how irrelevant all
predetermined head-pronoun relations are for the actual
working of anaphoric pronouns.   In this respect, anaphoric
pronouns differ also sharply from the bound variables of
quantification theory.   Notice, in this respect, that the following sentence can be treated in the same way as (80):

(83)   Susan met one of the ladies when bringing up the
              tea, whereupon she had some words with her.

Here one of the members of *I* is introduced by a quantifier
phrase ("one of the ladies") rather than by a proper name.
Yet the treatment remains essentially the same.

A little more has to be said here, however. Our
treatment means construing a sentence as a disjunction if it
contains in the same clause several pronouns of the same
kind, e.g., several occurrences of "he", "him" or "his".
The different disjuncts are obtained from the different assignments of members of *I* as values of the pronouns. For
instance, (80) is construed in effect as a disjunction of
(81) and (82).

This is in one sense quite natural. After all, (80) is
a grammatical sentence that is true if (81) or (82) is.
However, if someone utters (80) the audience normally assumes that (81) or (82) is what the speaker "means" or
"has in mind". Consequently (80) is often said to be, not
disjunctive, but ambiguous.

It might be thought, however, that the assumption
that an utterer of a sentence like (80) "means" (81) or (82)
represents merely a conversational expectation that is not
part of the basic semantics. For instance, if the Delphic
Oracle had uttered a sentence that is "ambiguous" for the
same reason as (80), it would not make much sense to ask
which alternative was "intended". There is more to be said
here, however. The decision between (81) and (82) does
not belong to the kind of semantics we are dealing with in
this section, but it is nevertheless a legitimate semantical
problem that can be assigned its proper niche and otherwise
dealt with by game-theoretical semantics. We shall return
to this matter in sec. 17 below.

Because of the filtering out of some disjuncts, it would
perhaps be more appropriate to speak of coordinated applications of rules like (G.he) to all occurrences of the
appropriate pronouns ("he", "him", "his") in the same
clause than to speak of simultaneous application. Such coordinated applications are not unknown in other cases.
Jaakko Hintikka has shown how the applications of the game
rule for the past tense (it involves a choice of an earlier
moment of time) to different past-tense verbs in the same
sentence many either be condensed into one or coordinated
with each other (see Hintikka and Kulas 1983, chap. 5.)
The principles governing this coordination are in fact

similar to the ones governing the coordination of multiple applications of pronoun rules. For instance, in the same way as the order of the values of pronouns tends to reflect (other things being equal) the order of their potential "heads", in the same way the order of the past-tense verbs is sometimes used to reflect the temporal orders of the past momemt of time correlated with them. The former is illustrated by the greater naturalness, ceteris paribus, of (81) over (82) as capturing the force of (80). The latter is illustrated by pairs of examples like the following:

(84)   Bill fell ill, and took medicine.
(85)   Bill took medicine, and fell ill.

13. The Exclusion Principle and Reflexive Pronouns

In English, an anaphoric back reference of the kind ruled out by the Exclusion Principle (i.e., reference to an indi- vidual in a game by an expression in the same clause as the pronoun) is accomplished by means of reflexive pronouns. The game rule for a reflexive pronoun like "himself" is of course analogous to our game rule for "he" except for the definition of I. In the rule for reflexives, only such indi- viduals of the appropriate category are included in I as are referred to by proper names in the same clause as the reflexive pronoun in question at the time of the rule application. In other words, the choice set for reflexives is precisely the class of individuals ruled out by the Exclusion Principle from the old I involved in our rule for nonreflexive anaphoric pronouns in sec. 5 above.

One way of implementing all this is to have at each stage of a semantical game a choice set I determined in the way explained in sec. 4 above. This set I is partitioned into subsets according to whether its members are referred to by expressions in the same clause. (Of course, an allowance must also be made for members of I introduced by the nonlinguistic context.) In any application of a game rule depending on I, with the exception of the rules for re- flexives to an expression E whose value must come from I, the choice is restricted to partition classes different from the class – call it $i(E)$ – that corresponds to the clause in which E occurs, i.e., restricted to $I - i(E)$. In contrast, in rules for reflexives the choice is restricted to $i(E)$.

From this the following corollary ensues immediately:
A reflexive pronoun, say "himself", is acceptable, i.e., interpretable, only if the choice set i(himself) figuring in the
rule (G. himself) is not empty. For it not to be empty,
there must be proper names in the same clause at the time
of the application of the rule referring to certain individuals. One of them will be the value of "himself". The corresponding name is its "head" in the conventional sense.

What this means – what is implied by our game rule –
is, in the conventional jargon, that reflexive pronouns are
always pronominalized by a "head" in the same clause. We
cannot go to the wider context for the purpose of seeking
for the individuals they refer to.

This is in effect an account of one of the best-known
regularities governing reflexive pronouns, a regularity that
is usually expressed by saying that reflexive pronouns always have an anaphoric interpretation (cf., e.g., Wasow
1979, p. 26). We don't want to prejudice the issue whether the uses of nonreflexive pronouns that rely on the larger context should be distinguished terminologically from the
"anaphoric" pronouns that operate like reflexives. Subject
to this terminological qualification, however, we have accounted for this well-known fact.

Our account does not predict that the distribution of
reflexive and the corresponding nonreflexive pronouns
should be complementary. However, it seems to predict
that, e.g., "he" and "himself" occurring in the same place
in two otherwise similar sentences S_1 and S_2 cannot be
coreferential, for their values must come from mutually exclusive choice sets. Basically, we believe that this regularity holds in English, properly understood, even though
prima facie counterexamples to this generalization are known
from the literature.

In view of these apparent counterexamples, a general
remark is in order, which also throws interesting light on
the   Exclusion   Principle   itself,   and   shows   how
game-theoretical semantics allows for sharper formulations of
linguistic regularities than competing treatments.

In our theory, the Exclusion Principle comes into play
only when a game rule is applied to the operative expression. For instance, the question of what a given reflexive
pronoun can be coreferential with is determined by the set
I plus the clausemate relations at the time the appropriate
rule for reflexives is applied. These are not always shown
by the initial sentence of the semantical game in question,

as it is assumed to do in competing approaches, but depends also on what happens to the input sentence before
the reflexive pronoun is treated.   This means a large number of apparent counterexamples – that our approach allows
for simpler formulations of regularities for – obviously are
not genuine ones, and that others can be naturally treated
by analyzing the intervening rule applications.   In contrast, in the competing approaches, such seeming exceptions have to be accounted for by the sole means of the
structure of the input sentence, which is much more
difficult.

Prima facie counterexamples of this kind include a
number of apparent exceptions to the generalization that a
reflexive and the corresponding nonreflexive pronoun cannot occur in the same context and have the same reference.
They will be dealt with in sec. 23 below.   Other apparent
counterexamples will be dealt with later in sec. 25.   The
naturalness of these treatments is an argument for our
approach.

In virtue of the similarity between our rules for reflexives and for anaphoric pronouns, many of the same
points can be applied to them as have been applied to singular third-person pronouns above. Witness, e.g., the following examples:

(86)   Tom, Dick or Harry bought a bike for himself.
(87)   *Tom, Dick and Harry bought a bike for himself.

The unacceptability of (87) can be explained by considering the ordering principles that cover a rule for reflexive pronouns in relation of such rules as (G. or) and
(G. and).   Although "and" and "or" are syntactically on a
par, they are not completely analogous semantically.   In
particular, (G. or) may be applied before the rules for
anaphoric pronouns, while (G. and) must not.   Hence in
the game correlated with (87) there are three possible "antecedents" (members of I) when a game rule is applied to
"himself", making it trivially false (and hence anomalous).
In contrast, in dealing with (86) the players may first apply the rule for the phrasal "or", yielding a sentence like

(88)   Tom bought a bike for himself.

Here there is of course precisely one member in the relevant *I*. Hence the game rule for "himself" applies trivially,
making (86) acceptable.

We can also explain by means of the same (or similar)
assumptions why the following sentence is acceptable:

(89)   Tom, Dick, and Harry each bought a bike for
            himself.

"Each" marks Nature's move, and so does "and".   Why
should this duplication of commands make any difference?
It does because the game rule for "each" has priority over
the game rule for reflexives.   An application of the game
rule for "each" will again yield a sentence of the form (88).
As before, this means that the subsequent application of
the game rule for reflexives is nontrivial and that (88)
should therefore be acceptable, as is indeed the case.

For the same reason as applies to (89), the following
are acceptable sentences:

(90)   Tom, Dick and Harry each believed that he alone
            was suspected.
(91)   Each man believed that he alone was suspected.

The acceptability of e.g., (91) on this (context-independent) reading can be explained by the fact that (G.
each) precedes (G. believes) in (91).   This ordering is
prescribed both by the left-to-right order (see (O. LR) in
Part I, sec. 8 above, and sec. 20 below) and the ordering
principle for (G. each), which gives this rule the right of
way with respect to many of the other game rules.   Similar
remarks apply to (90).

Examples like (86) are interesting also for another reason.   They show how dangerous it is to speak of the
"heads" of anaphoric pronouns, reflexive or not.   Earlier in
this section, we said that a reflexive pronoun has a head in
the same clause with which it is coreferential.   This is not
true without qualifications, as (86) shows.   Which expression in (86) is the coreferential "head" of "himself"?   Not
"Tom", "Dick", or "Harry", for each one can fail to be
coreferential with "himself" even when (86) is true.   Not
"Tom, Dick or Harry" for this expression does not refer to
any one individual.   Of course, this does not mean that
there is anything wrong with our approach, only that the
results it yields are hard to formulate in the superficial

traditional terminology of "heads", "coreference", etc. More criticisms of these superficial concepts will be offered in secs. 19 and 20 below.

Moreover, when it is said that a reflexive pronoun has a "head" in the same clause, this does not mean that there is a syntactically determined unique expression in the same clause serving as such a head or antecedent. Examples to illustrate this underdeterminacy include the following:

(92)   The doctor told Nicholas certain important medical facts about his wife and himself.

Here "himself" can obviously refer either to Nicholas or to the doctor. The former reading is sometimes denied by grammarians. We don't find that actual usage supports such claims at all.

Witness also such examples as the following:

(93)   Shaw and Wells left the members of the Fabian Society angry with themselves.
(94)   John saw Mary and introduced himself to her.

Here the treatment of (94) will introduce "John" to (a descendant of) the elliptical second clause, e.g., by a suitable rule for the phrasal "and". The output sentence of such an application (by Nature, of course) will be either

(95)   John saw Mary

or

(96)   John introduced himself to her.

This shows why the reflexive pronoun "himself" is needed in (94): in (96) "John" and "himself" occur in the same clause. In contrast, no nonpronominal reference to Mary will appear in the second clause. Hence we have "her" instead of "herself".

It may also be of interest to consider here a sample sentence whose meaning is explained by our rules:

(97)   Only Ernest admires himself.

This clearly means something different from

(98)   Only Ernest admires Ernest.

Why?   An application of (G. only) to (97) gives rise to a
sentence of the form

(99)   Ernest admires himself, but Scot does not admire
            himself.

Here "Scot" and "himself" are in the same sentence and
hence must refer to the same individual.   In contrast to
this, an application of (G. only) to (98) yields a sentence
of the form

(100)   Ernest admires Ernest, but Scot doesn't admire
            Ernest.

Hence (97) cannot have (98) as one of its readings.   This
explains the meaning (97) in fact has.
       Additional examples can easily be found to illustrate
the explanatory power of the exclusion principle.   Here are
a few instructive ones:

(101)   John asked Mary to shave him.
(102)   *John asked Mary to shave himself.
(103)   John promised Mary to shave him.
(104)   John promised Mary to shave himself.

In (101), "John" and "him" can be coreferential, but not in
(102).   The difference between (101)-(102) and (103)-(104)
lies in a semantical difference between "ask" and "promise".
A suitable game rule for "ask" might take us from (101) to

(105)   Mary shaves him

while a rule for "promise" would take us from (103) to

(106)   John shaves him.

Because of the Exclusion Principle, "him" can be
coreferential with "John" in (105) but not in (106).
       By reference to the behavior of reflexive pronouns we
can clarify further the nature of Exclusion Principle.   As it
has to be formulated, it says that any two different NPs in
the same clause, except for reflexive pronouns (plus a few
other exceptions that we shall not discuss here), must refer

to different objects.   Thus formulated, the principle does
not say anything of different occurrences of one and the
same NP in the same clause.   It is sometimes thought that
the Exclusion Principle must be extended to occurrences of
the same NP in one and the same clause, in that they are
not admissible unless the two occurrences refer for some
reason to different objects.   This is not the case, however,
as is shown by the following pair of examples due to
McCawley (1970, unpublished),

(107)   Only Lyndon pities Lyndon.
(108)   Only Lyndon pities himself.

Not only is the former acceptable.   It cannot be considered
as a mere stylistic variant of the latter, for the two mean
different things as was shown above.

14. The Exclusion Principle is Semantical in Nature

The Exclusion Principle introduced above in sec. 11 needs a
few additional comments.   As was mentioned there, it is essentially a special case of a more general regularity that
says that any two NPs occurring in the same clause (i.e.,
dominated by the same S-nodes) must refer to different individuals.   The same goes also for different occurrences of
the same NP in one and the same clause.
     One interesting point about this generalization of the
Exclusion Principle is that it speaks of the references of
different expressions (or of different occurrences of the
same expression) in the same clause.   In other words, it is
semantical in nature.   This can be confirmed by additional
evidence.   What our formulation implies is that there can be
two occurrences of one and the same nonreflexive pronoun
in the same clause, provided that they refer to different
individuals.   This is easily confirmed in the case of
third-person pronouns which often can have several referents.   That such a pronoun occurs instead of a reflexive
one thus is a guide to the intended reading.   This can be
seen, e.g., from the following examples:

(109)   Tom told Dick that he would have to shave him.
(110)   Tom told Dick that he would have to shave him-
           self.

This phenomenon is rarer with first-person pronouns, for there is normally only one person available for the role of "I" in any given speech situation. However, this uniqueness is not inevitable. For instance, the speaker or writer may be presenting a possible situation in which there are several counterparts to himself. We don't even need philosophers' and linguists' invented examples for the purpose of finding instances of such scenarios. Here is Robert B. Parker's sleuth Spenser watching the door of a hotel room with a gun in hand and considering what he would do if he were the bad guy trapped inside:

(111)   That's what I would do. Or would I? Maybe I'd dive out of the door and get an angle on me across the corridor, try to be too quick for the guy who's been standing there hypnotized by staring at the door. (*The Judas Goat*, Dell Books, 1983, p. 51.)

Notice that this would be turned into nonsense if "on me" would be replaced by "on myself". The use of the nonreflexive pronoun serves to indicate that Spenser is distinguishing from each other his two counterparts in the scenario he is considering.
     Thus there cannot be any syntactical rule forbidding the use of "I" (and/or "me") more than once in the same clause, as distinguished from "myself", as little as there is a rule forbidding the use of "he" (and/or "him") more than once in the same clause. In the latter case, all that happens is that different persons are picked out by the different occurrences of the pronoun:

(112)   He pointed the gun at him.
(113)   He pointed the gun at himself.

By the same token we cannot mark the first of the following sentences by an asterisk, i.e., consider it unacceptable:

(114)   I would point the gun at me.
(115)   I would point the gun at myself.

The only difference is that in the case of (114) it is harder than usual to think of a context in which "I" and "me" would have different references. However, the actual example we gave shows that this is in principle possible, e.g., in an imagined scenario.

Examples similar to (111) have occasionally been considered by linguists. Here is a case in point:

(116)   If I were you, I wouldn't marry me.

They have not been taken seriously, however, and have typically been dismissed as being somehow deviant or in some other way nongeneralizable. We don't find any valid reason for dismissing such examples, however. Dismissing them means merely falling prey to the fallacy of restricting in effect one's range of examples to conform to an a priori assumption.

Although these observations are fairly straightforward, they are not devoid of methodological implications. For instance, much of the evidence Chomsky marshals for his views on anaphora concerns reflexives. Now reflexives are used when coreference is impossible according to the Exclusion Principle. Hence, if the Exclusion Principle is semantical in nature, then so are the conditions on which reflexives are to be used. And if so, there are good reasons to think that the search for hard-and-fast syntactical criteria of admissibility (and necessity) of reflexives is going to be a wild-goose chase. No wonder, therefore, that much of the most recent discussion has been as inconclusive as it has.

If one tries to express this observation in the framework of generative syntax, one clearly will have to say that the reflexivization transformation is not obligatory, contrary to the views of many linguists. Moreover, there does not seem to be any hope whatsoever of capturing those cases in which reflexivization is obligatory (i.e., cases where two nonreflexive pronouns in the same clause cannot be coreferential) by means of any syntactical generalization. Such a possibility depends (as we have in effect seen) on the semantics of the sentence in question, which in turn depends on many things besides the syntactical form of the sentence, such as the lexical items it contains, semantical relations that don't effectively depend on its syntax, etc. We don't see any hope of maintaining that any reflexivization transformation is obligatory, in the unlikely event that such a transformation exists.

It is worth noting that our objection to the obligatoriness of reflexivization is different from the objections found, e.g., in Helke 1970. These objections will be discussed briefly below (see sec. 23); they pertain primarily to the behavior of prepositional phrases, not reflexives. We don't see that they are conclusive objections to the obligatory status of reflexivization.

If the use of reflexive pronouns is, syntactically speaking, optional, then even more so is the use of nonreflexive pronouns. Admittedly it has sometimes been claimed that in certain contexts the use of a pronoun is obligatory. It has sometimes been claimed that a similar principle applies more widely. For instance, it has been claimed that only the first of each pair of the following examples is acceptable:

(117)   What Lola wants, she gets.
(118)   What Lola wants, Lola gets.
(119)   Oscar is unhappy. He has discovered that no one admires him any longer.
(120)   Oscar is unhappy. He has discovered that no one admires Oscar any longer.

It is nevertheless unmistakable, in our opinion, that the difference between the two is merely stylistic. It is in fact easy to find a large number of examples from ordinary educated English prose violating the putative obligatoriness of pronouns.

It is here interesting to contrast (117)-(120) to the following examples, where we are dealing with genuine applications of the Exclusion Principle that justify the occurrence of the reflexive pronouns:

(121)   Oscar is unhappy. He no longer admires him.
(122)   Oscar is unhappy. He no longer admires Oscar.

Coreference is clearly impossible in (121)-(122), whereas we don't see that it is at all impossible in (120).

The semantical nature of the Exclusion Principle is important because, among other things, the regularities codified in it are essentially those governing reflexive pronouns. But if reflexive pronouns are governed by semantical principles, the prospects of the numerous recent attempts to formulate syntactical rules for the contexts in which they must be used appear rather dim.

CHAPTER IV

GENERAL THEORETICAL ISSUES

15. Anaphoric Pronouns and Quantifier Phrases

One of the accounts competing with ours assimilates anaphoric pronouns that have quantifier phrases as their antecedents to the bound variables of quantification theory. It is therefore in order to discuss such uses of anaphoric pronouns.

In many cases, our treatment and the bound-variable treatment yield the same result. Take, for instance, Evans's example of bound pronouns:

(123)   Every man loves his mother.

Here the first game rule to apply is (G. every), which yields a sentence of the form

(124)   Billie loves his mother if Billie is a man.

Here Billie is chosen by Nature.

When "his" is dealt with by means of (G. he), obviously the choice set $I = \{Billie\}$. Hence the force of (125) is on our interpretation

(125)   (Ax) (x is a man $\rightarrow$ x loves x's mother).

This is the same result as is yielded by the bound-pronouns treatment.

The bound-pronouns idea is nevertheless based on totally different theoretical assumptions than our theory. The most important general assumption is that quantifier phrases of natural languages operate logically speaking like the quantifiers of formal logic, i.e., have some variable-like expressions "bound" to them. Even though this assumption is widely shared, it is rarely argued for and, prima facie, rather implausible. If more natural models are sought for from modern formal logic for the quantifier phrases of English, surely conceptualizations like Hilbert's epsilon-terms are much more plausible candidates that the more usual quantifiers. (It is hard to suppress a suspicion here that those philosophers and linguists who have proposed to assimilate English quantifier phrases to quantifiers have not appreciated sufficiently the claims of such techniques as Hilbert's use of his epsilon-terms.) Among other things, a treatment relying on such techniques squares much better than the quantifier treatment with the fact that scope (as distinguished from rule ordering) is not marked in any way in natural languages. And if the so-called quantifier phrases of natural languages are treated as terms rather than as quantifiers, the same goes a fortiori for pronouns apparently bound to quantifier phrases.

Here we shall not argue for our theory on such an abstract general level. Rather, we shall mention a few specific shortcomings of the bound-pronouns view. One such shortcoming is illustrated by the so-called donkey sentences, i.e., sentences like our (28) and its relatives, e.g., (30).

(28)   If Bill owns a donkey, he beats it.
(30)   *If Bill owns every donkey, he beats it.

No half-way satisfactory treatment of such sentences exists that would be based on the bound-pronouns idea and that is not based on such theoretically totally unmotivated ideas as the ambiguity of the indefinite article. There just is no way of construing "a donkey" as an existential quantifier and "it" as a variable bound to it and of assigning the right reading to (28). Thus sentences like (28) have the important role in our discussion of ruling out the bound-pronoun idea as a viable way of handling the semantics of anaphoric pronouns.

The precise mechanism that assigns to (28) the right reading in our theory was explained in sec. 8, para. (iii), above. What is important for our present purpose is that this account turns on evaluating the quantifier phrase "a donkey" and the pronoun "it" independently of each other. In other words, each of them is construed as a term, not as a quantifier. The pronoun "it" is not "bound", as the usual terminology goes, to "a donkey". On the contrary, one clearly cannot reach the intended interpretation of (28) if one thinks of "it" as being bound to the "existential quantifier" "a donkey". Hence the "donkey sentences" serve as telling counterevidence to the idea of "bound pronouns", i.e., to the assimilation of anaphoric pronouns to the bound variables of quantification theory, even when the putative antecedent is a quantifier phrase.

This result is important enough to deserve a few further comments. Our treatment of the "donkey sentences" has been criticized by LePore and Garson (1983) on grounds that relate to the behavior of anaphoric pronouns. It is instructive to see what their objection is to our treatment and how it can be met.

In reality, the objection itself turns out to be based on a misunderstanding. It is the allegation that the Progression Principle makes it impossible to handle backwards anaphora in cases where the principle is in operation. This is simply a misunderstanding, due undoubtedly to inadequate exposition in the original paper by Hintikka and Carlson, where the Progression Principle was first formulated. Applied to (say) a conditional "If X, Y", the Progression Principle does not say that a subgame G(X) has to be played on X before any rules are applied to Y. Rather, it says merely that when the game rule for conditionals is applied to "If X, Y", the two subgames that this rule prescribes are played in the left-to-right order. It says absolutely nothing whether some other rule can be applied to "If X, Y" before (G. cond). Whether such applications are possible or not, is determined by the usual ordering principles. The same goes of course for the other rules that prescribe a division of a semantical game into subgames.

The examples LePore and Garson offer against our account involve an anaphoric pronoun occurring in the antecedent whose "head" is in the consequent. The following is a case in point:

(126)   If a man can find the money to pay for it, he will buy a fancy car.

A simpler example illustrating the same point is, e.g.,

(127)   If Bill owns it, he will beat a donkey.

According to what was just said, the only thing needed to account for (127) is to find a reason why a rule should be applied to "a donkey" in (127) before (G. cond) is applied to "if". This reason is obvious. On the most natural assumptions concerning the syntactic structure of conditionals, "a donkey" occurs in (127) in a higher clause than "if". Hence the reason we need is (O. comm).

This observation can be confirmed in different ways. One of them is the fact that in (127) "a donkey" has an existential force.   This means that it is evaluated before a subgame is played on the antecedent of (127), instead of evaluating it as a part of this anterior subgame.   Furthermore, we can understand, by the same token, why the following sentence is acceptable (unlike (30)) and why it has the force it does:

(128)   If Bill owns it, he beats every donkey.

Likewise we can deal with the following example:

(129)   If he finds it, a man will beat a donkey.

In particular, we can see why "a man" and "a donkey" have an existential surface force in (129).

The only complicating factor in (126) is that the value of "it" depends on that of "a man", on the reading of (126) which   allegedly   is   a   problem   for   a   game-theoretical treat-ment.

There is nevertheless no problem here.   Even if "a fancy car" cannot be evaluated before "a man" is in (126), surely the most natural order of applications is to allow (G. a(n)) to be applied to "a fancy car" as it were in the middle of the subgame played on the antecedent of (126) as soon as a rule has been applied to "a man".   (Surely this is the way (O. comm) naturally works here.)   This explains (126) without any new assumptions.

Another kind of example which LePore and Garson use is not even a conditional:

(130)   When   a   parent   speaks   to   him,   a   child   should
           listen.

Here the first rule to apply is (G. when).   The proposition expressed by (130) receives its generality, not from the same mechanism as (28), but from the fact that (G. when) can be applied by Nature.   Hence this example is scarcely relevant here.

Thus the phenomena LePore and Garson discuss speak for our theory and not against it.

16. Pragmatic Factors

A further qualification might seem to be needed in our rules for anaphoric pronouns. The rule (G. he) (as modified in the course of the discussion) is apparently sometimes relaxed in normal English use in that the uniqueness requirement is frequently dropped. This might prima facie seem to create an asymmetry between anaphoric pronouns and anaphoric the-phrases, which seemingly presuppose uniqueness. Consider, for instance, the following sentence:

(131)   The umpire warned John, whereupon he walked off the court.

Here the umpire need not be a woman (or a computer) in order for (131) not to be trivially false. But the same underdetermined character (multiplicity of possible references) is in principle present in (131), too, as was found, e.g., in (15). It is only our collateral knowledge of what is likely to happen on a tennis court that leads us to unique reading of (131). If the example had been instead

(132)   The coach warned John. Then he walked off the court,

the ambiguity (if that's the right word) would be felt even more keenly.

      This phenomenon is nevertheless not completely foreign to anaphorically used the-phrases. Witness, e.g., examples like the following:

(133)   When Jimmy protested about another call to the umpire, the angry man became angrier still.

Here "the angry man" can in principle refer to either Jimmy or to the umpire, and both of them can be angry even if (133) fails to be trivially true.
      Thus the sometime absence of the uniqueness requirement does not break the analogy between anaphoric pronouns and anaphorically used the-phrases, which we have used as a heuristic guide in this paper.
      What really happens in examples like (133) is that the apparent exceptions to the uniqueness requirement are merely apparent. In interpreting sentences like (132)-(133)

they are taken to be part of some longer discourse that takes place in some specific context. For instance, in (133) the uniqueness of the definite description may be guaranteed by the situation. Indeed if both Jimmy and the umpire are angry, (133) would be unnatural to utter. In general, there is nothing wrong about the uniqueness condition merely because it is enforced by deictic or textual factors.

The same point can be put by saying that by uttering a sentence like (128) the speaker is airing an assumption concerning the situation, more specifically, concerning the attributes that the bearer of the definite description must have for the uniqueness to be unique. In this respect, these uses of definite descriptions are rather like the uses mentioned in sec. 8, para. (vii), above. They are closely related to the epithetic uses discussed in Part II of this study. Such uses are not only compatible with the uniqueness requirement. Their way of functioning semantically presupposes the uniqueness requirement.

The following is an instructive example, where, in the absence of uniqueness, the speaker signals by means of an emphatic stress that she is referring to an individual that figures prominently in the earlier discourse:

(134)   "Oh, you thought these three [men] had spent
           the night on the moors, did you?"
           "No, only the one you want me to describe."
           "Ah, only the one you think stole the anorak and
           the rucksack. Now, madam, what did he look
           like?"
           ". . . He was a lot older than the other two.
           They would have been in their early twenties, I
           dare say, and quite well-spoken and just the de-
           cent, quiet type we like to have. Did *his* share
           of the chores, too, as well as their own, before
           they left this morning." (Gladys Mitchell, *The
           Death Cap Dancers*, St. Martin's Press, N.Y.,
           1981, p. 61; emphasis in the original.)

Here "his" does not have only the force of "the man's", but also that of "the man's whom you want me to describe".

Thus such uses of anaphoric pronouns as are illustrated by (131) don't really constitute counterexamples to the uniqueness requirement that is included in (G. he) and other similar rules. There is no reason to give up the uniqueness requirement as an ingredient of the basic semantics of anaphoric pronouns.

What follows is that the interpretation of utterances that contain anaphoric pronouns will depend on the linguistic and pragmatic context. Even though this does not imply any changes in our basic semantics of pronouns, it means that in interpreting particular sentences we have to look at the presumed context and for this purpose rely on pragmatic considerations; for they are needed to decide what the intended context is likely to be like.

These observations have consequences for the head-anaphor relation that has traditionally dominated discussions about the interpretation of pronouns. For if the choice set *I* and the attributes of its members depend on the context, the intended choice of a member of *I* in rules like (G. he), i.e., the choice that is part of a winning strategy of Myself, will likewise be determined by the context. This introduces a heavy apparent pragmatic element into the theory of anaphoric pronouns, even though they don't affect our semantics.

Our observations show also that the "head" of an anaphoric pronoun is in principle never determined purely syntactically and that often it can only be obtained pragmatically.

It might seem that relaxing the uniqueness requirement (sec. 12 above) enables us to deal with a variety of phenomena pragmatically. Instead of trying to decide what the respective "heads" of different anaphoric pronouns are, we can use instead our knowledge of the situation in question to decide what the intended reading is. The following pair of examples illustrates this:

(135)   John beat Jim in the first set, but he was not discouraged.

(136)   John beat Jim in the first set, but he was not elated.

These are of the same syntactical form. If the "head" of "he" were determined syntactically, it would therefore have to be the same in both cases. Yet the so-called head of "he" is unmistakably "Jim" in (135) but "John" in (136).

It might be thought that in the examples (135)-(136) the choice of the preferred reading is determined by the respective meanings of the operative words "beat", "discourage", and "elate". However, other examples show

that the information needed to select the intended reading
is pragmatic rather than semantical. For instance, the following pair of sentences shows how one's factual knowledge
of the situation influences the preferred force of a sentence
containing anaphoric pronouns:

(137)   John Doe gave a gift to Richard Roe, which led
             him to emphasize its modesty.
(138)   Kuniyoshi gave a gift to Haranobu, which led him
             to emphasize its modesty.

In (137), "him" is naturally taken to refer to John
Doe, while in (138) "him" naturally picks out Haranobu.
The reason is that it is a custom in the Japanese culture
(we are told) for the receiver of a gift to praise its modes-
ty, whereas in our culture the inverse is expected. There
in no a priori derivation, and cannot be, of this preference
in interpretation; it is a matter of the hearer's knowledge
of the social context of the statement. It looks extremely
hard to try to get hold of all such information on the basis
of merely linguistic clues.

Even when the prima facie semantical meaning gives us
a way of assigning the right "heads" to the right pronouns,
and so to interpret a sentence, such prima facie clues may
be cancellable. To illustrate, we would not use example
(24) (above, sec. 8) in San Francisco. These difficulties
are relevant among other things to the prospects of machine
translation. In so far as the improvements in machine translation are based on more refined syntactical and semantical
clues only, they are bound to be frustrated in the long
run.

Among other niceties of the semantical interpretation
which find a natural niche in our theory there are the
following:

(i) In a discourse, there is some leeway concerning
how many successive subgames generated by successive
sentences are to be combined in one and the same
"supergame". Other things being equal, either an
anaphoric pronoun or an anaphoric definite description is
likely to have its "head" in the nearest earlier sentences.

(ii) It was noted earlier that all anaphoric pronouns
(ranging over the same class of entities) in the same sentence or segment of discourse may be evaluated at the same

time.   It should be added that in the same sense all
anaphoric pronouns and all anaphoric definite descriptions
(with overlapping ranges of entities) in the same sentence
or in the same segment of discourse may be evaluated
together.

Both these points are illustrated by the following pas-
sage from Dick Francis, *Rat Race*, Pocket Books, New
York, 1978, p. 8:

(139)   A Ford ... stopped about twenty feet away,
           and two men climbed out. The larger ... went
           around to the back. ... The smaller one walked
           on over the grass. ... He stopped a few paces
           away, waiting for the larger man to catch up.
           He was dressed in faded blue jeans. ... All his
           bones were fine and his waist and hips would
           have been the despair of Victorian maidens.

Here the fourth and sixth sentences exemplify (i) and the
fourth exemplifies (ii).
        Things are complicated further by the possibility that
members of *I* are dropped when the players move from sentence to sentence in discourse (see sec. 5 and Part II, sec.
4 above).   Such changes in *I* may for instance, reflect
changes in the speaker's focus of attention. Here is the
excentric Mr. George Manciple calling Sir John Adamson,
Chief Constable of Fenshire, about his neighbor and enemy,
Mr. Raymond Mason who has been found shot to death in
his driveway:

(140)   Sir John swallowed.   "Why," he said, "did Dr.
           Thompson advise you to call [police] Sergeant
           Duckett?"
           "Well, he can't have shot himself, can he?   It
           stands to reason."
           "Are you talking about Raymond Mason now?"
           "Of course I am. ... "
           (Patricia   Moyes,   *Murder   Fantastical*,   Holt,
           Rinehart and Winston, New York, 1984, p. 9.)

Here by the usual syntactical rules of thumb, "he" would
be expected to be Dr. Thompson or Sergeant Duckett, as
Sir John recognizes.   He recognizes also from collateral information that neither of them can be referred to, and

correctly resorts to the assumption that Mr. Manciple is changing his choice set *I* according to his unpredictable changes of attention.   This example also illustrates how easily concellable the normal syntactical clues for choosing the "head" of a pronoun are in discourse.

17. Semantics and Strategy Selection

What was said in the preceding section has to be put in wider perspective, however. It would be mistaken to relegate all the problems discussed there to "the pragmatic wastebasket". What we have here is a general feature in the way the actual force (meaning) of natural-language utterances is determined. Whether we label it "semantics" or "pragmatics" is of lesser importance. It is brought out especially clearly by game-theoretical semantics.

In order to understand it, we have to go back to the basic ideas of game-theoretical semantics, especially to our game-theoretical truth-definition. The truth of a sentence S is defined in game-theoretical semantics as the existence of a winning strategy for Myself in the game G(S) correlated with S. Here we have to make a sharp distinction between the "existence" of a winning strategy for Myself, and Myself's "actually having one in the sense of knowing one. Both have to be distinguished from the speaker's knowing such a strategy. Whatever connection there is between these three is mostly conversational. For instance, whoever utters "S_1 or S_2 is asserting that there is a winning strategy for Myself in $G(S_1$ or $S_2)$. In other words, the speaker believes that Myself can choose either S_1 or S_2 and verify it, i.e., have a winning strategy in the game connected with it.   However, if he knew the first move in Myself's winning strategy, i.e., knew the winning choice of a disjunct, i.e., knew which disjunct is true, he or she would be unlikely to utter the disjunction (instead of the true disjunct).

This shows that knowing what Myself's winning strategy is like conveys extra information over and above knowing that there exists one, i.e., knowing that S is true. Now sometimes there are clues in a given sentence S, or in the context in which it is uttered, concerning what the winning strategy is. Such clues convey meaning to a hearer in a way different from the way semanticists are normally considering. We shall call the former "abstract meaning" and the latter "strategic meaning". One of the merits of our game-theoretical approach is that it enables us to make the distinction between the two and hence to do justice to strategic meaning as a separate semantical phenomenon. By so doing, game-theoretical semantics once again illustrates that meanings are many-splendored things to a far greater extent than is realized in current theories.

It is to be noted that our game rules are calculated to help capture the abstract meaning of the sentences on which semantical games are played. At the same time, they form the basis of strategic meaning. For what strategic meaning typically does is to filter out some of the strategies that the game rules leave open.

Strategic meaning is a frequent component in our se-mantical intuitions. These intuitions thus turn out to be even more of a mixture of essentially different things than has been spelled out in the literature. This shows once again that it is hopeless to try to capture such intuitions, even if they were more reliable than they in fact are, by means of one set of generalizations, as many linguists are still trying to do.

Notice that strategic meaning, too, is in a sense truth-conditional. If I know that the certain strategy codi-fied by a certain function f can serve as Myself's winning strategy in G(S) then I know certain things "about the world", more about the world than merely that S is true on the basis of the conditions of abstract meaning, i.e., that there exists a winning strategy for Myself. I know also that the world is such that the particular strategy f can in it serve as the appropriate winning strategy.

This is illustrated by the disjunction example above. If I know which is the beginning of Myself's winning strate-gy, I know more than that "S_1 or S_2" is true. I also know which disjunct is true.

In some of the simplest cases, strategic meaning relies on knowledge of what strategies are likely to work – intui-tively, what alternatives are true or false. Thus, if one says,

(141)   The witness is lying or I'm a Dutchman

the force of the utterance is to assert that the witness is indeed lying. This may be taken to be an instance of strategic meaning based on the audience's collateral knowl-edge that the speaker is not a Dutchman. Notice that if

the speaker were Dutch (or likely to be suspected to be),
he could not utter (137) with the intended meaning (strategic meaning).

Strategic meaning comes to competent speakers even
more naturally in connection with quantifiers. It is also
unmistakable that it constitutes a perfectly legitimate
variety of meaning. Here is a case in point:

(142)   Susan ignored this. She said, "You'd suppose,
           Gerald, that someone who was living somewhere
           at someone else's expense would be even more
           considerate, don't you think?"
           "Well --."
           "If you mean me," said David, "why not say so.
           Someone!   Somewhere!   Someone else! For
           Christ's sake, stop wrapping it up. ... " (Mi-
           chael Gilbert, *End-Game*, Penguin Books, 1983,
           p. 16.)

Here Susan, Gerald, David, and the reader all know perfectly well who is "meant". Equally clearly, the meaning in
question is strategic in nature. We know which person,
which flat, and which other person have to be chosen to
carry out the winning strategy that Susan unmistakably has
in mind.

The example (142) is somewhat complicated by the "generic" (generalizing) element in the use of existential quantifiers. However, examples without this complication are
also easy to find:

(143)   Her seat, naturally, was the wrong one. She had
           definitely been given to understand that she
           would have a cover seat, facing the engine.
           "I can only say, Arthur," she said, her eyes
           fixed on Henry, "that reservations seem to mean
           absolutely nothing to *some people.*"
           (Patricia Moyes, *Dead Men Don't Ski*, Holt,
           Rinehart and Winston, New York, 1984, p. 9.)

There are two main classes of clues to strategic meaning. They are (i) collateral information that helps to rule
out some of Myself's strategies as not being winning ones;
(ii) the syntactic structure of the sentence S uttered. The
latter set of clues includes the syntactical order of the ingredients of S to which a game rule can be applied and the

similarity of the syntactical constructions in which they occur.   The order of the syntactic parts of S operates as a
clue to the order in which game rules are applied to them
and the similarity of two syntactical constructions suggests
that the game rules are likewise to be applied to them in a
similar fashion.   Furthermore, the order in which the members of a choice set *I* have been introduced into it can
serve as a clue as to the order in which they are to be selected to be values of anaphoric pronouns.   That the syntactical indicators are clues to strategic meaning only is
shown by their being cancellable by other factors.

Such uses of quantifiers as illustrated by (142)-(143)
are often dismissed as having merely stylistic interest.   We
can now see that this stylistic device has a solid semantical
basis.

Indeed, it is the very same strategic meaning that
forms the background of the idiomatic use of "somebody" as
meaning an important person.   For such a person is precisely one who is likely to figure as a choice in Myself's
winning   strategies   associated   with   people's   everyday
statements.

It is not very difficult to see why strategic meaning is
particularly important to keep in mind in the theory of
anaphoric pronouns.   Whenever there is more than one
member in the choice set *I* in applying a rule like (G. he)
or (G. she), there is more than one way in which the rule
can be used by Myself.   In the usual jargon, there is more
than one possible head for the pronoun in question.   If only one such way of applying the rule (i.e., only one kind
of strategy on the part of Myself) is a part of a winning
strategy, the "head" is uniquely determined.   However, it
is normally not determined by the rules of the game and the
rest of the paraphenalia of game-theoretical semantics; it is
partly determined by the facts.

An example of this situation was offered in sec. 12
above:

(80)   Susan met Mrs. Carstairs when bringing up the
            tea, whereupon she had some words with her.

Here either (i) "she" refers to Susan and "her" to Mrs.
Carstairs, or (ii) "she" refers to Mrs. Carstairs and "her"
to Susan.   (Contextually provided references are not considered here, and the identity of the two references is
ruled out by the Exclusion Principle.)   In the conventional

terminology, either (i) the head of "she" is "Susan" and
that of "her" "Mrs. Carstairs" or (ii) vice versa. How are
we to view these two alternatives? The important fact is
that the difference between the two is a matter of strategic
meaning, not abstract meaning. You may call (80) ambiguous, if you want to highlight strategic meaning, or unambiguous, if you prefer to emphasize abstract meaning. In
the sense illustrated by these observations, we can thus
say that the relation of an anaphoric pronoun to its head
belongs to the realm of strategic meaning rather than abstract meaning. What is unsatisfactory about the approaches to anaphora that rely on this head–anaphor relation is
therefore not that this relation somehow is totally irrelevant
or otherwise illusory, but that they confuse strategic meaning with abstract meaning. There are regularities governing either type of meaning, but they cannot both be
captured by the same generalization. A clear distinction
between the two is therefore vital in the study of
pronominal anaphora, even though it is absent from the recent literature. Notice, for instance, that the acceptability
of a sentence S in the sense of the interpretability of S
goes together with its having an abstract meaning, even if
S does not have a unique strategic meaning. (Again, (80)
offers an example of this.) Yet the emphasis on the
anaphor–head relation in recent literature easily leads one
to expect, mistakenly, that if the head of an anaphoric pronoun is not determined, the meaning of the sentence in
which it occurs is not determined, either.

Another example is offered by (17). It is understood
and accepted even though the linguistic properties of (17)
do not determine whether it is Gail or Billie who is a he,
i.e., whether it is "Gail" or "Billie" that is the so-called
head of "he" in (17). Moreover, the hearer of (17) does
not have to know it, either, for him or her to find (17) acceptable (in a way in which, e.g., (15) is not). These are
all symptoms of the status of the head–anaphor relation as
belonging to the realm of strategic meaning.

It is now seen that the "pragmatic" factors considered
in the preceding section are largely instances of strategic
meaning. Hence, they should probably be called semantical
rather than pragmatic phenomena after all, even though
terminology is not important here. For instance, the reason
why "he" is normally taken to pick out John in (136) but
Jim in (135) is that this is likelier to make the sentence in

question true, i.e., likelier to be part of Myself's winning strategy.

Even where the regularities governing strategic meaning are not hard-and-fast, it is easy to see what theoretical issue is involved. For instance, it was noted in sec. 12 above that whenever there is more than one way of coordinated application of a rule like (G. he) to several pronouns in the same clause, there is an expectation that collateral factors should filter out all but one of the different disjuncts that result from different assignments. Now we can see that this expectation is an expectation that the sentence in question has a unique strategic meaning.

If there are no clues to filter out all but one of the disjuncts, the strategic meaning of the sentence is undetermined, and the sentence is felt to be a deviant one, at best ambiguous. It does not violate abstract meaning, however, not even to the extent being ambiguous on the level of abstract meaning.

The different clues that help to filter out unwanted disjuncts (due to different coordinated applications of pronoun rules) thus are indications of the mechanisms that strategic meaning relies on. It is not our purpose here to present an exhaustive survey of these mechanisms. A few remarks may nevertheless be helpful.

One clue is the syntactical order of potential "heads". However, it is not a very strong clue. It was already noted in sec. 12 above that a sentence like (80) can have either the force of (81) or that of (82).

Indeed, if the order of available antecedents prejudged the evaluation of pronouns, there could not be any need of the locutions "the former" and "the latter".

Another clue to strategic meaning in connection with pronouns is similarity of grammatical structure. This is what determines the evaluation of pronouns in sentences like the following

(145)   John knows that Bill likes to read computer magazines. He also likes to read chess magazines, but John doesn't know that.

However, the fact that we are here dealing with strategic meaning rather than abstract meaning is shown that this clue can be cancelled by others. The following is a case in point:

(146)   John knows that Bill likes to read computer maga-
             zines. He also likes to read computer magazines,
             but Bill does not know that.

        It seems to us that there probably are genuine,
rule-governed syntactical clues to strategic meaning in connection with anaphoric pronouns. It may even be that the
head-anaphor relation as a syntactical relation comes into
play in this sub-department of the semantics of pronouns,
after all. (We shall argue for its irrelevance on the level
of abstract meaning in the next section.) Further work
needs to be done here. What is important to realize is that
we are dealing with a semantical phenomenon of an essentially different nature from the ones our game rules and ordering principles are calculated to capture.
        The nature of strategic meaning is illustrated further
by a phenomenon that is predictable on the basis of our
theory. Whenever there are several potential "heads" NP_1,
NP_2, ... for a given pronoun P, i.e., several members i_1,
i_2, ... in I introduced as values of NP_1, NP_2, ...
respectively, then a choice between them is a matter of
strategic meaning, not of abstract meaning, which is neutral
with respect to different members of I. In order for the
strategic meaning to have a foothold to operate independently of the pragmatic context, there must be some asymmetry or difference between NP_1, NP_2, ... to provide a
"sufficient reason" for one of them to be preferred as a
part of the strategic meaning of the sentence containing P.
Such a sentence would then be trivially false, and hence
likely to be thought of as unacceptable, unless the value of
P is thought of as being provided by the context. The following examples illustrate this:

(147)   John told Bill that he was responsible.
(148)   John and Bill admitted that he was responsible.
(149)   George Will and Reagan agreed that he had done
             well in the debate.
(150)   All orchestra members thought that he had played
             well.
(151)   All orchestra members, including the first violin,
             thought that he had played well.

In (147) "he" can be "coreferential" (as far as strategic
meaning is concerned) with either "John" or "Bill", but in
(148) the value of "he" must be provided contextually. Yet

in (149) he is likely to refer to Reagan, given a suitable political and historical context. In (150) "he" is unlikely to refer to one of the orchestra members, whereas in (151) it can very well refer to the first violin. All these facts are explained by the observations made above.

What is striking about the examples (145)-(151) is that they show the extent to which strategic meaning is part of the surface force of anaphoric pronouns. This observation is important because it shows that strategic meaning, and not just abstract meaning, influences the possibility of various coreference relations. These relations, as they surface in our intuitions about sundry examples, are thus the combined product of several essentially different factors. In view of this, there are good reasons to think that it is completely hopeless to try to formulate adequate constraints on coreference as straightforward generalization from examples, as many linguists are currently trying to do.

These observations can help to understand further semantical phenomena. One rare but amusing dialectal use is illustrated by the following example (to the likes of which our attention was first directed by Dr. Eve Clark):

(152)   Clan Campbell prospered, but himself was still not satisfied.

This example of Highlands usage prima facie seems to be parallel with examples like (150), in which coreference is frustrated by the lack (as it were) of a "principle of sufficient reason" to select one individual rather than another as Myself's choice in a winning strategy. However, in the case of a Scottish clan there is a designated individual that stands out among the members of the clan, viz., its chief. And in fact that is what "himself" refers to in (152).

18. Irrelevance of the Head-Anaphor Relation, and the Semantical Character of Pronominal Anaphora

After having discussed these specific features of our theory of anaphora, we are in a position to discuss a few wider theoretical issues. They include the irrelevance of the head-relation (i.e., the relation of an anaphoric pronoun to its head), the unsatisfactory nature of the concept of coreference generally employed by linguists, and the nature of the restrictions on the relation of an anaphoric pronoun to its so-called "head" (when this notion makes sense).

As was noted in the beginning of Part III of this work, on the treatment suggested here no special working role is played by the relation of an anaphoric pronoun to any particular antecedent noun phrase. What plays the crucial mediating role in determining the reference of an anaphoric pronoun is the totality of individuals chosen by the players up to the pronominal move in question in a semantical game, plus individuals otherwise accessible to the players. The expressions that serve to introduce these individuals (in so far as these individuals are introduced by reference to any particular grammatical expression) form a totality of, as it were, potential antecedents for the pronoun. What is usually labelled the antecedent is merely that particular potential antecedent (if any) whose reference yields a winning strategy when chosen by Myself. However, the question of which potential antecedent (if any) is liable to do so is not determined merely by the grammatical relations that obtain between the various ingredients of the sentence in question, but depend also on de facto questions pertaining to the references of the other potential antecedents as well.

Examples of this phenomenon will be given later. It can be described by saying that on our theory pronominal anaphora is essentially a semantical rather than syntactical phenomenon. One aspect of this fact is that pronominal anaphora in natural languages operates in a way essentially different from the variables of quantification, where the syntactical identity of the variable letter serves to determine the syntactical entity called the quantifier to which it is bound, whereupon the identity of quantifiers determines the identity of reference. The mechanism that is relied on by natural languages is so different from formal quantifiers that it seems to us to prejudice the theoretical situation in favor of a wrong approach to refer to the subject matter of pronominal anaphora by the term "binding".

Another aspect of the same phenomenon is that the member of *I* that ends up serving as the "antecedent" of a pronoun may not have been introduced by an one antecedent expression that would be "coreferential" with the pronoun or otherwise bear a fixed syntactical relation to it. This is illustrated in different ways by what was found above in sec. 8, paragraphs (i), (vi), and (vii).

Further examples are easily found of sentences in which an individual is introduced into the choice set *I* without using any one expression that would refer to this individual and hence could serve as the syntactical antecedent of a pronoun.

The following remarks may help to put the whole matter into perspective. What is (or at least can be) determined by general linguistic considerations about the force of an anaphoric pronoun is the choice set I. If this set contains more than one member, however, Myself's choice between them is free, and is constrained only by the idea that Myself has a winning strategy if the sentence in question is true. Hence to anticipate the intended choise is to anticipate what Myself's winning strategy might be. Now it is this optimal choice that determines, on the apparently syntactical level, what the "antecedent" or "head' of the pronoun is. Hence we reach the conclusion that the notion of "head" or "antecedent" belongs in the last analysis to the theory of strategic meaning characterized in the preceding section rather than to the theory of abstract meaning. For it is the theory of strategic meaning that deals with the question of how the choice of a winning strategy can be anticipated. This incidentally also illustrates the importance of the notion of strategic meaning.

The irrelevance of the alleged head-anaphora relation as an operative factor in explaining anaphora also means that anaphora is in a sense assimilated to deixis. This sense is that the reference of an anaphoric pronoun is not provided in the first place by its alleged head, but by the total situation, summed up in the choice set I. What differentiates pronominal reference from garden-variety deixis is that the situation in question is not the speech situation but a situation in a semantical game, viz., the situation the players have reached by the time a pronoun rule is applied. As a slogan, we might thus say that anaphora is deixis in a semantical game. This illustrates further the fundamental similarity of different kinds of pronouns that was pointed out in sec. 7 above.

Another general observation is in order here. There is nothing in the rule (G. he) (or in its analogues, with the exception of the rules for reflexive pronouns) that can exclude such carry over from the discourse context of the sentence in which a pronoun like "he" occurs. In principle, the possible values of "he" are never restricted to entities referred to in the sentence in which "he" occurs. This observation is closely related to the so-called anaporn relation of Dougherty (1969). He claims that any anaphoric pronoun can have what he calles a nonanaphoric

interpretation.   By an anaphoric pronoun, he means a
pronoun whose "antecedent" is in the same sentence.   For
this reason, his thesis comes closer to our observation that
extrasentential entities can never be in principle excluded
from the choice set *I*, except for reflexive pronouns.

It seems to us that our observation represents the
true gist of Dougherty's thesis.   It is nevertheless important to realize that ours is strictly an "in principle" observation.   There is nothing in our approach that prevents the
filtering of outside entities from *I* by some special feature
of its linguistic context.   Hence our position does not entail
that the anaphoric relation is exceptionless (even when restricted to nonreflexives).   Dougherty's claim may thus
turn out to be correct in spirit rather than in letter.

In any case, some of the putative counterexamples to
Dougherty seem to us to illustrate merely the lack of semantical imagination on the part of the cited linguists.   For
instance, the following type of example is frequently used
here:

(153)   The doctor lost his head.

It is nevertheless not hard to spin a tale about a primitive
tribe whose life revolves around an ancestral father figure
whose mummified head is the most important object of wor-
ship for them.   In such a context, speaking of the great
ancestral figure, it makes perfect sense to say:

(154)   One day, a terrible   crisis struck the tribe wor-
             shipping The Great Ancestor.   The shaman lost
             his head.

where "his" does not refer to the shaman but to the re-
vered ancestor.

The only way of excluding the extrasentential antecedent completely in (153) is to construe "losing one's head"
as an idiom.   But then it cannot generate counterexamples
to the behavior of pronouns at large.

Another group of arguments for the semantical character of pronominal anaphora can be derived from agreement
phenomena.   It is usually said that a pronoun must agree
with its antecedent in person, gender and number.   Since
the status of the antecedence relation is dubious, the same
goes for the agreement requirement.   Here are some exam-

ples that illustrate the impossibility of construing agreement as a hard-and-fast requirement:

(155)   John told his wife that they had been evicted.

(156)   John bought a Veg-o-matic after seeing them advertised on TV.

(These two examples are from Wasow 1979, p. 75.)

(157)   "I'm sorry, Dame Maud. I don't quite follow."
          "But you must. You must know. It was an OGPU safe house. Everyone knows that."
          "They do?"
          (Julian Rathbone, *A Spy of the Old School*, Pantheon Books, New York, 1984, p. 132.)

(158) = (24)   A couple was sitting on a bench. He stood up and she followed his example.

(159) = (39)   If Stewart buys a car or a motorcycle, he will take good care of it.

(160)   If Stewart buys a car and a motorcycle, he will take good care of them.

(161)   "Are we?" Emmy gave him a rueful smile. "Just pure coincidence that we're going to the hotel which Interpol thinks is a smugglers' den?"
          "It was just my luck to pick that particular place," said Henry. ... "Interpol knows you're going to be there, though, don't they?"
          (Patricia Moyes, *Dead Men Don't Ski*, Holt Rinehart and Winston, New York, 1984, p. 10.)

It is fairly obviously hopeless to try to capture such examples by any strictly syntactical generalization. Pronominal agreement, like pronominal anaphora in general, is an essentially semantical phenomenon.

It is not just a matter of abstract meaning, though. Rather, agreement is a syntactical device that serves to facilitate strategic meaning. For it helps to see what the "head" of a pronoun is - which head-anaphor relation was earlier seen to belong to the province of strategic meaning.

For an additional example of a failure of the usual pronominal agreement, see (371) below (sec. 33).

19. Shortcomings of the Notion of Coreference

A closely related phenomenon is the failure of the concept of coreference as an explanatory tool in dealing with anaphoric pronouns. Examples of its shortcomings can be seen from what was found in sec. 8, paragraphs (v)-(vii) above. For instance, if "a car" and "it" can be "coreferential" in (39) (=(159)), why can't they be so in (41) so as to make (41) acceptable? Again, the relation of "she" and "night life" in (43) is scarcely one of coreference. One way of putting the main point is to say that the notion of coreferentiality is not a grammatical one. Which expressions in a given sentence or segment of discourse refer to the same entity is not determined by their grammatical (syntactical) relations alone, but may depend on what happens in a given play of a semantical game – and even on the facts of the situation. Hence the relation of coreferentiality should not be used as a primitive in semantical or grammatical conceptualizations.

There are many other reasons for being suspicious of the usual notion of coreference. The linguists who employ this notion usually realize that actual coreference is not what is involved. Hence they resort to the idea of "intended" coreference. Intended by whom? By the speaker or writer, of course. (Who else is there to intend anything in the first place?) But consider the following sentence:

(162)   Jocasta wondered who her husband's mother was. One day she would meet her, Jocasta hoped.

Here the writer – whether he or she is Sophocles or a critic explaining the plot – of course intends "she" and "her" to be "coreferential". Yet coreferentiality in our sense is excluded by the Exclusion Principle discussed above. Hence the usual construal of coreference as intended coreference deprives us of the possibility of formulating interesting regularities in natural languages.

In contrast, this does not reflect on our treatment in the least. On it, in treating the clause "one day she would meet her" we have to evaluate it in a world compatible with everything Jocasta hoped. In such worlds, "she" and "her" will pick out different individuals. (Whatever hopes she had, her being the mother of Oedipus was not compatible with them.) Hence on our account no exception to general principles is implied by the acceptability of (162).

This phenomenon may at first seem rather arcane. However, it is not completely uncommon. In fact, we will present further examples of it later.

There are of course other ways of illustrating the hopeless confusion involved in the usual notion of coreference. For instance, it is sometimes said that indefinite NPs occurring in the same sentence or the same segment of discourse cannot be coreferential (in the traditional sense of intended coreference). But witness the following:

(163)   Three women were sitting in the room. One woman was dressed in white, one in black, and one in grey. One woman was knitting, one cooking, and one was reading.

Here some of the indefinite noun phrases must be coreferential in order for the sentences to be true, and this is normally "intended" by the speaker. What can be meant here by saying that the indefinite noun phrases in the example must not be coreferential?

Similar examples can also be constructed where the coreference takes place in one and the same sentence. There are also examples of the following kind:

(164)   A young man decided that he would become a violinist.
(165)   One of the football players is a lawyer.
(166)   Ernest recognized one of the men as a famous painter.
(167)   A fellow of King's was dismissed because his colleagues disapproved of an agnostic and a pacifist.

Of these examples, (167) can be explained in our approach by means of the idea of strategic meaning (cf. sec. 17 above). It is clear from the context who the agnostic is who can be chosen by Myself, in order to have a winning strategy in the game associated with (167). Of course, this explanatory strategy is not available to our competitors.

Examples like (167) have been objected to (in their role here) by claiming that "an agnostic" and "a pacifist" are used in (167) generically – whatever that means. We do not agree.   Whatever presumed "generic" is due to strategic meaning, not vice versa.   The sentence (167) can be true even though there is no general policy on the part of the fellows of King's to disapprove of any and all agnostics,   any   and   all   pacifists,   any   and   all agnostic-cum-pacifists,   or   any   and   all   agnostics   and/or pacifists.   (Which of these is supposed to be the generic force of (167), anyway?)   The function of the attributes "agnostic" and "pacifist" is to indicate what the reasons of the good fellows of King's were in this particular case, but not necessarily to state a general rule.   What this means is that the primary force of (167) is due to strategic meaning, just as we asserted.

Examples like (165) are sometimes dimissed because "a lawyer" allegedly is in (165) not a referring expression at all, wherefore the notion of coreference is supposed not to be applicable here.   Rather, "is" is a part of the copula "is a".   This line of thought presupposes the idea that "is" is ambiguous between the "is" of identity and the copulative "is".   This presupposition has been criticized by Jaakko Hintikka (Hintikka and Kulas 1983, chap. 7).

Some linguists restrict the claim of the alleged impossibility of coreference by different indefinite NPs to the shared scope (in the sense of the scope of formal quantifiers, sometimes called by linguists the "domain") of the indefinite NPs in question.   But even then we seem to have counterexamples at hand.   For instance, the following examples are acceptable:

(168)   A young man decided that he would become himself again.

(169)   One of the football players in the picture is himself.

(170)   Ernest recognized one of the men in the picture as himself.

According to the theorist relying on the notion of "domain", the admissible occurrence of the reflexive pronoun "himself" suffices to show that it is in the "domain" of its so-called head.   Hence (168)-(170) should show that (164)-(166) are genuine counterexamples to the noncoreference thesis.

These critical remarks are especially relevant to a discussion of anaphora for the following reason.   As was mentioned in sec. 2, one of the main current types of approach to   anaphora   operates   essentially   with   the   notion   of

coreference as one of its primitives. The hopeless confu-
sions that beset this notion make it virtually impossible to
discuss whether this approach is correct or not, except for
saying that it needs better understood primitives.

There nevertheless are even more striking
counterexamples to the explanatory value of the received
notion of coreference. Consider the following sentence,
used by Peter Geach:

(171)   Bill is the only man who loves his wife.

It has two readings, which are perhaps seen even more
clearly from the corresponding negative sentence:

(172)   Bill is not the only man who loves his wife.

On one reading, (172) says that there are other uxorious
men than Bill; on the other reading, (172) makes Bill a
cuckold.

In (171), the two readings are presumably reached on
the basis of a traditional treatment by assigning two different "heads", viz. "Bill" and "the only man", to the
anaphoric pronoun "his". But (171) is true only if Bill is
the only man who loves his wife, i.e., only if "Bill" and
"the only man" are coreferential in the traditional literal
sense. Hence the difference between the two possible
heads should not matter. Thus the received notion of
coreference leads to the false predication that (171) ought
to be unambiguous.

Later in this work it will be shown how our treatment
explains the ambiguity of (171) and (172) in a perfectly
natural manner. (See sec. 22 below.)

Another example of the impossibility of giving clear
theoretical meaning to the notion of coreference employed in
the literature is the following:

(173)   Both Jill and Jane told Jim about herself.

Here "Jill" and "herself" must obviously be coreferential.
(Otherwise the reflexive pronoun would be out of place.)
Likewise "Jane" and "herself" must be coreferential. But
the relation of coreference does not make any useful sense
unless it is transitive. Hence Jill and Jane must be the
same person in (173), which is absurd.

Furthermore, the traditional notion of coreference does not even apply in all the cases where the syntactical notion of a head (antecedent) makes at least prima facie sense. For instance, consider one of our earlier examples again:

(37)   If you extend an invitation to every friend of yours, someone will disregard it.

Here "it" has "an invitation" as its antecedent in some fairly obvious sense.   But this sense cannot be explained by saying that the two expressions refer to the same entity, for neither one refers to any one particular object.   Nor, for that matter, can it be explained by saying that "it" picks out the same "arbitrary" individual as "an invitation", for "an invitation" picks out an object for each friend, whereas "it" only picks out someone's particular invitation.
    Another instance of the shortcomings of the received notion of coreference is provided by the following bit of dialogue:

(174)   "Did you hear that Greta Garbo has been seen in public?"
             "Who is she?"

Here "Greta Garbo" and "she" are undoubtedly "coreferential", as the term is currently being used in the literature. But what is the force of saying so?   The second speaker is not referring to anybody at all, but rather trying to find out what the reference of the name "Greta Garbo" is.   What possible explanatory sense can it make to say that such a use of a pronoun is "coreferential" with an earlier NP?
    It is important to realize, moreover, that our criticisms cannot be dismissed as merely pointing out discrepancies between linguists' technical sense of the word "coreference" and its concrete semantical meaning as standing for the same entity.   For one thing, linguists frequently rely in their argumentation on a presumed approximate equivalence between the two.   What we have seen demonstrates that the two cannot possibly go together in a way that would preserve the explanatory value of linguists' technical notion, unless a great many further explanations are given.   Second, it can be shown that in some cases it is the intuitive semantical notion that allows for better generalizations than the technical one (see, e.g., secs. 14 and 33 of this work).   Third, more than one recent linguist has in effect

emphasized the importance of giving an explicit semantical sense to the technical notion of coreference. For instance, Reinhart (1983, p. 144) writes that "the major problem for the anaphora model outlined above is that there is no explicit semantics for its complex indexing system". Similar views are expressed, e.g., by Bach and Partee (1980). At the very least, our observations show the great difficulty of this task.

CHAPTER V

GTS EXPLAINS COREFERENCE RESTRICTIONS

20. Game Rules and Their Order as Explanation
for Coreferentiality Restraints

The inadequacies of the received notion of coreference do
not, of course, imply that all its uses in the literature are
worthless. However, the legitimate uses can in many cases
be captured by our theory, given a deeper foundation, and
in some cases improved on.

One of the easily legitimized uses of the notion of
coreference – perhaps the only one – is in speaking of
possible coreference. In order to see what it amounts to,
let us assume that E_1 and E_2 are expressions in a sentence
S to which a game rule can be applied. Assume further
that E_1 involves a choice of an individual that need not
have occurred in the play of the game before. (Quantifier
rules are cases in point.) Assume that E_2 involves the
choice of an individual i from a choice set I. Now if a rule
can be applied to E_1 (before one is applied to E_2) so as to
introduce i and if i can be a member of I, then in an
obvious sense E_1 and E_2 can be "coreferential". In
contrast, if no rule can be applied to E_1 (to introduce i
into I) before one is applied to E_2, in an equally obvious
sense E_1 and E_2 cannot be coreferential. Ditto if i cannot
occur in I for some other reason.

Notice that this explains what can be meant by
"possible" and "impossible" coreference. It does not enable
us to speak of coreference simpliciter. Even though we can
go beyond this and vindicate certain other uses of the
notion of coreference (cf. sec. 28 below), there is little
reason to believe that this notion can be saved in its
totality as it has been used in the recent literature.

The notion of coreference can be given a literal sense
by relativizing it to some particular play of a semantical
game. Only then can we speak of different phrases as
literally referring to the same entity or to different
entities. But this relativization is quite different from
current usage and probably impossible to reconcile with it.

These explanations nevertheless suffice for several
important purposes. Indeed, what undoubtedly are the
most important problems, and some of the most interesting
results, in the recent literature concerning the semantics of

157

anaphora deal with limitations of when an anaphoric pronoun can be "coreferential" with a given nonanaphoric NP. Even though the concept of coreferentiality used here is dubious, the explanations just given show what its cash value is. We shall argue that such regularities that hold here not only can be captured within our conceptual framework but are predicted by our theory. In other words, we shall try to raise the existing discussion of the limitations on coreference to a new level. Instead of thinking of the regularities concerning possible coreference as empirical generalizations (generalizations from data), we shall consider them as special cases or consequences of certain more general assumptions that are part of our overall semantical theory, quite independently of the treatment of anaphora. These assumptions thus can have evidence in support of them independent of anaphora. They concern mostly, but not exclusively, the order in which the rules of semantical games are applied.

Admittedly, some of the competing theorists make general assumptions that go beyond direct data. In particular, several linguists, for instance, Reinhart, Higginbotham, May, et al., assume that the conditions on possible coreference are the same as the conditions defining the "scopes" of quantifiers. This enables them to bring indirect evidence from the behavior of quantifiers to bear on conditions on coreference. However, the identification of the two kinds of conditions, though plausible, does not have any deeper theoretical foundation in competing approaches, and is instead made initially suspect (in those approaches) by the inapplicability of the traditional logical concept of scope to natural languages.

Our basic idea here is the following: Consider an application of (G. he) to an anaphoric pronoun P in a sentence S. Let NP_1 be a noun phrase occurring in the same sentence S, and let us assume that NP_1 is of the same category as P in the sense that the values of NP_1 (entities referred to by the names substitutable for NP_1 in a semantical game) come from the same subdomain as the values of P. Assume further that our ordering principles entail that (G. he) has to be applied to P before the appropriate rule is applied to NP_1 to introduce an individual, say b, as the value of NP_1. Then b will not be in the set I from which the value of P is chosen. In such circumstances, P and NP_1 cannot be "coreferential" in the sense that is presupposed in the recent literature.

More generally, there may be some other principle that excludes b from I, even if a rule has been applied to NP_1 so as to introduce b by the time (G. he) is applied. By the same token P and NP1 cannot then be coreferential. Our Exclusion Principle offers an example of this phenomenon.

In order to utilize these ideas fully, we must realize that a special rule (G. name) is needed. What it does was explained above in Part I. Applied to a proper name, it assigns an individual as its reference. This is not unnatural, for in interpreting a sentence S one of the steps needed is to ascertain what individuals its proper names stand for. Obviously, this rule can, and should, usually be applied early in the game. This is the reason why we have not been forced to formulate it earlier. However, there are occasions on which the relative order of (G. name) as compared with other rules matters.

The main theoretical burden nevertheless falls on the ordering principles that govern the choice of the rule that is to be applied next at each stage of the game.

Now what are these ordering principles? They were discussed briefly in Part I, secs. 8-9, of this study. The main features of the situation are the following: There are two kinds of ordering principles, general and special. General ordering principles deal with the influence of syntactic structure on rule ordering. Special ones govern the relative order of two particular rules.

A general ordering principle (O. comm) was formulated above in Part I. It governs the order of application of the game rules. It can be overruled by special ordering principle characteristic of certain special kinds of expressions. This (O. comm) says the following:

(O. comm) A rule must not be applied to a node N_1 if some rule applies to another node N_1, when N_1 s-commands N_2 but not vice versa.

Roughly speaking, a node N_1 is said to s-command another node N_2 iff the s-node most immediately dominating N_1 also dominates N_2.

Another general ordering principle (C. LR) says that in one and the same clause and in co-ordinated clauses our game rules are applied left to right.

These general ordering principles can be overruled by special ones. They nevertheless imply a number of

approximate predictions that can be compared with the
evidence – and with the generalizations from evidence that
can be found in the literature.   As was pointed out, our
predictions are consequences of an overall theory and not
merely generalizations from data.   Hence they provide a
theoretical explanation of the data and not just a summary
of them.   They also admit indirect evidence in a way
straight generalizations from examples do not.   For any
evidence for our ordering principles yields further support
for their consequences concerning pronouns even when the
evidence has nothing to do with anaphora.

The ordering principles that govern game rules for
anaphoric pronouns will emerge in the course of our
analysis.   By way of anticipation, the following principles
can be registered already:

(a) (G. he) and similar rules are restricted by (O.
LR) but not by (O. comm).

(b) (G. he) and similar rules can apply before (G.
the) and (G. genitive) but need not do so.

Thus, according to our account, what prevents
"coreference" (in the cases we are concerned with here) is
the absence of the reference *i* of the potential "head" from
the choice set *I*.   From this it follows that if this reference
i is somehow forced back into *I*, no matter however post
hoc and ad hoc, the possibility of coreference can be
restored.   In this sense, the coreference restrictions we
are dealing with here are cancellable, as our theory
predicts.   This prediction is supported by evidence from
perfectly normal and acceptable usage.   Here's an example:

(175)   "What's her name?   The nun who knew all the
time where she was and never told." (Antonia
Fraser, *Quiet as a Nun*, Penguin Books,
1978, p. 23.)

Here it is clear to the reader (and to the fictional character
to whom the question is addressed) that the value of "her"
is the nun who knew etc.   Further examples are provided
by Bolinger (1979).

21. Ordering Principles and the Langacker-Ross Restriction

As an example of the consequences of our general ordering principles, it follows from (O. comm) and (O. LR) that, other things being equal, a denoting phrase NP_1 cannot pronominalize another noun phrase, say NP_2, if NP_2 precedes and s-commands NP_1. For, in such circumstances, a rule cannot be applied to NP_1 in one and the same sub-before a pronoun rule is applied to NP_2 because of (O. comm). Moreover, the assumption that NP_2 precedes NP_1 rules out the possibility that a rule should be applied to NP_1 in an earlier subgame than the one in which NP_2 is handled, for one of our ordering principles, the Progression Principle, says that subgames are played left to right (see Part I, sec. 8, and cf. Hintikka and Carlson 1979).

The restriction on coreference we have thus arrived at is closely related to a generalization known from the literature. It is the famous Langacker-Ross restriction on backwards anaphora (see here Langacker 1969 and Ross 1967). At first blush, the consequence of our ordering principle just formulated might seem to be precisely the Langacker-Ross condition. Thus we have placed this familiar condition on anaphoric coreference in a wider theoretical perspective. It is in terms of our theory but a consequence of the general ordering principles (plus, of course, certain other overall features of our approach). Since (O. comm), (O. LR) and the Progression Principle governing the order of subgames all have a great deal of independent evidence, our observations in effect serve as a partial theoretical justification of the Langacker-Ross restraint.

It is to be noted that our reconstructed version of the Langacker-Ross condition presupposes that (G. name) is subject to the same general ordering principle (O. comm) as other rules. For if it were not, and if NP_1 were a proper name, (G. name) could be applied to NP_1 before the appropriate pronominal rule is applied to NP_2, so as to introduce the entity named by NP_1 as a potential value of NP_2 (i.e., as a member of the choice set I used in applying this pronominal rule).

This is already an example of the power of our approach to put earlier discussion into a wider perspective. At the same time, the set of restrictions on backwards anaphora like the Langacker–Ross condition (suitably qualified, as discussed below) that can be derived from our theory is an illustration of a regularity that in virtually all competing analyses is treated as an empirical generalization but which in our approach can be shown to be explainable on the basis of more general laws.   For instance, in Chomsky 1981 restrictions on backwards pronominalization are treated as independent filters without any general theoretical backing.   This shows vividly the sense in which we are offering a genuine theory of anaphoric pronouns, unlike many of our competitors.

It is known, however, that the Langacker–Ross condition is only an approximative one, admitting a large number of counterexamples.   Do they tell also against our theory?   No, they do not, for there are subtle differences between the Langacker–Ross restriction on coreference and the implications of our general ordering principles.   Here we can register three important differences:

(i)   The Langacker–Ross condition is a consequence of our general ordering principles.   These can nevertheless be overruled by special ordering principles, as was already mentioned.   These special ordering principles may therefore cause exceptions to the Langacker–Ross condition, too.

Notice that such exceptions would not tell against our approach, even if they are counterexamples to the Langacker–Ross condition.   For it is part of our overall theory that general ordering principles are "weaker" than (subject to being overruled by) several special principles, e.g., (O. any) governing "any".

In the Langacker–Ross situation, the possibility of an exception depends on the game rule that applies to NP_1. One kind of exception to the unreconstructed Langacker–Ross rule can be expected to come about when this rule is not governed by the ordering principle (O. comm).   For most types of NP_1's, this does not seem to be the case.   The closest we have come to exceptions (exceptions, that is to say, to Langacker and Ross, not to our theory) are examples where the rule in question is (G. Russellian the):

(176)   It pleases him that best known doctor in the town finally got the recognition he thought he deserved.

(177)   It amused him that the most famous scientist in
               the world was not always recognized in shops
               and restaurants.

.(ii) We have already noted the Exclusion Principle
(see secs 11 and 13-14, above).   Likewise, we have given
reasons why the Exclusion Principle should be construed as
a principle largely independent of the syntactical structure
on which such general ordering principles as (O. comm) are
based.   The Exclusion Principle necessitates further
exceptions to the Langacker-Ross generalization.

(iii) In practice, the most important factor that drives
a wedge between our general ordering principles and such
approximative conditions restricting coreference as the
Langacker-Ross restraint is a matter of timing.   The
Langacker-Ross condition is usually formulated in terms of
the syntactical structure of the input sentence S_0 of an
entire semantical game.   Our ordering principles are
formulated so as to depend on the sentence S_1 reached in
the semantical game at the stage of the game at which a
rule is applied to a particular constituent of S_1.   The
syntactical structure of S_1 is of course derived from that of
S_0, but it is a part of the structure of S_0 only if the
intervening applications of game rules that took the players
from S_0 to S_1 don't change this structure.   It is obvious,
however, that they sometimes do change relevant aspects of
the syntactical structure of the sentences involved.
When the possibility of these three types of
discrepancies is realized, several well-known types of
exceptions to the Langacker-Ross condition are seen to be
explicable on the basis of our theory.   All these three ideas
will in fact be invoked in our discussion.   We shall begin
with (iii), which is probably the most important of the
three points.

22. The Timing of Rule Applications

The point (iii) can be generalized.   It is true in general
that the rules and principles of our theory (especially the
definition of I and the ordering principles) are brought into
play at the time when a rule for anaphoric pronouns is
applied and in the way determined by the sentence S_1 so
far reached in the game.   In contrast, the customary

accounts are based on what for us is the input sentence S_0 of an entire game. This can make a difference, for the intervening applications of game rules can for instance change the syntactical structure of S_0 in the transition to S_1.

On the basis of this observation, we can save not only the Langacker-Ross criterion (partly), but also other generalizations.

In doing so, we always have several different cases to consider depending on what the intervening game rule is that changes the structure of the input sentence. In one of them the operative rule is (G. genitive). Its influence serves to explain away, among other things, a class of apparent exceptions to our Exclusion Principle. They are illustrated by the following sentences:

(178)   Jane saw her sister.
(179)   Jane remembered her misfortune.

These look like exceptions to our Exclusion Principle in that "her" and "Jane" can be coreferential in (178)-(179), even though they occur in the same clause. As was pointed out in Part II, sec. 10, above, these exceptions are nevertheless merely apparent. For in (178)-(179) the game rule (G. genitive) has priority over (G. she) and yields sentences of the following forms:

(180)   Jane saw Jill, and Jill is a sister of hers.
(181)   Jane remembered the accident, and the accident is
           the misfortune of hers.

Here "hers" and "Jane" are in different clauses, and can hence be coreferential without violating the Exclusion Principle. What we have to assume, though, is that (G. genitive) can precede (G. she).

Here (G. genitive) can be formulated roughly as follows:

(G. genitive) If the game has reached a sentence of the form

X - Y's Z - W,

an individual b may be selected by Myself, whereupon the game is continued with respect to

X - b - W, and b is a(n)/the Z of Y.

Here the choice between "a(n)" and "the" is left to unspecified further factors, and small adjustments in Y for pronouns must be allowed.

This rule may be applied before our rules for anaphoric pronouns, but apparently does not have to be applied before them (optional order).

Apparent counterexamples to (G. genitive) as a viable game rule are created by a number of propositional-attitude verbs. The following is a case in point:

(182)   She remembered Jane's name.
(183)   She remembered Jane's accident.

Accordingly, the game rule (or rules) for "remember" must be formulated so as to allow (182) to be dealt with as if it were

(184)   She remembered what Jane's name is.

Otherwise, an application of (G. genitive) can yield a nonsensical sentence like

(185)   She remembered "Jane".   "Jane" is the name of Jane's.

When this need is taken into account in formulating rules for "remembers" there is no need to modify (G. genitive).

One reason why it is important to note this peculiarity of constructions with verbs like "remembers" is that otherwise we would have to countenance unwanted exceptions to the Langacker-Ross rule in the form in which we are espousing it. For in (182) "she" precedes but does not s-command "Jane's". Hence coreference is not ruled out by the Langacker-Ross rule, whereas it is clearly impossible in (182). For us, after we have noted how the game rule or rules for "remembers" have to be formulated in any case, there is no problem here, as little as there is a violation of the Langacker-Ross condition in (184), where this condition forbids coreference.

By taking into account the effects of (G. genitive), we can also dispose of some of the putative counterexamples that have been offered in the literature to the Langacker-Ross condition and which have been instrumental in attempts to improve on it. The following are cases in point:

(186)   I told his wife that John should consume less cholesterol.

(187)   Mary looked after his cat while John was on vacation.

Coreference should be ruled out here by the Langacker-Ross condition. Yet it is unmistakably possible. This can be predicted on the basis of the (optional) priority of (G. genitive) over (G. he), as in earlier examples.
        Notice that the situation is different if we don't have a genitive pronoun present:

(188)   I told him that John should consume less cholesterol.

(189)   She was taken care of by Mary while Jill was on vacation.

Even though some speakers seem to accept coreference in (188)-(189), this seems to be a marginal reading. In any case, the clear difference between (188)-(189) and (186)-(187) has to be explained, which we have just done.
        As will be explained in sec. 23 below, a prepositional construction can here have the same effect as the genitive, for instance, in the following example:

(190)   I saw from a single look at him that John ought to go on a diet.

        It has been claimed in effect in the literature that there are counterexamples to the power of (G. genitive) to change the left-to-right order of a pronoun and its potential "head". For instance, coreference is said to be impossible by some linguists in the following:

(191)   His mother hates John.

However, whatever is wrong with (191) does not have to do with its structure, including the role of the genitive pronoun "his", as has been pointed out by Bolinger 1979,

p. 293.   For instance, coreference is perfectly possible in
the following:

(192)   His mother hates John when he behaves that way.

(This example is Bolinger's.)   Hence we don't see any
reason to qualify our comments on the role of (G.
genitive).   Incidentally, the relation of (191) and (192)
reinforces Bolinger's points of how treacherous intuitive
evidence is in this area.   Linguists should really put more
faith in theoretical considerations like our ordering
principles and less on the examples that happen to occur to
them.
       It is worth noting here that our explanation of the
impossibility of coreference in (188)-(189) depends on the
assumption that (G. name) is subject to the general
ordering principle (O. comm).   For why can't we first
apply (G. name) to "John" in (188) and to "Jill" in (189) to
have the bearer of the name in *I* when the pronoun is
handled?   Because the proper name to which (G. name) is
to be applied is in a lower clause and hence (by (O.
comm)) inaccessible to an application before an application
of (G. he) or (G. she).
       Another instructive group of examples is the following:

(193)   Bill disgraced himself.
(194)   Bill disgraced him.
(195)   Bill's brother disgraced himself.
(196)   Bill's brother disgraced him.
(197)   Bill's brother's book disgraced him.

We leave the details of these examples for our readers to
work out.
       A slightly more complicated example of the explanations
our theory yields is the unacceptability of the following (cf.
Kuno 1983, p. 267):

(198)   John found Mary's picture of himself in the
             gallery.

Coreference is impossible here.   We can explain this easily.
An application of (G. genitive) yields something like this:

(199)   John found "Interior with Husband" in the gal-

> lery, and "Interior with Husband" is a picture
> of Mary's of himself.

Here "himself" is obviously out of place, and a fortiori the
same is true of (198).

It is distinctly encouraging to see that we can explain
away in one and the same way apparent exceptions to two
entirely different and (if we are right) unrelated
generalizations, namely, to the Exclusion Principle and to
the Langacker–Ross condition (more properly, to its
reconstructed counterpart in our theory).

In the same way, we can explain why there are no
genitive reflexive pronouns in English.   Our theory shows
that such a form would be redundant, for an ordinary
anaphoric pronoun in the genitive form can do the same job
as a genitive reflexive would (see sec. 13 above).   For
instance, consider the sentence

(200)   *John polished himself's car.

If "himself" is interpreted here in the same way (i.e.,
subjected to the same game rule) as this reflexive pronoun
is normally interpreted, (187) would turn out to mean the
same as

(201)   John polished his car.

on the context-independent reading of (200).   In other
words, we can see that a genitive reflexive pronoun would
be vacuous in English.   The treatment we have outlined
thus explains why genitive reflexive pronouns are missing
from English: they are not needed.

Our explanation presupposes that the rule for
genitives (G. genitive) can be applied before the rules for
personal pronouns.   If this ordering principle did not
obtain, there would be room for reflexive genitives.   This
seems to be the case with other languages, e.g., Swedish.
There coreference is possible only in the first of the
following two examples, the first of which has a reflexive
genitive, the second a nonreflexive third-person genitive
personal pronoun:

(202)   Stig såg sin lärare.
            (Stig saw his own teacher.)

(203)   Stig såg hans lärare.
          (Stig saw his, i.e., someone else's, teacher.)

Indeed, if a rule for genitives is applied first in (202)-(203), we obtain something like

(204)   Stig såg Gustav. Gustav är sin lärare.
          (.. Gustav is his teacher.)

and

(205)   Stig såg Gustav. Gustav är hans lärare
          (... Gustav is his teacher.)

Here (204) is not fully acceptable without the addition of a word like "egen" (own). But such an addition assigns (204) a sense incompatible with (202), and (205) assigns to (203) the sense (202) in fact has. In contrast, if the pronoun is evaluated first, we obtain something like the following:

(206)   Stig såg Stigs lärare. Stig är en man.
(207)   Stig såg Peters lärare. Peter är en man.

These assign the right sense to (202)-(203). Thus in Swedish the rule for genitives does not have a priority over rules for anaphoric pronouns. This shows that the presence of a genitive reflexive in Swedish is in fact correlated with a different ordering principle, just as was suggested.

Our observations concerning a class of apparent counterexamples to the Langacker-Ross condition were seen to apply because and in so far as the rule (G. genitive) is to be used before the rule (G. he). This is the normal order of application of the different game rules. But it is to be noted that if there are rules that can be used besides (G. he) and (G. genitive), the effects of their application can affect the prima facie anaphoric relations (the so-called relations of pronouns to their heads). This can make an inverted anaphora (in the conventional sense of the word) impossible. It can likewise affect all sorts of other prima facie anaphoric relations. For instance, we already noted in sec. 19 above that two different relations of forward anaphora are possible in the following sentence:

(208)   Bill is the only man who loves his wife.

On one of the resulting readings, Bill is the sole virtuous husband; on the other, Bill is merely not a cuckold.   How do these two readings come about?   They cannot have anything to do with the genitive in (208), for we have the same situation in examples like the following:

(209)   Gauss was the only mathematician who did not be-
             lieve that he could solve every problem.

On one of its readings, (209) says Gauss was the only moderately modest   mathematician; on the other, it says that Gauss was the only mathematician who doubted Gauss's problem-solving omnipotence.[4]
     It appears that the first game rule to be applied to (208) is (G. name) followed by (G. the) or by (G. he). The rule (G. genitive) cannot apply because of (O. comm), for "his" occurs in (208) in a lower clause.   In applying the rule (G. the), Myself's best hope for a winning strategy obviously is to select Bill (who has just been introduced by (G. name)).   This yields

(210)   Bill is Bill, Bill is a man, Bill loves his wife, but
             Tom is not a man who loves his wife.

Here Tom is assumed to have been chosen by Nature after Myself has chosen Bill in (210).   (G. and) applies and can yield

(211)   Tom is not a man who loves his wife.

This results in the "sole virtuous husband" reading (208). However, instead of applying (G. the) the players could have applied (G. he) because of the ordering principle mentioned above in sec. 20.   This yields obviously

(212)   Bill is the only man who loves Bill's wife.

This results in the "no cuckold" reading of (208).
     In contrast to (208), the following sentence has only one natural reading:

(213)   The only man who loves his wife is Bill.

Why is this the case? In (213), (G. name) does not apply before (G. the) or (G. he) because of (O. LR). Since the rule applicable here is clearly the rule (G. the) governing the Russellian use of "the", its applicability is not hampered by Bill's not having been picked out in the game. However, (G. he) does not apply to (213), because the choice set is empty. Hence the next sentence making its appearance in the game is like (210), which explains the readings (213) has and doesn't have.

The example (209) can be dealt with in the same way.

These examples illustrate strikingly the advantages of our dynamic approach, which takes into account the order of rule application, over a static account that relies only on the coreference relations in the given initial sentence. The only way that a static theory has of accounting for the difference between (208) and (213) is to say that in the former "his" can be coreferential with either "Bill" or "the only man" whereas in (213) it can be coreferential only with "The only man". It is not perhaps very hard to formulate purely technical rules for possible coreference on which this is the case. However, then the notion of coreference does not make any sense, for the brute fact remains that both in (208) and in (213) "his" is coreferential both with "Bill" and "the only man" in the natural sense of coreference possible here. This criticism is lent especially acute bite by the practice of many linguists (cf., e.g., Radford (1981), pp. 368, 370) of identifying possible coreference (possibility of proper binding) with interpretability, can at least interpretability independently of context. The only way of interpreting (208) and (213) is to take "his" to be coreferential with "Bill" and "the only man" in both of them.

The explanation we gave turned essentially on the question whether another rule, viz. (G. name), can apply in our approach to the given sentence before (G. he) is applied to it. Thus we can understand several things about (208) by taking into account what can happen to it before (G. he) is applied: (i) Why it makes a difference in (208) whether "Bill" or "the only man" is the so-called head of "his" even though they refer to the same individual (if (208) is true); (ii) Why (208) has the readings it in fact has; (iii) Why only one of the two possible "heads" is possible in (213) as distinguished from (208).

Our explanation also predicts that if there is some other way of introducing Bill as a member of the choice set

I in (213), the other reading would become possible. Since such an introduction can be contextual, there are discourse examples to confirm this prediction. For instance, in the following example the reading that was missing in (213) is in fact possible:

(214)   Bill is a happily married man. The only man who loves his wife is indeed Bill.

This serves to support our diagnosis of (208) and (213).

23. Rules for Prepositional Phrases

In a similar way, we can handle another class of apparent counterexamples to the Exclusion Principle. In them, the intervening rule is not (G. genitive), but a rule for one kind of prepositional phrase or another. They are illustrated by the following sentences:

(215)   Near him, Ernest saw a snake.
(216)   Ernest brought Mary with him to the party.

Here "Ernest" and "him" should not be coreferential, says the unreconstructed Exclusion Principle. Yet they can clearly be coreferential. The way to deal with these is fairly clearly to have separate game rules for "near" and "with". The former can be formulated as follows:

> (G. near)   If the game has reached a sentence of the form
> X – near Y – Z
>
> one of the players may choose a location, say one named by "b". The game is then continued with respect to
>
> X – prep+b – Z, and b is near Y.

Here prep+b is "b" with the appropriate prepositional construction, such as "in b", "on b", etc.

Notice that in (G. near) the players do not enjoy the same privilege of choosing the order of the two clauses or sentences of the output as they have in many of the other more "propositional" rules, such as the quantifier rules.

The effects of this new rule can be illustrated by an application of (G. near) to (215), which can yield the following sentence:

(217)   On the lawn, Ernest saw a snake, and the lawn is near him.

For vividness of example, we are here (and in what follows) treating definite descriptions like "the lawn" as if they were names. We shall not try to attempt an explicit formulation of (G. with). It is sufficiently explained by seeing how it applies to (216). It will yield

(218)   Ernest brought Mary to the party, and Mary was with him.

In both cases, "Ernest" and "him" end up in different clauses. Hence the Exclusion Principle, in conjunction with the rest of our theory, does not rule out their coreferentiality.

The same assumptions allow us to deal with certain apparent exceptions to the Langacker-Ross condition. They are exemplified by such sentences as the following:

(219)   I was near him when Jack was hit.

Here the Langacker-Ross condition seems to rule out a coreference of "Jack" and "him". Yet such a coreference is clearly possible.

This is explained by noting that, an application of (G. near) to (219) can yield

(220)   I was on first base when Jack was hit.   First base was near him.

There is nothing here to rule out the coreferentiality of "Jack" and "him".

In contrast to (215), coreference is not possible in the following sentence

(221)   Near Ernest, he saw a snake.

The explanation is the same as applies to (215). An application of (G. near) moves "Ernest" to a later clause or even a later sentence, yielding something like

(222)   On the lawn, he saw a snake. The lawn is near
            Ernest.

Here Ernest is not normally available as a member of *I* when
(G. he) is applied.   This explains the impossibility of
coreference in (221).
    Notice also that the mechanism that explains the
coreference restraints in (215) and (221) is subject to
interference by other game rules.   For instance, consider

(223)   Near him, each soldier found a loaded weapon.

Coreference is clearly possible here. Why? The rule (G.
each) has priority over most other rules, presumably
including (G. near).   Hence it has to be applied first in
(223).   Now an application of (G.every) to (223) yields,
with the proper choice of order of clauses,

(224)   If Victor is a soldier, then, near Victor, he
            found a loaded weapon.

Here coreference is obviously possible, explaining why it
was possible in (223), too.
    The need of game rules for such prepositions as
"near" and "with" shows also certain interesting things
about the semantics of prepositions.   One thing we can see
is that there is a difference between the occurrences of
prepositions where they are part of the verb construction
and where they are part of adverbial phrases.   The latter
are treated by means of game rules of the kind we have
formulated.   The former are dealt with by means of lexical
rules applying typically to the end-point sentences ("atomic
sentences") of semantical games.
    This contrast is known from the literature, and is not
at all ad hoc.   It is usually referred to as a distinction
between a prepositional phrase (PP) that is "verb-phrasal"
and a PP that is "sentential".   Linguists use various tests
to distinguish these two types.   Without going into great
detail here, let us consider some of the linguistic evidence
invoked by Reinhart (1976):

(225)   Rosa is riding a horse in Ben's picture.
(226)   Rosa found a scratch in Ben's picture.

The PPs in (225) and (226) are of different type. First of all, notice how pseudo clefting affects acceptability:

(227)   *What Rosa did was ride a horse in Ben's picture
(228)   What Rosa did was find a scratch in Ben's picture.
(229)   What Rosa did in Ben's picture was ride a horse.
(230)   *What Rosa did in Ben's picture was find a scratch.

Only VP material can occur in the predicate of a pseudo-clefted sentence, while only non-VP material can occur in the what-clause.
Finally, only non-VP material can be interposed between subject and VP (keeping the meaning constant), as the following show:

(231)   John probably came.
(232)   *John by bus came.
(233)   Rosa, in Ben's picture, is riding a horse.
(234)   *Rosa, in Ben's picture, found a scratch.

These observations show the reality (and interest) of a distinction between verb-phrasal and sentential PPs. Our game-theoretical treatment shows what the semantical difference between the two really is.
This contrast need not be thought of as being completely black-or-white, however. The later a preposition like "near" is treated in a semantical game, the closer its semantics comes to being essentially lexical. What is important here is the relative order of prepositional rules like (G. near) and rules like (G. he). Hence, as so often, the crucial question turns out to be one of rule ordering.
In some of their occurrences, prepositions can be treated in either way. Then the difference between the two can be manifested by the presence or absence of reflexive pronouns. The reason is that since applications of rules like (G. near) move the bulk of the prepositional phrase to another clause, the applicability of such rules may make the use of a reflexive pronoun dispensable. On the other hand, treating the preposition as a part of the verbal construction may necessitate using reflexive pronouns. If both treatments are possible, both reflexive and nonreflexive pronouns may be possible in the same environment. This phenomenon is known from the

literature, and is illustrated by such examples as the following (cf. Wasow 1979, p. 24):

(235)   Mrs. Cabot wrapped the stole around her.
(236)   Mrs. Cabot wrapped the stole around herself.
(237)   It annoys John that a picture of him is hanging in the post office.
(238)   It annoys John that a picture of himself is hanging in the post office.

These exemplify the apparent counterexamples to the mutual exclusion of reflexive and nonreflexive pronouns in the same environment that was mentioned above in sec. 13 above.   Now we can see that in the last analysis these are not genuine counterexamples to the (correctly understood) exclusiveness of reflexive and nonreflexive pronouns in the same environment.   For at the time the pronoun is dealt with in (235) and in (236) it occurs in a different environment in the two cases.   In brief, we don't have here instances of two different ways in which anaphoric pronouns can work but of two different ways in which prepositions can work.

     This difference can create subtle differences in meaning between analogous sentences containing reflexive and nonreflexive pronouns.   We can even predict what the differences will be.   Treating the preposition as verb phrasal obviously presupposes or suggests a closer semantical relationship between the reference of the pronoun and what is said about it.   Kuno (1983) discusses this matter in a most perceptive fashion, and formulates the following generalization:

(239)   Reflexives with clausemate antecedents require that their referents be the direct targets of the actions or states represented by the verb phrases.

This is exemplified by the following:

(240)   John put the blanket under him.
(241)   John put the blanket under himself.
(242)   Descartes commissioned the portrait of him by Hals.
(243)   John Doe has a snapshot of himself in his wallet.

In (242), the famous painting has, as it were, a life of its own. That it is a portrait of Cartesius is not particularly important to its aesthetic qualities and other important attributes. In contrast, a snapshot of John Doe is just a snapshot of John Doe – nothing more, nothing less. Indeed, the right generalization seems to be more like Zribi-Hertz's (1980), whose formulation is essentially the same as ours. He puts it as follows: "The more direct the semantical relationship established by the predicate between the referent of NP_1 and that of NP_2 (where the two are coreferential), the better the reflexive form and the worse the nonreflexive." Neither Zribi-Hertz nor Kuno offers any theoretical motivation for their respective rules. In our treatment, however, the regularity Zribi-Hertz notes is not merely an empirical generalization, as it is in Zribi-Hertz and as the narrower generalization (239) is in Kuno. These generalizations are predicted by our theory, other things being equal. This leads to the generalizations put forward by Kuno and Zribi-Hertz and lends them additional theoretical respectability. The derivability of their empirical generalizations from an overall theory shows that they are not recording mere stylistic devices or conventional usages, but regularities at least partly based on interesting semantical rules of language.

The following are additional examples illustrating the same general point:

(244)   I told John about myself.
(245)   I told John about me.
(246)   Tom was beside himself.
(247)   Tom had a book beside him.

It is unmistakable that the more intimate my message to John is, the more appropriate (244) is in contrast to (245). In (246), Tom is beside his very own temperamental self, whereas in (247) the book is merely beside his body.

It is interesting to see that the very same theoretical observation enables us to explain other phenomena that prima facie have nothing to do with the distribution of reflexives. If some prepositional phrases have to be dealt with by means of a rule application and others as a part of the semantics of the verb in question, this difference will predictably show up also, e.g., in the conditions on backwards anaphora. This is illustrated by the following pair of examples from Jackendoff (1972):

(248)   In John's picture of Mary, she looks tired.
(249)   In John's picture of Mary, she found a scratch.

In (248), the force of the "in" phrase depends on the construction with the verb, and has to be dealt as a part of the lexical semantics of "looks". (Looking X in a picture is not the same as looking X and being in a picture.) Hence the first rule to apply to (248) is (G. genitive), which yields something like

(250)   "Interior with Wife" is a picture of Mary of John's. In "Interior with Wife", she looks tired.

Coreference is all right here and hence in (248). In contrast, in (249) we have a normal adverbial use of an "in" phrase. Hence the rule (G. in) applies first, yielding something like

(251)   In the dark area, she found a scratch. The dark area is in John's picture of Mary.

Coreference is unnatural here, and by the same token in (249). This explains the difference between (248) and (249) on the basis of the two roles that prepositions can play semantically.

In the usual treatments, attempts have been made to capture the contrast between the two ways of construing prepositional phrases by postulating a difference in the syntactical structure in the two cases. The difference is in terms of what the prepositional phrase "modifies", more explicitly, whether it "modifies" the verb (verb-phrase prepositions) or the entire clause (sentential prepositions). For instance, in (215) it is supposed to modify "a snake", so that (215) could be paraphrased as "Ernest saw a snake that was near him."

This distinction is compatible with our treatment, and can do some of the same things as our conceptual scheme. It nevertheless involves commitment to syntactical assumptions of the kind we are trying to minimize. We prefer to leave open the question whether our semantical distinction is reflected in the details of syntactical structure.

The contrast we are finding here seems to be related also to the apparent exceptions to the ordering principle governing nested prepositional phrases that was noted above in Part I, sec. 8. The ordering principle mentioned there goes together with prepositions as a part of the verbal construction, whereas exceptions seems to go together with prepositions as being governed by a specific game rule. This contrast is illustrated by the following pair of examples:

(252)   Every ape near a tree ran for it.
(253)   Every single taxpayer in some rural town failed to
          vote.

Here the separate rule treatment is more natural in (252), and hence the back-to-front ordering principle less natural, than in (253).

24. Don't Try to Anticipate the Course of a Semantical Game

A supplementary methodological comment on the difference (iii) between our approach and its rivals (see sec. 21 above) may be in order. The changes that take place between the initial sentence S_U of a semantical game and the sentence S_1 to which a pronoun rule is actually applied are of course determined largely by the syntactical structure of S_0. So what's wrong with trying to formulate the rules for anaphoric pronouns in terms of S_0, as happens in the competing approaches, instead of S_1, since the structure of the former determines the latter, anyway? What is wrong, not absolutely but comparatively, is that an attempt to force the syntactical structure of S_0 to do all the work results in packing into pronoun coreference rules several different kinds of regularities. In effect, in trying to do so one must anticipate in these rules everything that might happen in the transition from S_0 to S_1, over and above covering the way pronoun rules apply to S_1. Such anticipation need perhaps not be impossible, but an attempt to force the coreference rules to do two entirely different kinds of job makes their formulation extremely awkward. What we have seen in the last few sections illustrates the variety of intervening factors and thereby the difficulty of keeping track of all of them. We have not even considered cases in which more than one intervening rule application changes the structure of the initial sentence before a generalization like the Langacker-Ross constraint or the Exclusion Principle is applied. Repeated applications would complicate

further the task of those who rely only on the structure of
the input sentence of a semantical game. This need to
anticipate intervening rule applications, more than anything
else, is the basic reason for the complications to which
other recent accounts of coreference restrictions in the
literature have been forced to resort.

The difficulties competing accounts face are not merely
complications, however. A matter of principle may be
involved. An application of a game rule is triggered by a
word or a phrase characterized by a certain lexical item.
The special ordering principles depend on these particular
lexical items, and hence are not completely determined by
the syntactical structure of the sentence in question.
Hence the regularities we are after here probably cannot in
the last analysis be captured by any formulation that relies
entirely on the syntactic structure of the sentences one is
dealing with.

This is illustrated by our treatment of prepositional
phrases in the preceding section. There, certain prima
facie exceptions to our generalizations were explained by
assuming an intervening application of a rule for some
preposition such as (G. near). Such rules are tied to a
particular lexical item, e.g., "near". If the account we
gave is basically correct, the presence of such lexical items
in the input sentence will make a difference to the
coreference restraints applying to it. But if so, these
restraints are not any longer likely to depend solely on the
syntactical structure of the input sentence.

In fact, there are differences in this respect between
different prepositions. It is to be expected that "X in Y"
expresses a closer relation between X and Y than "X near
Y". Hence, on the basis of what was said in sec. 23,
coreference without reflexives is somewhat rarer with "in"
than with other prepositions. This seems to be confirmed
by examples. Here are some:

(254)   In himself, John recognized some of his father's
          characteristics.
(255)   In him, John recognized some of his father's
          characteristics.

Coreference is not possible in the latter. Hence the
desired generalization, if it is to refer to the input
sentence, cannot be formulated by speaking of the

grammatical category of prepositional phrases. It has to mention particular prepositions.

We are not dealing here with a hard-and-fast regularity, however. One can, for instance, dissociate a person from his body sufficiently to say, e.g.,

(256)   Most of the soldiers were not wounded, but Bill still has a bullet lodged in him.

It may be noted that the same impossibility also results from the influence of special ordering principles – the impossibility, that is to say, of formulating coreference conditions solely in terms of the syntactic structure of the input sentence of a semantical game. For special ordering principles can be geared to specific lexical items, and can therefore introduce exceptions to generalizations that are based merely on the structure of the given sentence (the input sentence). (Cf. secs. 21 and 27.)

An illustration of these difficulties encountered by other approaches is offered by the examples (101)-(104) (above, sec. 13):

(101)   John asked Mary to shave him.
(102)   *John asked Mary to shave himself.
(103)   John promised Mary to shave him.
(104)   John promised Mary to shave himself.

Here we are not dealing with conditions on coreference, such as the Langacker-Ross rule, but with conditions on the acceptability and necessity of reflexives. These examples (101)-(104) show vividly how hard it is to formulate simple and realistic conditions in terms of the syntactic structure of what for us is the initial sentence of a semantical game. For, prima facie the syntactical structure of (101) and (103) as well as of (102) and (104) is the same. Moreover, it is natural to think that what makes the difference between the two pairs of examples is not a difference in syntactic structure, but the difference between the lexical items "ask" and "promise".

In our approach, there is no problem, for our pronoun rule applies not to the initial sentence of a semantical game, but to the sentence the players face when the application is made. Hence, what makes a difference between (101)-(102) and (103)-(104) is an antecedent application of a game rule for "ask" or for "promise", respectively. What the game rules governing such lexical items as "ask" and "promise" will look like is illustrated by means of examples in the next section.   The reason why applications of such rules are antecedent is the relative order of the different game rules, as governed by our ordering principles.   If that order could be changed, we would (so our theory predicts) get different results.   The following will perhaps illustrate, at least partially, this possibility:

(257)   Him, John asked Mary to shave.
(258)   Himself, John asked Mary to shave.

Here the presumption of a coreferentiality of "John" and "him" is weaker in (257) than it was in (101), and coreference is less objectionable in (258) than in (102). This is because our ordering principles now prescribe an application of (G. he) before "asked" is handled.
      Even if competing theorists should manage to find a way of dealing with such examples, it is inevitable (we believe) that the resulting account will be much more complicated than ours.   For then such an account will have to involve building into the presumed structure of the intial sentence of a semantical game an anticipation of all the different things that may happen to it in a semantical game. Even if this should be possible we do not see any advantages in doing so.
      Some competing theorists still face another, probably smaller, difficulty.   As we shall indicate they can try to capture in another way some of the effect as we are capturing by means of intervening rule applications.   The sequence of game-rule applications to S is (very roughly) a reverse mirror image of one possible generation process of S.   Generative theorists can therefore try to capture the right regularities by making these regularities depend on some earlier stage of the generation.   But, in many treatments, lexical insertions are not yet made at such earlier stages.   If so, it is most unlikely that theorists of this kind can capture the right generalizations.

25. Surface vs. Deep Structure

The problem we are discussing here - problem for others, not for us - has not gone entirely unnoticed in the literature.   It was noted in sec. 21 (iii) above (and anticipated in sec. 13) that our regularities apply at the time the operative rule is applied in a semantical game. In contrast, in the conventional approaches the relevant regularities have to be formulated by reference to the structure of the input sentence S of the entire game G(S). This means that the subsequent course of the game has to be anticipated on the basis of the structure of S. For this purpose, the surface structure of S does not always suffice, and some sort of deeper structure has to be invoked in order to save theoretically important generalizations. In contrast, in our theory the task is not to dig deeper into the syntactical structure of S but rather to formulate the intervening game rules.

A simple example here is the following, which takes us back to the problems mentioned in sec. 13 above:

(259)   John wants to see himself on TV.

Here the prima facie subordinate clause "to see himself on TV" has no head for "himself" to be pronominalized by. Hence the necessity of using a reflexive pronoun is apparently not explained by our rules for reflexives, sketched in sec. 13 above.

We shall not discuss here whether, and if so how, this example could be treated by means of further analysis of the syntactical structure of the example. What happens in our approach is obvious: we have to formulate a game rule for the construction "b wants to S". Such a rule will clearly look somewhat as follows:

(G. wants to)   When the game has reached a sentence of the form

(260)   b wants to X

and a world w_1, then a want-alternative w_2 to w_1 (with respect to b) is chosen by Nature. The game is continued with respect to w_2 and the sentence

(261)   b X'

where X' is like X except that the main verb is in the appropriate finite form, not in an infinitival form, as in X.

An application of this rule to (259) will yield the following sentence, considered by the players with respect to some alternative world:

(262)   John sees himself on TV.

Here the need of a reflexive is blatant.

In this way, we can explain a number of apparent exceptions to what was said in sec. 13 above.   It is important to realize that the motivation of such rules as (G. wants to) is completely independent of the specific problems concerning reflexives or anaphora.

Other verbs that behave as "want" does here with respect to reflexives include "like", "dislike", "need", "yearn", "hope", "will", "expect", "have", "try", "intend", "know", and "seek".

Even though we are not going to discuss in detail the question whether, and if so how, the same explanations can be reached in other approaches by analyzing further the syntactical structure of the input sentence, it is relevant to note the fact that this is not a trivial problem.   It is in effect discussed by linguists in the form of discussions about what level of syntactical generation the restraints on, and other rules concerning, anaphora should apply.   For instance, in interpretivist theories like Jackendoff's, reflexives are already present in the deep structure (Jackendoff 1972).   Hence the rules concerning their admissibility must apply on that level.

We are not concerned with Jackendoff's theory as such.   What we are interested in is first the fact that some of the counterexamples that have been put forward against Jackendoff illustrate the same general point we have argued in the last few secs: the need of considering the applications of game rules that intervene between the initial sentence and the stage of the semantical game at which the crucial rule is applied that determines coreference or the admissibility of reflexives – or some other such thing. Second, we note the fact that these counterexamples show the difficulty of doing the same job as our game rules and ordering principles do by means of the syntactic structure of the input sentence.

In the case of Jackendoff, instructive examples have in fact been produced by Harada and Saito (1971).   One of them is the following:

(263)   Bill believes himself to be hard for Max to under-
             stand.

Its syntactic deep structure is something like (264) (see the
next page).

        In (264) Jackendoff's original rules would lead him to
consider "himself" as coreferential with "Max", which of
course it is not.   In contrast, in our approach (263) has
"Bill" and "himself" in the same clause at the time when the
pronoun rule is applied to "himself".   We have to assume,
of course, that this happens before an appropriate rule for
"believes + to" is applied.   However, there is independent
evidence for this ordering of the game rules, in any case.

(264)

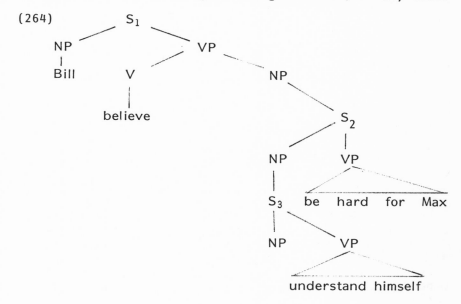

        The obvious motivation for this rule-ordering is that,
without such ordering, the rule (G. believes to) would
produce   an   ill-formed   output.   This   illustrates   the
explanatory strategy (iii) mentioned above in Part I, sec.
12, of this work.   In fact, by the same token, the game
rules for reflexives can be applied before any rule that can
likewise produce an ill-formed output.   This observation
applies   to   the   rule   that   applies   to   a   reflexive   R   in
comparison   with   any   other   rule   whose   output   includes

clauses (a) subordinate to the S containing r or (b) clauses derived from clauses subordinate to that S. This observation captures an important feature of the behaviour of reflexives.

In our own treatment, a related problem is to see why (263) has the meaning it has, i.e., why the person who is hard for Max to understand is Bill and not himself. In order to see whát the situation is, witness an approximate form of the requisite rule:

(G. believes to) If the game has reached a sentence of the form

(265)   b believes X to Y

and a world w_1, then a doxastic b-alternative w_2 to w_1 may be chosen by Nature. The game is then continued with respect to w_2 and

(266)   X – Y'

where Y' is like Y except that the main verb is in a finite form (determined by X).

This rule will not always yield a grammatical output, for – tentatively speaking – anaphoric back references to "b" in (265) may be lost in (266). In particular, any reflexive pronoun in X will become an orphan. Hence the rule for reflexive pronouns in X will have to be given priority over the rule (G. believes to).

With this rule-ordering, (263) receives the correct meaning. For, before (G. believes to) is applied, (G. himself) has to be applied. After the two applications, preceded of course by an application of (G. name), we obtain

(267)   Bill is hard for Max to understand.

In this case, the explanation our theory yields does not even need the postulation of any special ordering principles.

This also illustrates further how the merely apparent counterexamples mentioned in sec. 13 can be handled in our theory by taking into account what happens to a sentence in the course of a semantical game.

26. Other Intervening Rules

Yet another way in which intervening rule applications can affect the possibility of coreference can be seen from the following examples:

(268)   She admires everybody who works for Lola.
(269)   Everybody who works with Lola admires her.
(270)   Everybody who works with her admires Lola.

Here coreference is possible in (269)-(270) but not in (268). Of these three examples, (268) and (270) are immediately explained by our principles. For instance, in (270) (G. name) can be applied before (G. every), even though "Lola" occurs to the right of "Everybody", for (G. name) has a priority over other rules applicable to the ingredients of the same clause. Hence Lola is in *I* by the time "her" is treated.

However, (269) prima facie is not likewise explainable. For in (269) "Lola" occurs in a lower clause than "her", and hence apparently Lola is not available as a value of "her" when the latter is treated in the game.

An explanation is offered by the fact that the first move in the game connected with (269) is obviously an application of (G. every). It can yield a sentence of the following form:

(271)   If Jill works with Lola, Jill admires her.

provided that the order of clauses in the output sentence is chosen appropriately. Here coreference is obviously possible.

This explanation assumes that (G. every) is formulated in such a way that the players have a choice in applying it. The output sentence of this rule is a conditional. The choice we have assumed is between the two left-to-right orderings of the antecedent and the consequent of this conditional.

There are other prima facie problem cases connected with the Langacker-Ross restraint that can be discussed by means of our theory. Here are some examples (adapted from Reinhart):

(272)   The chairman hit him on the head before Linus
               had a chance to say anything.
(273)   Rosa won't like him any more, after Ben has lost
               all his hair.

The majority of linguists seem to believe that coreference is
possible in (272)-(273), even though it is ruled out by the
Langacker-Ross rule. However, this judgment is
questionable and has little to do with the syntactical form of
(272)-(273). For there are other examples of the same
syntactical form where coreference is not at all plausible,
e.g.,

(274)   Ali hits him on the head while the speaker merely
               drones on and on.
(275)   Rosa won't see him any more, after her husband
               has found out.

The situation is made murkier still by the claim voiced in
the literature that in sentences like the following, obviously
closely related to (272)-(273), coreference is not possible:

(276)   He was hit on the head by the chairman before
               Linus had a chance to say anything.
(277)   He won't expect Rosa to like him any more, after
               Ben lost all his hair.

But here, too, the syntactical structure does not seem to
be the crucial factor, as stressed by the following examples
in which coreference appears much more natural:

(278)   He was beaten up by gangsters because Clyde
               failed to pay his gambling debts.
(279)   He expected Rosa to admire him after Ben won a
               gold medal.

     Hence it seems to us hopeless to hypothesize some
difference in the syntactical structure between the instances
of acceptable and unacceptable coreference. The reasonable
course is to say that on the basis of the basic linguistic
(semantical) situation alone coreference should be impossible
in both (272)-(273). What remains to be explained then is
why in some cases there is a temptation, no doubt
encouraged by some variety of the principle of charity, to
allow coreference.

In the literature, examples like (272)-(273) are sometimes classified with others that are of a somewhat different nature. The following are cases in point (the first example taken from Reinhart 1983a, p. 34):

(280)   We finally had to fire him since McIntosh's weird habits had reached an intolerable stage.
(281)   If he owns it, Bill beats a donkey.

The syntactic structure of (281) is (partially):

(282)   [[If he owns it] Bill beats a donkey]

Hence the order of the relevant rules applicable here is, because of (O. comm), (G. name) (applied to "Bill"), (G. an), (G. cond) (introducing the division into subgames), (G. he) (applied to "he"), and (G. it) (applied to "it"). What this means is that the last two rules are applied in the first subgame only after values have been assigned to "Bill" and "a donkey". Hence suitable values are available for "he" and "it" after all, which means that they can be "coreferential" with "Bill" and "a donkey".

Notice that the only assumptions we need here are trivial assumptions about the syntactical structure of (281) plus (O. comm), applied in a reasonable way in the context of subgames, viz., in the way most directly suggested by the syntactic structure.

This explains the possibility of coference in (281). In (280), a different explanation is in order. Without going into the details of the semantics of since-constructions, we can say that there is some pressure to reverse the left-to-right subgame order in the case of sentences with "since" like (280). If the reversal is carried out, "him" has a value (to wit, McIntosh) in the game G(We finally had to fire him). This serves to explain why there is some tendency to allow coreference in (280). This explanation turns on one particular lexical element in (280), viz., that of "since".

Whatever the details of this explanation, the comparative point is clear. There does not seem to be any realistic hope of explaining the differences between (272)-(275) (with respect to the admissibility of coreference in them) by reference to their syntactical structure. In comparison, some partial explanation along the lines we have indicated flows naturally from our general theory.

27. Coreferentiality and Special Ordering Principles

One of the empirical generalizations that has been proposed in the literature as governing anaphoric pronouns is the following:

(283)   If a definite pronoun is to the left of an NP, the NP may be coreferential with the pronoun only if it is definite.

(See, e.g., Postal 1970.)   What can we say of this putative generalization from the vantage point of our theory? Basically, it says that rules for indefinite NPs do not have priority over rules for anaphoric pronouns like (G. he). The usual examples listed in support of (83) also support this ordering principle in many cases.   Here are some of Postal's examples:

(284)   The man who lost it needs to find something.
(285)   The man who lost something needs to find it.
(286)   The fact that he lost amused somebody in the crowd.
(287)   Somebody in the crowd was amused by the fact that he lost.

Coreference is possible only in the second member of these pairs of examples.
       There is in fact further evidence that rules like (G. some) do not have such priority over rules like (G. he) as would overrule (O. LR).   However, there is no deeper theoretical reason why this priority relation should hold between (G. he) and all rules for indefinite NPs.   Indeed, there is a quantifier phrase that notoriously tends to have wider scope but that is nevertheless indefinite.   This quantifier expression is "a certain".   Hence it may be expected that counterexamples to (274) can be found among sentences containing "a certain".
       Such counterexamples are known from the literature; cf., e.g., Wasow (1979) and Reinhart (1983a).   Here are some of their examples:

(288)   After Bill kissed her, a certain young lady blush-
             ed repeatedly.
(289)   That he was not elected upset a certain leading
             politician.

The same applies also to some extent to the quantifier words "a" and "any". Consider such examples as the following:

(290)   The woman he loved betrayed a man I know.
(291)   The fact that he is being sued should worry any businessman.

Now we can locate these examples on a theoretical map of the marvelous land of anaphora. They can be predicted, on the basis of our theory. What happens in them is that (O. comm) enables the players to introduce an individual into *I* before the pronoun is handled.

28. Different Explananda

The theoretical superiority of our approach is also shown by the fact that it rises to the interesting challenge recently issued by Tanya Reinhart (1983a). She points out that in dealing with coreference, we have to distinguish three cases from each other: (a) obligatory coreference; (b) impossible coreference; (c) optional (possible but not required) coreference. She emphasizes that a satisfactory theory of anaphora should explain the triple distinction – explain not only the possibility or impossibility but also the necessity or nonnecessity of coreference.

Admittedly, we have so far given a sense only to the idea of possible coreference. However, in certain restricted cases we can also give sense to the idea of obligatory coreference. We cannot have such a relation between a nonreflexive pronoun and a potential "head" in a given clause or sentence, for there is nothing in the rules for nonreflexive pronouns that would prevent a member of the choice set *I* coming from the outside of the clause or sentence in question, even from the discourse context. We can have an obligatory coreference only in the case of reflexive pronouns, where the choice set is restricted to entities ruled out by the Exclusion Principle and hence picked out by phrases in the same clause as the reflexive pronoun. If this choice set has only one member, we have an instance of "obligatory" coreference.

It is of some interest to note that this explanation does not assign a definite sense to the notion of coreference simpliciter, only to the notion of obligatory coreference.

On the basis of these observations, we can nevertheless offer in many cases different explanations of the kind Reinhart wants. For instance, consider Reinhart's own examples of the three phenomena (a)-(c):

(a)
(292)   Zelda bores herself.

(b)
(293)   Zelda bores her.
(294)   She adores Zelda's teachers.

(c)
(295)   Zelda adores her teachers.
(296)   Those who know her adore Zelda.

All these types of example have in effect been dealt with above. For (292), see sec. 13, and for (293), sec. 11. Coreference is unlikely in (294) because application of (G. genitive) moves "Zelda" to another, later sentence. Because of (O. LR) and/or the Progression Principle, Zelda is not available as a member of I when a rule is applied to "she". In contrast, the rule (G. name) is applied to "Zelda" before any rule is applied to "her" in (295) because of (O. LR), and in (296) because of (O.comm). In neither case is there any way of excluding other members from I, which explains (295)-(296).

Reinhart proposes to capture the differences between different cases (a)-(c) by means of different kinds of indexing (coindexing and counterindexing). While not involving any outright mistake, this procedure tends to hide the radical dissimilarity of the underlying mechanism in the different cases. For instance, in (292) it follows from the Exclusion Principle that there is only one member in the choice set involved in the game rule for "herself". Indeed, this set is simply {Zelda}. This accounts for the obligatoriness of the coreference in (292).

In contrast, in the case of nonflexive pronouns there is nothing restricting the choice set to individuals that are values of expressions in the same clause (dominated by the same s-nodes) as the pronoun. Hence, for them we cannot have obligatory coreference.

However, in the case of reflexive pronouns, too, obligatory coreference is merely the result of certain particular features of the clause in which the pronoun

occurs.   It is important to realize, for instance, that the
mechanism that gave rise to obligatory coreference in (292)
does not always do so.   This is exemplified by examples
like the following:

(297)   Jane or Jill told Jim a story about herself.
(298)   Jill helped her mother to enroll herself in the
           college.
(299)   John told Bill a story about himself.

(This last example is from Jackendoff 1972, p. 132.)

     In contrast to the Exclusion Principle, the restrictions
on coreference resulting from ordering principles cannot
enforce obligatory coreference.
     Here we also are in a position to make a correction to
what was said earlier.   In sec. 20 above, we showed how
the game-theoretical approach enables us to make sense of
the idea of possible coreference.   It was said there also
that this provides a way of speaking of impossible
coreference.   Now we can see that the resulting notion
cannot be understood literally.   As an example, take a
violation of the Langacker-Ross restrictions on backwards
anaphora.   What is strictly speaking impossible here is not
a coreference in a concrete semantical sense between the
anaphoric pronoun and its putative head (occurring in a
lower clause), but the possibility that the referent of the
pronoun be introduced into a semantical game as a value of
the head.   Coreference is perfectly possible between the
two.   However, then the shared referent of the head and of
the pronoun must have been introduced in some other way,
e.g., by an NP occurring earlier in the discourse.   But
from this it does not follow that the reference of the
pronoun cannot be identical with that of its putative head,
for the latter can of course be introduced in principle in
one of the alternative ways.   Hence, in the literal sense of
the word, coreference cannot be ruled out in such cases.
Failure of "possible coreference" in our sense does not mean
that coreference is literally impossible.
     Here's an example of such a situation (modified from
Dick Francis, *Forfeit*, Pocket Books, N.Y., 1975, p. 7):

(300)   Why didn't I write for the *Sunday Times*, Agatha,
           my wife's mother, always said, instead of a rag
           like the *Sunday Blaze*?   One thing she ignored

was that the *Blaze* paid twenty-eight per cent
more than the *Times* and that Agatha's daughter
was quite expensive.

In the last sentence of (300), "she" and "Agatha" cannot be
coreferential if the sentence is considered alone.   For
"Agatha" will not be handled in time for its bearer to be in
the choice set I for "she".   But of course Agatha could
have been introduced into I earlier in the discourse – which
is precisely what happens in (300).

We have found thus yet another flaw in the
contemporary concept of coreference.   (The idea discussed
here is virtually the same as Evans's notion of "referential
dependency"; see Evans 1980, pp. 358 ff.   Cf. also
examples like (214) above in sec. 22.)

This observation is not merely another curious
counterexample.   It has implications for the formulation of
generalizations like the Langacker-Ross restraint.   Even
though the underlying mechanism is the same in all cases,
it can now seem that prima facie exceptions must be made in
the case in which the putative antecendent NP_0 of an
apparently anaphoric pronoun P_1 is itself a pronoun.   For
then NP_0 (the head) can typically be interpreted only by
reference to the extrasentential context.   But the very
same context can then supply the reference also for P_1
making it "coreferential" with NP_0.   Hence the very same
mechanism that explained the ceteris paribus validity (with
qualifications)   of   the   Langacker-Ross   constraint
automatically explains also a certain prima facie exception to
it, víz., the case in which the potential "head" itself is a
pronoun.

This exception is made in the recent formulations of
the Langacker-Ross constraint in its improved versions,
e.g., the formulations given by Reinhart (1983a, 1983b).
It introduces another improvement to our initial approximate
formulation of the Langacker-Ross restriction.   It is not an
ad hoc correlation, however, but an inevitable corollary to
the general ideas of our theory.   In contrast, the need of
making an exception in the case in which the putative
"head" is itself a pronoun is not explained at all in the
competing approaches, even if there is no intuitive reason
for it in those approaches.   Our theory shows a sense in
which such "exceptions" are not really exceptions to the
underlying true law.

This mechanism is not even restricted to cases where the putative head is a pronoun.   Earlier, we found a related example (213) (as contrasted to (208)) in which the potential "head" is a *the*-phrase.   There we were not dealing with "exceptions" to the Langacker-Ross restraint, but with other regularities.   The underlying mechanism is the same, however.

It has been thought that there are other cases than those covered by the Exclusion Principle (in the form we have given to it) or by the consequences of our ordering principles where coreference is impossible.   For instance, in sentences like the following coreference seems to be excluded:

(301)   Amanda feared that the wretched girl had no chance.

Here Amanda apparently cannot be the wretched girl, even though we have so far put forward no rules or principles to explain why not.

The apparent impossibility of coreference in (301) is nevertheless not representative of the actual theoretical situation.   In other words, (301) does not seem to be a genuine counterexample.   There are other examples with the same structure where coreference is in fact possible. Whatever factor it is that serves to explain the apparent unnaturalness of coreference in (301), coreference is perfectly possible, for instance, in

(302)   It amused Einstein that the best known scientist in the world was not always recognized in stores and restaurants.

There are in fact other examples in which the "antecedent" to a the-phrase is not in the subject position and in which coreference cannot be ruled out.   Here we have a few:

(303)   It bothered Amanda that the wretched girl had no chance.
(304)   It annoyed Mondale that the former V.P. was portrayed as a weak leader by the press.
(305)   His aides assured Walter that the former V.P. was not a weak leader.

Hence there does not seem to be any reason to change our theory because of examples like (301).

For further work on the problems discussed here, see Lauri Carlson, "Reference in Dialogue Games" (forthcoming).

CHAPTER VI

COMPARISONS WITH OTHER TREATMENTS

29. Comparisons: General Perspectives

The three differences (i)–(iii) listed above in sec. 21 between our theory and most other approaches enable us to make certain comparisons here. In historical perspective, it is perhaps not entirely unfair to say that one of the aims of recent treatments of anaphora has been to explain such exceptions to the Langacker–Ross condition that from our perspective are caused by (i)–(iii), especially by (ii)–(iii). One theoretical difference between our theory and some of the other current theories is that, in these competing theories, an attempt is made to account for the exceptions by reference to the syntactical structure of the input sentence S_0 of a semantical game. From our perspective, this may be expected to be doubly misleading (a) because some of the exceptions are caused by factors that are essentially semantical, not syntactical, such as the Exclusion Principle; and (b) because the relevant syntactical structure is not that of S_0, anyway, but that of some different sentence making its appearance at a later stage of the semantical game that originally started from S_0. Furthermore, exclusive reliance on the syntactical structure of S_0 will not help us in connection with the problems (c) caused by special ordering principles, either. These problems were discussed in sec. 27 above.

Because of the differences (a)–(c) between our theory and its rivals, a detailed comparison with the competing treatments is difficult. It may nevertheless be helpful to indicate some of the overall differences in explanatory strategy. This will, we hope, also help the reader to appreciate our own explanatory strategy. Since point-by-point comparisons between other treatments and ours are not possible, we propose to follow here roughly the same strategy we used in discussing the Langacker–Ross restraint above. In other words, we shall try to reconstruct a certain competing thesis within our own framework, seeking to preserve the spirit of the competing view. This approach enables us to bring the resources of our own theoretical framework to bear on the pros and cons of the alternatives.

30. Comparisons: Chomsky

One aspect of Chomsky's approach that can be compared with ours can be seen from the following pairs of examples:

(306)   I told his wife that John should exercise more.
(307)   I told him that John should exercise more.

Here coreference between "his" and "John" is possible in (306), but coreference between "him" and "John" is impossible in (307). The explanation in our approach is that (G. genitive) can be applied before (G. be) in (306). Such an application yields something like

(308)   I told Jill that John should exercise more. Jill is
          his wife.

Coreference is possible in (308) and hence in (306) because (G. name) will be applied to "John" before (G. he) is applied to "his". In contrast, there is no rule that could be applied to "him" in (307) to move it to a clause later than "John".

   In Chomsky's approach there is nothing like the possibility of an intervening application of a rule such as (G. genitive) that would change the structure of the sentence in question. All the work has to be done by the labelled tree structure of the input sentence, e.g., (306) or (307). In order to capture the relevant regularities, a linguist representing an alternative approach to ours can try to do two different things. First, he or she can try to refine the general ordering principles in order to reach the proper formulations of observable regularities. Most of the competing theorists do this, usually by means of the idea of c-command, to be discussed in the next section.

   Our examples strongly suggest that this alone will not do the trick, and detailed evidence quickly bears this out. For from (306)-(307) we can see that what makes the difference and opens the door to an intervening rule application is not a difference in structure of the kind that is relevant to rule ordering, but the occurrence of a certain kind of NP (in (306), one containing a genitive pronoun) to which a rule can be applied. If such possibilities of rule application are to be discerned from the structure of an input sentence like (306) or (307), attention must be paid what kind of labels occur in the sentence (tree) and what kinds of other labels they govern. This is no mean task, for it was seen above that certain prepositional constructions can trigger intermediate rule applications similar to, but not completely analogous with, the applications of (G. genitive). Indeed, the treatment of the following example is (as we saw above) parallel to that of (306):

(309)   Near him, John saw a snake.

Moreover, the same contrast (from the vantage point of our theory) as was found between (306) and (307) is also found between the following:

(310)   Penelope grabbed his cane and beat Peter with it.
(311)   Penelope cursed him and slandered Peter.

What this line of thought suggests is therefore the necessity of introducing into a competing approach distinctions between different phrases relevant to possible antecedence relations (in our approach, relevant to membership in *I*). This is clearly the source of Chomsky's notion of governing category and, more generally, his entire idea of government. It is clearly also predictable, in the light of the arguments of the preceding chapter, that the details of any full account of such notions as government, whose mission is to account for the changes which intervening rule applications impose on the structure of the initial sentence, is bound to be intricate. It is not even clear that such an account can be given, for reasons spelled out earlier. But even if it can, what is obtained is bound to be merely an account much less uniform and much less perspicuous of phenomena that we can account for in simpler terms. For this reason, we shall not discuss the details of Chomsky's theory of government here.
One can say more than this, however. There is another facet of Chomsky's approach whose spirit can be captured by reconstructing his ideas – admittedly somewhat freely – within our theoretical framework. Consider, the following putative generalizations put forward by Chomsky (1981, pp. 58-61):

> *Nominative Island Constraint*: A nominative anaphor cannot be free in S.

> *Opacity*: An anaphor in the domain of the subject
> of a phrase cannot be free in that phrase.

Some explanations are in order here.   By "anaphors",
Chomsky means reflexive pronouns and certain other
expressions (e.g., "each other") exhibiting similar
behavior, not anaphoric pronouns in general.   Being bound
to an expression means having it as an antecedent.   "Free"
means not bound to any expression (in the context in
question).   The "domain" of phrase N_1 (node in a tree)
consists of all nodes c-commanded by N_1 that do not also
dominate N_1.   What c-command means will be explained in
the next section.   For the purposes of the present section,
we do not have to distinguish c-command from the notion of
command involved in our ordering principle (O. comm).
        One striking thing about Chomsky's principles is that
there is an obvious way of trying to explain the Nominative
Island Constraint and Opacity within our framework (or
something like our framework).   It amounts to modifying
our ordering principles to give the right of way to rules
applying to nominative NPs in S over other NPs in it or to
give priority to rules that apply to an NP in the subject
position in a phrase.   Such additional ordering principles
would explain the Nominative Island Constraint and the
Opacity Principle in the context of our overall theory in the
same sense in which our good old ordering principles
explain the Langacker-Ross constraint (cf. above, secs.
20-21.)   Hence we may consider the proposed new ordering
principles as a partial "rational reconstruction" of some of
Chomsky's leading ideas within our framework.   Even if
there is a good deal of "yield" between Chomsky's
principles and their putative reconstruction within our
theory, Chomsky's ideas are put in interesting light by our
"rational reconstruction".
        But are the putative new ordering principle true - the
principles which would explain the Nominative Island
Constraint and the Opacity Principle?   They don't seem to
be.   If we try to apply the modified ordering principles to
sentences containing quantifier phrases, we obtain wrong
results.   Consider, for instance, the following examples:

(312)   On every lot, someone has built a house.
(313)   Every single phone booth - someone is occupying
           it!

In both cases, "someone" has narrower scope than "every" even though it is the subject of both sentences. It is a little hard to find knockdown evidence here because in English the subject phrase usually precedes the others in the left-to-right order.   Hence the predictions of the modified ordering principles don't normally differ from the predictions of (O. LR).   However, in languages in which the word order is relatively free, it is in most cases conspicuous that the relative logical order of quantifier phrases is determined by their left-to-right order and not by their status as object terms or subject terms, so much so that one is tempted to see in this possibility of varying the logical order of operators a partial functional explanation of the free word order.

When we are dealing with anaphoric pronouns, the same difficulty comes up.   For instance the subject of a phrase is usually to the left of any anaphor in the same phrase.   Hence it must be treated before the anaphor in virtue of (O. LR) in order to introduce an individual into the choice set *I* of the anaphor.   This anaphor accordingly cannot be "free" in the phrase.   Hence the predictions of the Opacity Principle are not so different from what we get automatically from our general theory.

There are some differences, however, between the predictions yielded by the two treatments.   For instance, the Nominative Island Condition prevents a reflexive pronoun from occurring as the subject of a tensed clause. This restraint may be true in letter, but it seems to be quite wrong in spirit.   It is true that we cannot say

(314)   *Himself is Dick's worst enemy.

However, we can say

(315)   He is himself Dick's worst enemy.

and even

(316)   He himself is Dick's worst enemy.

Here we can see what's wrong with (314): it's not that a reflexive pronoun as such occurs as the subject, but that "himself" is in the wrong case.   Hence we have to use "he himself" instead of "himself" alone.

The OED lists an example from 1619 that goes further than (316):

(317)   Sir Edward Villiers told him himself was the man.

If there is anything wrong with (315), it is that (O. LR) calls for us to evaluate "he himself" before "Dick" is evaluated. Even though (O. LR) is not exceptionless, it is strong enough to cause a minor awkwardness about (315).

Notice that the phenomenon illustrated by (314)-(316) is largely independent of a reflexive pronoun's occurring in the subject position. It is likewise less natural to say

(318)   Dick's worst enemy is himself

than to say

(319)   Dick's worst enemy is Dick himself.

It is even less than completely clear that the asterisk in (314) is absolutely necessary. A recent historical novel by Jean Plaidy is called *Myself My Enemy* (Putnam, 1983), and we suspect that even more direct counterexamples can be found in contemporary educated English prose.

As for the Opacity Principle, the very term seems to us to betray a mistaken diagnosis of the situation. The phenomena that the principle is designed to explain – in the main, the obligatory coreference of a reflexive pronoun and the subject of the clause it occurs in – have nothing to do with referential opacity in Quine's sense. They are due to the Exclusion Principle and the relation of reflexive pronouns to it. Even though explicit counterexamples are not easy to come by, the Opacity Principle does not even seek to be correct in that it assigns a special place to the subject of a sentence vis-à-vis reflexive pronouns. The following examples, which seem to be acceptable in some idiolects, tell against the alleged special status of subject terms:

(320)   Sue compared in her mind Tom with himself
            twenty years ago.
(321)   The catastrophe put Dick beside himself.
(322)   His wife gave Nelson a portrait of himself.

These are not counterexamples to the Opacity Principle, but they show that the role assigned in it to the subject term is highly dubious.

Hence the consequences of our reconstructed versions of Chomsky's principles seem to be dubious in so far as they differ from the implications yielded by our theory without any special assumptions.

31. Comparisons: Reinhart

Chomsky's treatment uses certain ideas originally proposed by Tanya Reinhart. These ideas can be discussed by means of the same strategy as was used in the previous section to discuss Chomsky. Expressed in our terms, her basic idea is essentially to change the ordering principles to take into account nodes other than S-nodes. This modified ordering principle can be expressed as follows:

(O. CR) A game rule must not be applied to a node N_2 if one can be applied to N_1, where N_1 c-commands N_2.

A node N_1 is said to c-command a node N_2 iff the closest branching node dominating N_1 dominates N_2, but neither N_1 nor N_2 dominates the other.

This reconstruction of Reinhart's ideas and general ordering principles seems to be in the spirit of her own treatment. She emphasizes herself the generality of her basic ideas as governing the ordering of various different operations. For instance, she claims that the scopes of quantifiers are determined in the same way as the "scopes" of potential heads of anaphoric expressions (see, e.g., Reinhart 1983a, sec. 9.2).

This leads to the following approximate coreference restriction which Reinhart formulates in effect as follows:

(CR) A noun phrase NP_1 can be coreferential with another noun phrase NP_2 if and only if (i) one of them c-commands the other and (ii) the c-commanded one is a pronoun.

However, both (O. CR) and (CR) are open to objections. Some objections were mentioned in Part I, sec.

9. We shall cover some of the same ground here. The following is a counterexample to (O. CR):

(323)   For every child, someone had brought a present.

Here the bracketing should go as follows, showing that (O. CR) predicts the wrong order of quantifiers:

(324)   [[For every child] [someone]$_{NP}$
           [had brought a present]$_{VP}$]$_S$

Some might argue that there should be another S-node in this structure, presumably as follows:

(325)   [[For every child] [[someone]$_{NP}$
           [had bought a present]$_{VP}$]$_S$]$_S$

But if this were the correct structure, (O. CR) would not yield a wrong prediction here (for the closest branching node dominating "someone" would not dominate "every".) This cannot be right, for the following is acceptable:

(326)   For himself, John had bought an old print.

If (325) were correct, (326) would have the following structure, by parity of structure:

(327)   [[For himself] [[John]$_{NP}$
           [had bought an old print]$_{VP}$]$_S$]$_S$

But then "himself" and "John" would not be in the same clause, and the reflexive pronoun would be impossible. Hence the acceptability of (326) shows that the structures (325) and (327) are wrong.

But if so, that is, if (324) is the right structure, (O. CR) predicts a wrong logical order of quantifiers, as we asserted, and must therefore be rejected.

The intended consequences of (CR) can be seen from examples like the following:

(328)   Bill met him when Dick was in town.
(329)   He met Bill when Dick was in town.
(330)   He saw a snake near John.
(331)   Near him John saw a snake.

Coreference is possible between "Dick" and "him" in (328) but not between "Dick" and "He" in (329). Coreference is likewise possible in (331) but not in (330). All these facts are explained by (CR), as the reader can easily ascertain, assuming a suitable syntactic structure for (328)-(331).

The same examples are likewise explained by our theory. Indeed, examples like (330)-(331) were discussed already in sec. 26 above. In examples like (328)-(329) it suffices to see how our ordering principles work in them. Given that the general structure of (328) is

(332)   [[Bill met him]$_S$ [when Dick was in town]]$_S$

Here the order of the first two applications is (G. name) (to "Bill") and (G. when), which can take us from (328) to something like

(333)   Dick was in town yesterday, and Bill met him yesterday.

Here "Dick" and "him" can be coreferential.

In contrast, in (329) the first rule to be applied is (G. he) to "He". Since I is empty at this stage of the game, "He" and "Dick" cannot be coreferential in (329). This explains the difference between (328) and (329).

Hence (328)-(331) don't favor Reinhart's theory at the expense of ours. Moreover, (CR) does not help us with other examples. Consider, for example, the following sentences:

(334)   In Ford's home town he is considered a genius.
(335)   In Ford's home town he built a house.
(336)   About Hugh he keeps many girlfriends.
(337)   About Hugh he has much to tell.

Here (CR) does not account for the difference between (334) and (335), for it allows for coreferentiality in either case. Reinhart has tried to take care of the difference by further changing her analysis. Without discussing the details of these changes, we can see what the story is. In our theory, one natural explanation why coreference is more awkward in (335) than in (334) is the following: In (335), coreference is ruled out by the fact that in its surface form "Ford's" and "he" are in the same clause. Furthermore, the construction with "in" is so simple that it is naturally handled as a part of the verb construction rather than as introducing an adverbial phrase (cf. sec. 24 above). In contrast, in (334) we are obviously dealing with an adverbial phrase. Accordingly, an application of the game rule (G. genitive) to (334) can have the effect of changing it into something like

(338)   Grand Rapids is Ford's home town.   In Grand
             Rapids, he is considered a genius.

For in (G. genitive), unlike, e.g., (G. near), Myself can change the order of sentences or clauses in the output. Now in (328) Ford is in / for the game rule (G. he), because he has been introduced by (G. name) before the other rules are applied.

Our account of the contrast between (336)-(337) is predicated on an assumption of the two kinds of uses of prepositions mentioned above in sec. 24.   For reasons explained there, a special game rule (G. about) is much likelier to be applied in (336) than in (337). Accordingly, "Hugh" and "he" can perhaps be coreferential in (336) but certainly not in (337).

A further example of a phenomenon similar to the one illustrated by (334)-(335) is the contrast between the following two examples:

(339)   Near John he saw a snake.
(340)   Near John's girlfriend, he saw a snake.

Coreference between "John" (or "John's") and "he" is possible in (340) but not in (339).   This is in keeping with our theory.   An application of (G. genitive) to (340) yields something like the following, when the order of sentences in the output is selected appropriately:

(341)   Jill is a girlfriend of John's.   Near Jill, he saw a
             snake.

In (341), (G. name) is applied to "John's" before (G. he) is applied to "he".   Hence coreference is possible in (340).

In contrast, in (339) (G. near) applies first, because of (O. LR).   Since in (G. near) there is no option concerning the order of clauses in the output, the players will obtain something of the same form as

(342)   On the lawn, he saw a snake. The lawn is near
             John.

(We have chosen to overlook the role of tense here, for it
is immaterial for our present purposes.)   Coreference is
impossible in (342), and hence in (339).   Once again, the
crucial point in our explanation is the difference in the way
such rules as, e.g., (G. genitive) and such rules as,
e.g., (G. near) operate.   The former allows Myself some
leeway concerning how the sentences or clauses of the
output are ordered; the latter do not.   This distinction,
while entirely natural within the game-theoretical
framework, clearly is extremely hard to capture by sole
reference to the syntactic structure of the input sentences.
Hence it is not surprising that examples like (334)-(337)
should have presented difficulties to other approaches.
     Our diagnosis of examples like (334)-(337) is further
confirmed by observing that one can use a reflexive
pronoun only in those sentences in which the anaphoric
pronoun and its possible "head" are not moved to different
clauses or different sentences before a rule is applied to
the pronoun.   Thus we can have examples like the
following:

(343)   In Ford's home town he built a house for himself.
(344)   About Hugh, he himself has much to tell.

In contrast to these, there are no natural "reflexivized"
counterparts to (334) and (336).
     Counter-examples to Reinhart's amended analysis seem
to be offered by the following sentences:

(345)   About Hugh, Gay denied that he has any intrigu-
             ing secrets to reveal.
(346)   In Percival's bed, Guinever found him.

According to Reinhart's improved analysis, there should not
be anything wrong about coreference in these sentences.
Yet coreference is extremely awkward in both (cf. here
Carden 1981).
     Furthermore, in the course of our discussion we have
in effect dealt with all the different kinds of examples
Reinhart lists in (1981) in support of her approach, i.e.,
in support of (O. CR) and (CR) as distinguished from (O.
comm) and (O. LR).

Thus it appears that our theory throws more light on coreference restrictions than some of its closest competitors. Quite apart from the ability of the competing approaches to deal with particular examples and apart from the detailed changes that can be made to improve on them, our theory predicts what the main difficulties are that they are subject to and provides a treatment of its own of some of the problem cases. Moreover, the concepts which our approach operates with are obviously more realistic psycholinguistically than the purely syntactical relations relied on by its rivals. For instance, an application of (G. near) to (339) can be thought of as a natural step in the interpretation of (339) in the situation in which it is uttered. In contrast, the alternative explanation that complicates the already involved definition of c-commanding uses relations that prima facie are not likely to have much psycholinguistic reality.

32. Exclusion Principle is Clausebound

As was noted above in sec. 11, suggestions have been made in effect to extend the Exclusion Principle to apply also outside the boundaries of a single clause, i.e., outside the class of nodes dominated by the same s-nodes. If so, our arguments in the preceding sec. would no longer be conclusive. Hence a brief comment on attempts to extend the Exclusion Principle is in order. The following examples have been listed by Chomsky to motivate such an extension (1981, p. 144, note 79):

(347)   Which pictures of John did he like?
(348)   Which pictures of the woman John married did he like?
(349)   Which people who John liked did he meet?
(350)   He attacked someone who John likes.
(351)   Someone who John likes, he attacked.
(352)   He attacked a friend of John's.

Chomsky says that it is much more natural to take "John" and "he" to be coreferential in (348) and (349), and that they are disjoint in reference in (350) and in (352), but not necessarily in (351).

Of these, the possibility of coreference in (348) and (349) might seem to go against the fact that (G. name) is

subject to (O. comm), and hence can introduce John into *I*
only after "he" has been interpreted. In reality, however,
"John" occurs in (348) and (349) in a phrase which is
essentially like a quantifier phrase and hence has to be
dealt with first. In fact, we might as well have, instead of
(348), an example like

> Some pictures of the woman John married were liked
> by him.

This application of a quantifier rule moves "John" from a
lower clause and hence makes it possible to introduce John
into *I* before "he" is handled. In contrast, in examples like
(347), the game rule for a propositional construction in
questions threatens to move "John" to a position after "he"
and hence to make coreference impossible, according to the
general ideas explained in sec. 21.

In contrast, an application of (G. some) to (351) puts
"John" in an earlier clause than "he" in the output
sentence, assuming that the appropriate order is chosen.
Therefore there is nothing in (351) that prevents an
application of (G. name) to "John" before (G. he) is
applied.

In (352), (O. LR) prescribes an application of (G. he)
before (G. name) is applied. Accordingly, John is not in *I*
when (G. he) is applied, and coreference between "John"
and "he" is therefore awkward.

These explanations do not involve any extension of the
Exclusion Principle beyond a single clause. We do not find
any other evidence in the literature, either, that would
indicate that the Exclusion Principle should be applied
beyond the boundaries of a single clause.

The same sort of explanation (evoking (O. LR) or the
Progression Principle for subgames) works in the following
examples (due to Langacker):

(353)   Penelope cursed him and slandered Peter.
(354)   Penelope cursed Peter and slandered him.

33. The Exclusion Principle and Different Methods of Identification

The Exclusion Principle (see sec. 11 above) deserves a few
additional comments. For one thing, there are apparent

exceptions to the principle. In reality, they merely offer more grist to the mill of our theory. They are illustrated by such examples as the following:

(355)   I am Dr. Livingstone.
(356)   One of the suspects is you.
(357)   [Caller on the phone:] "I'd like to speak to Mrs. Bell." [Answer:] "I'm she."

(This example was suggested to us by Professor Merrill Hintikka.)
     Apparently, the only genuine exception is the case in which the operative clause is an identity statement. Compare (355)-(357) with the following:

(358)   I admire Dr. Livingstone.
(359)   One of the suspects saw you.
(360)   I saw her.

In (358) the "I" cannot be Dr. Livingstone (even though it is possible for a person to admire himself or herself). In (359), you cannot be one of the suspects. In (360) I cannot be "her".
     This exceptional case seems to be easy to take care of. We can at the same time see that identity is not just like any old two-place predicate, but exhibits a logical behavior different from that of other predicates.
     The same phenomenon is reflected on the syntactical level by the choice of pronouns (reflexive vs. nonreflexive) possible in different contexts. The pronoun choice is illustrated by the following examples:

(361)   You are looking for Dr. Livingstone?
           Dr. Livingstone is *him*. [Pointing to a person.]
(362)   I am me.

With other verbs, a reflexive pronoun would be required for identity:

(363)   Dr. Livingstone forgot himself.
(364)   Dr. Livingstone forgot him.

The contrast between (361) and (362) also seems unexplainable by means of Reinhart's rule without further syntactical assumptions concerning "is".

However, this is not quite the whole story. For one thing exceptions are not restricted to sentences containing the verb "to be". The following is an example:

(365)   He has become a more mature person.

The connection between (365) and our earlier examples is nevertheless obvious. The verbs "to be" and "to become" are related to each other semantically. In a sense, (365) can still be considered a kind of identity statement.

Second, (365) is not only a counterexample to a simple-minded formulation of our Exclusion Principle. It is also a counterexample to Reinhart's generalization. Indeed, all the requirements of her principle are satisfied, and hence "He" and "a more mature person" should not be coreferential according to her lights.

The relevant question is how to capture the exceptions. This brings us to a third point. The exceptions seem to be determined semantically rather than syntactically. Even in what appear to be relatively simple identity statements, the possibility of coreference may depend on the intended semantical interpretation. If a prima facie identity sentence is used as a roundabout way to attribute a property, the Exclusion Principle is applicable again, and coreference is possible only when reflexives are used. The following examples illustrate this:

(366)   John is himself again.
(367)   John is him. [Pointing to a person.]

Thus no syntactical reformulation of Reinhart's rules is likely to take care of the exceptional cases.

It is worth noting that the semantical character of the exceptions to the Exclusion Principle indirectly supports our diagnosis of the phenomena the Exclusion Principle is calculated to explain. Reinhart tries to capture these phenomena by means of a generalization concerning the syntactical structure of the sentence in question. We have seen that there is much to be said for such an explanatory strategy in many cases: syntactic structure determines the order of applications of different game rules, and the order of game rules determines which individuals are available for coreference. However, the Exclusion Principle uses a different explanatory strategy. The cases it covers are assimilated to the exclusive interpretation of quantifiers, which is by any token an operative phenomenon in natural languages. If an exclusive interpretation is what is going on here, it is almost predictable that exceptions to the Exclusion Principle should arise in connection with identity statements, for they just cannot be formulated without violating the exclusive interpretation of quantifiers, quantified variables, and quantifier phrases. Hence the observations just made definitely favor our account of the phenomena the Exclusion Principle covers over Reinhart's.

It is to be noted that the Exclusion Principle is in operation even in identity statements where the pronoun in question (or other NP to which a game rule could be applied) is one of the two sides of the identity. This is illustrated by the following pair of contrasting examples:

(368)   He is Dr. Livingstone.
(369)   He is Dr. Livingstone's secretary.

In (368), "He" and "Dr. Livingstone" can be coreferential, while in (369) "He" and "Dr. Livingstone's" cannot be. This fits of course in very well with our diagnosis of the situation.

All these prima facie exceptions to the Exclusion Principle are perhaps in the last analysis no exceptions at all. Earlier, in sec. 13 above, it was pointed out that a nonreflexive pronoun may very well be possible in the same clause as its "head" provided they refer to different individuals. Of course, this is rare, but not impossible, for the presupposed reference may take place in possible situations different from the actual one.

Now such alternative situations or scenarios are always involved in contexts dealing with knowledge. They include contexts involving questions. Hence apparent exceptions to the Exclusion Principle can perhaps be explained though their tacit involvement with knowledge, doubt, or questions.

It is not hard to find examples where this is in fact the case. Here is an actual example from Catherine Aird's mystery story *Henrietta Who?*, whose title indicates its theme, which is a young lady's search for her natural parents (p. 73):

(370)   "When I was a little girl," said Henrietta, "I used
           to ask myself, 'Why am I me?' Now I'm grown up
           I seem to be asking myself, 'Who am I?'"

"Philosophy is so egocentric," complained Bill
Thorpe. ...
"I am me," declared Henrietta.
"And very nice, too, especially your ..."
"I know I am me, but where do we go from
here?"

On page 56 of the same book we read:

(371)   Henrietta looked up at him in astonishment ...
          and said "Why?"
          "I thought it was me."
          "You thought what was you?"
          "The reason why your mother wouldn't let us get
          married."

In the former quote, we have "I" and "me" in the same
clause (not "I" and "myself") and in the latter we have
prima facie coreferential "it" and "me", not "it" and
"myself". In both quotes, questions are raised about the
identity of the referents or else the operative clause occurs
explicitly governed by such words as "I know", "I
thought", etc., just as was suggested.[5]
    Thus the apparent exceptions in reality serve only to
highlight the semantical nature of the Exclusion Principle.
If this tentative conclusion is correct, then it is hopeless to
try to capture the effects of the exclusion principle by
means of syntax-based generalizations, as most competing
approaches strive to do.
    But even the discovery of an epistemic element
underlying the apparent exceptions to the Exclusion
Principle does not get us to the bottom of the problem.
However, by showing that several different scenarios
("possible worlds") are involved in these apparent
exceptions to the Exclusion Principle, it opens the door to a
much simpler explanation. There is a far stronger sense in
which the prima facie exceptions to the Exclusion Principle
we have listed are not genuine exceptions at all in the first
place: the coreference that seems to contradict the principle
is not there, because the entities referred to are in reality
different.
    This looks like a bold assertion, but it has a solid
theoretical foundation. We have in fact two different kinds
of cases to cope with. The less striking examples include
(365). In such cases, the two apparently coreferential

expressions really refer to different temporal stages of what
we normally think of as the "real", i.e., persistent,
individuals. In order to spell out this point, we would
have to formulate an explicit semantics (model theory) for
temporal concepts, which task lies beyond this work. But
even without such an explicit semantics, our point is not
difficult to appreciate as applied to examples like (365).

The other class of examples is instantiated by
(355)-(357), (361)-(362), (367), and (368). At first sight,
there does not seem to be any hope in denying that the two
sides of such equations refer to the same entity. But let's
look at (344) again:

(355)   I am Dr. Livingstone.

Here Dr. Livingstone, the entity referred to by the
right-hand side of (355), is presumably to be identified by
means of such information as might be included in *Who's
Who* or *The Dictionary of National Biography* or perhaps, in
the case of less upright characters, in his FBI file. In
contrast, the entity referred to by the indexical "I" is
identified by reference to the situation in which the speaker
finds himself, e.g., by pointing. Hence, even though the
two entities coincide in the situation envisaged in (355),
they are to be identified in different ways and hence are in
a very real sense different entities. Hence there is no
genuine coreference in (355), and hence it is not a valid
counterexample to the Exclusion Principle.

This claim might at first sight seem ad hoc. It
nevertheless has a solid theoretical basis in Jaakko
Hintikka's theory of two different types of methods of
cross-identification, the descriptive methods and the
perceptual and ostensive methods (more generally methods
relying on acquaintance). (See Hintikka 1969, 1975a,
1975b.) These methods define what counts as the same
entity in different "worlds" (it is nowadays in fashion to
call them "situations"). By doing so, they define what the
values of quantifiers are, and since in a very real sense
"to be is to be value of a bound variable" (Quine), they
define what an entity is. ("No entity without identity", to
quote Quine again.) Since there are two different ways of
doing all this, there are two kinds of entities. Some of
them identified by reference to a general public framework;
the others are identified by reference of the same person's
perceptual or epistemic context, as it were by means of a

coordinate system created by some person's first-hand relations to persons, objects, places, etc. The paradigm case of the latter mode of identification is by pointing.

This is precisely the contrast that comes up as a special case in (355). A survey of the other examples mentioned shows that in all of them a contrast is present between identification by reference to public framework (e.g., by name) and by reference to a concrete situation. In some cases, the contextual ("indexical") identification is brought in by first or second-person pronouns, which often rely on the speech situation. (It is not accidental that so many of the examples involved first-person pronouns.) In some of the other cases, e.g., (361), an explicit mention has to be made of an act of pointing. Hence all of them exemplify Hintikka's duality of identification methods, and hence turn out not to be genuine counterexamples to the Exclusion Principle.

This prompts a couple of general theoretical comments. First, we have here a new kind of indication of the insufficiency of the received notion of coreference. In order to apply it, we have to know what the entities are that are being referred to. What we have found here is that this problem is much more complicated than first meets the eye. And yet, without solving it we cannot hope to formulate truly exceptionless generalizations, such as, in the present case, the Exclusion Principle.

Second, the natural way in which the distinction between different methods of identification saves the Exclusion Principle serves as a forceful reminder of the theoretical interest of Hintikka's distinction.

One of the many subleties present here is the fact that personal pronouns like "I" and "you" can be used to refer either to the contextually identified entity or to the publicly ("descriptively") identified one. This was illustrated by the examples (370) and (371), where in sentences like "I am me" the first "I" is descriptive but the second "me" is contextual. (Otherwise one would have to use a reflexive pronoun.) The same phenomenon is seen even more clearly in the contrast between the following examples:

(372)   A typed note was found: "I can no longer hide from the community that I have lost my vocation. ... Please don't try to find me. I want to find myself."

> "I want to find myself!" I echoed. It was the phrase Rosa had used to me years ago in our teenage discussions about our future. ... (Antonia Fraser, *Quiet as a Nun*, Penguin Books, 1978, pp. 22.)

(373)   I am me.

In the latter, we may imagine the speaker as pointing to himself. In the former, the entity involved cannot be a contextually identified one, for that entity is always there and presents no search problems. In the example, the entity Rosa was trying to find is different from the entity her community might have tried to find, for Rosa would not have had any difficulty in finding her perceptually or otherwise contextually identified self, unlike her fellow sisters. Hence what is involved in such cases is the abstract noncontextual ego, one's very own psychological or even religious self. Since this is also clearly the "I" in (372), one must use a reflexive in (372), unlike (373).

This diagnosis is confirmed further by the following observation: When an identity is asserted, not between a descriptive (public) individual and a perceptual object (object of acquaintance), but between (say) two public individuals, our theory predicts that a reflexive pronoun becomes possible. This is confirmed by examples. Here is one:

(374)   ... the man at the desk asked if he could help me. "The cultural attache?" I said. I've an appointment."
The gray-haired man moved gently like a lily in the wind and said that the cultural attache happened to be himself. (Dick Francis, *Trial Run*, Pocket Books, N.Y., 1980, p. 59.)

Here the grey-haired man is not considered only or primarily one of the narrator's perceptual objects. He is very much an official, a member of the staff of Her Majesty's Embassy. Hence we have here a case in our point, for the narrator is in fact using a reflexive pronoun.

34. Apparent Exceptions: Pronouns of Laziness

Various prima facie exceptions to our theory can be found in the literature.   Here we shall discuss two of them. There are undoubtedly other apparent exceptions, but it lies in the nature of things that we cannot anticipate all of them.   For instance, there may be discourse-determined factors which affect anaphoric pronouns but which can only be discussed against the background of more discourse theory (discourse semantics) than we can presuppose here.

The issue we shall discuss in this section is the phenomenon known as pronouns of laziness.   We are no longer entirely happy with the earlier treatment of the pronouns of laziness by Hintikka and Carlson.   It now seems to us that a better account is possible, even though there is nothing basically wrong with the earlier treatment, as far as it goes.   This new account is based on suggestions by Lauri Carlson.

What is the mechanism governing the semantics of "it" in a typical "pronoun of laziness" sentence like (3) (above)?   We have already uncovered the way the operative pronoun works in certain closely related sentences, such as

(375)   If a man gives his paycheck to his wife, he is
           wiser than any man who gives it to his mistress.

The subgame played on the antecedent involves a choice of a man by Nature (playing the verifier's role) and after that (among other things) a dependent choice by Myself of an object whose name replaces "his paycheck". This dependent choice is governed by a strategic function that is "remembered" by the players in the subgame connected with the consequent.   Applied to the individual chosen in the second subgame as the value as of "a man", it yields an object as its value.   This object is available as the value of "it".   The object must be a paycheck, because the game would not go to the second subgame unless the remembered function yielded always a paycheck as its value.   This explains how the allegedly special "pronoun of laziness" "it" in (375) has the force it has without any new assumptions.

This account squares well with the fact that we obtain a "pronoun of laziness" even if we replace "his paycheck" by "a paycheck" in (375).

Likewise, example (49) in sec. 9 above would probably be taken to be a garden-variety instance of pronouns of laziness. Yet we saw that it can be explained easily in our general theory without postulating any differences between different kinds of pronouns.

What such observations show is that some of the typical examples in the literature of alleged "pronouns of laziness" do not involve any unusual mode of semantical behavior on the part of anaphoric pronouns different from what we have charted in this work. As a brief – and oversimplified – slogan, we can say that pronouns of laziness are pronouns relying on remembered strategies like the ones discussed above in sec. 6, paragraph (iii).

This account is not exhaustive, but it suggests a more general one. The intuitive reason why "it" can pick out the intended object in (375) is that when the time comes in the game to apply (G. it) to "it", the players have available to them not just some reference for the second "a man", but also a function which, when applied to this reference as an argument, yields a paycheck of his as a value. Now where do such functions come from? Our observations concerning (375) show that in some cases they are supplied to the players simply by our general rules and ordering principles. The crucial insight here is that even when they are not automatically available in this sense, they may still play a legitimate role in semantics. What we have then is an instance of strategic meaning explained in sec. 17 above. (Indeed, here we have another example of the importance of the notion of strategic meaning.) In other words, there are various indirect ways in which a choice strategy (choice function) can be available to the players and to the hearer of a sentence other than being given by the straightforward game rules.

It lies in the nature of strategic meaning that the regularities governing the availability (and prominence) of earlier choice functions (strategies or parts thereof) are less clear-cut than the game rules. Thus it is not surprising that the very phenomenon of pronouns of laziness or "sloppy identity" is somewhat amorphous. It is nevertheless not difficult to see something of what is going on in typical instances of pronouns of laziness. The strategy functions on which sloppy identity relies are not just to be gathered from sundry clues. They are strategy functions used earlier in the sentence (or discourse). Hence the operative question here is, How are such

strategies signaled linguistically?   Where do they come from?
No single general answer is possible.   One can nevertheless
locate some ways in which the "remembered" strategy might
have been introduced.   A frequent source is genitives.
They involve a choice of an individual, governed by a
strategy function.   In so far as strategic meaning is
operative, the idea is close at hand that the same prominent
strategy might be used again by the players somewhere else
in the sentence, too.   This helps us to understand the way
sentences like (3) functions.   It also explains the difference
between examples like these:

(376)   Carl keeps the front-door key under the mat, but
           Carol always carries it with her.
(377)   Carl carries a book in his briefcase, but Carol
           keeps it in a drawer.

In the first clause of (376) one naturally assumes (in a
context of normal collateral information) a rule-governed
way of moving from Carl to his front-door key.   This rule
or function will yield as its value, when applied to Carol,
the intended object.   In contrast, there is no normally
simple functional dependence between a bookowner and her
or his book, that would enable a hearer to treat (377) in
the same way as (376).

        In sum, our suggestion is that the so-called pronouns
of laziness do not always rely on abstract meaning, but can
also operate by a means of strategic meaning (explained in
sec. 17 above).   It is important to realize that even though
strategic meaning often relies on ad hoc clues, our
suggested account nevertheless yields a number of
predictions, based on the rest of our rules and principles –
and their consequences.   For instance, the argument value
of the strategy function, however it might be given, must
be available when the function is to be applied.   This is
illustrated by the fact that, even though the
pronouns-of-laziness reading is all right in (376), it is
unnatural in, say,

(378)   Carol keeps the front-door key in her purse, but
           it always falls out of Carl's pocket.

        Here "it" occurs in the left-to-right order before the
argument value (Carl) of the strategy function that is

supposed to give "it" its value comes up.   No wonder,
therefore, that (378) doesn't make the same sense as (376).
        There is in any case some evidence that pronouns of
laziness represent a phenomenon which is not governed by
the basic semantics of anaphoric pronouns but by some
secondary kind of meaning like our "strategic meaning".
One kind of such evidence consists in the cancellability of
the laziness reading.   Here is an example of such
cancellability modified from *Sports Illustrated*, January 30,
1984:

(379)   Asked how badly he wanted to win the Super
           Bowl Washington Redskin left guard Russ Grimm
           replied, "I'd run over my mother to win it."   The
           quote was repeated to Los Angeles Raider inside
           linebacker Matt Millen, who answered, "I'd run
           over her, too, - I mean Grimm's mother."

        Even though this will not yet amount to a full analysis
of pronouns of laziness, we have seen enough to make it
likely that they do not involve a semantical mechanism
different from the ones we have diagnosed.   At the same
time, we can see how the idea of strategic meaning can do
some real explanatory work for us.

        35. Apparent Exceptions: Syntactical Control or Not?

The problem discussed in this section is posed by the claim
by Hankamer and Sag that "there are anaphoric pronouns
that must be syntactically controlled" (Hankamer and Sag,
1976).
        As far as the question of syntactically controlled
anaphora is concerned, we do not want to argue in absolute
terms that it does not exist.   We have argued that in many
examples of what looks like an anaphoric pronoun relying on
a syntactical relation to its head, the relation in question is
really pragmatic.   However, these arguments do not cover
all different types of anaphora.
        Hankamer and Sag argue that there obtains in general
a contrast between two different kinds of anaphora: the
syntactically   controlled   and   (as   they   call   it)   the
pragmatically controlled.   We have argued above that many
cases of the so-called pragmatically controlled anaphora are
controlled partly by semantical rules, not merely pragmatic

ones.   The evidence Hankamer and Sag assemble for syntactically controlled anaphora concerns mostly types of anaphora other than anaphoric personal pronouns, which are what we have been concerned with here.   And whatever evidence there is concerning anaphoric personal pronouns in their paper, we don't find it convincing.   What we have discovered in this work shows that some of the assumptions they are basing their evidence on are in fact questionable. If we had to venture a guess at this time, we would conjecture that syntactically controlled anaphora is found only in propositional anaphora, never with anaphoric personal pronouns.   Take, for instance, the following examples used by Hankamer and Sag:

(380)   I've never ridden a camel, but Ivan's ridden a
            camel, and he says it stank horribly.
(381)   I've never ridden a camel, but Ivan has, and he
            says it stank horribly.

Their argument is essentially that, in order to provide an antecedent for the anaphoric pronoun "it" in (381), we must assume that (381) must have been derived from some intermediate structure like (380) by deletion.   Hence the pronoun "it" in (381) must be syntactically controlled, just as in (380).
       However, we have seen that an anaphoric pronoun does not always need a syntactical antecedent for its operation (cf., e.g., (43) or (140) above).   All we need for the right interpretation is a set I that contains the camel Ivan rode.   And that presumably is available to the players by the time "it" is handled on any reasonable treatment of the elliptic clause.
       Presumably, the ellipsis must have been restored before the pronoun comes into play.   But this is not necessitated, if it is, by the treatment of the anaphoric pronoun as such.
       For the sake of comparison, consider the following pair of examples:

(382)   As New York has its night life, so Tallahassee
            has its night life.   Unfortunately this weekend
            she is in Tampa.

(383)   As New York has its night life, so does Talla-
            hassee.   Unfortunately, this weekend she is in

Tampa.

Here (383) must presumably be derived from some such intermediate form as (382), but not to restore an anaphoric relation, for there is no natural head for "she" in (382), either. The mechanism that gives "she" its force in (383) is the same as in (382). Hence (by parity of the two cases) such examples as (380)-(381) are not convincing as evidence that we must distinguish two entirely different kinds of anaphora operating by means of essentially different mechanisms.

Other examples also show that the argument based on (380)-(381) is not persuasive:

(384)   I have never ridden a camel, knowing that it would smell horribly.

Here "a camel" not only can serve as the antecedent of "it" in our restricted sense, but can be "coreferential" with it, in linguists' usual sense of the term. The fact that we can happily say that in (384) we have a case of possible coreference does not change the theoretical situation and force us to consider "it" in (384) to be syntactically controlled. For what happens is that speaking of knowledge brings in the situations not ruled out by the knowledge in question. In some of them, "a camel" and "it" are coreferential in our treatment. Hence a semantical account is possible here, and there is no theoretical reason to think of the pronoun "it" as a mere placeholder for its antecedent in (384).

NOTES

[1] This point has been emphasized by (among others) Peter Geach. See his *Reference and Generality*, Cornell U.P., Ithaca, N.Y. 1962; "Referring Expressions Again", in *Logic Matters*, Blackwell, Oxford, 1972; "Back-Reference", *Philosophia* 5 (1975), 193–206. For a discussion of Geach's views, see Gareth Evans, "Pronouns, Quantifiers and Relative Clauses", *Canadian Journal of Philosophy*, 7 (1977), 467–536; Gareth Evans, "Pronouns," *Linguistic Inquiry* 11 (1980), 337–362.

[2] Examples like (37) and (38) seem to be originally due to Lauri Karttunen.

[3] With apologies to Cyril Hare for taking the names of some of his characters in vain; cf. *An English Murder*, Harper & Row, New York, 1978, pp. 160–161.

[4] Examples of this kind are not all linguists' and philosophers' artifacts. Here is an example from ordinary fiction:

(385)   Cargill recollected that Lady Kitti Bridge was not the first person he had interviewed who had read only the parts that concerned her and none of the rest. (Julian Rathbone, *A Spy of the Old School*, Pantheon Books, New York, 1984, pp. 184–185.)

[5] Likewise, a reader of Antonia Fraser's Jemima Shore mystery, *Cool Repentance*, Methuen (paper), London, 1983, is told on pages 155–157 the following:

(386)   The person who had thought all along that Christabel could not just come back like that and expect to get away with it knew that she was alone. ... The person decided that the right moment had at last come to put an end to Christabel. ... Oh, it would be terrible, the most dreadful pity, for the person's plan to kill Christabel to be ruined at the very last moment!

If the Exclusion Principle is applied here in the most straightforward manner, the reader could conclude that the murderous person in question cannot have been Christabel herself. Yet when the reader eventually finds out that she was, he or she is scarcely likely to claim to have been tricked by bad grammar. According to the conventions of mystery stories, the reader is not supposed to know who "the person" was, even to the exclusion of Christabel. In other words, there is a scenario compatible with the reader's knowledge in which Christabel and the murderer are different persons.

Notice that this case is unlike the Jocasta case, for here Christabel of course knows that she is herself the murderer. It is the reader who is nescient.

Bibliography

Bach, Emmon and Barbara H. Partee: 1980, "Anaphora and Semantic Structure", in Kreiman and Ojeda, 1980, pp. 1-28

Beth, E. W.: 1964, *The Foundations of Mathematics*, North-Holland, Amsterdam.

Bolinger, Dwight: 1979, "Pronouns in Discourse", in Talmy Givon, ed., *Discourse and Syntax* (*Syntax and Semantics* 12), Academic Press, New York, pp. 289-310.

Bosch, Peter: 1980, "The Modes of Pronominal Reference and Their Constraints", in Kreiman and Ojeda 1980, pp. 64-78.

Bresnan, Joan: 1970, "An Argument against Pronominalization", *Linguistic Inquiry* 1, 122-124.

Bresnan, Joan, ed.: 1982, *The Mental Representation of Grammatical Relations*, MIT Press, Cambridge.

Carden, Guy: 1981, "Blocked Forward Coreference and the Surface Interpretation Hypotheses", paper presented at the 56th Annual Meeting of the Linguistic Society of America, New York.

Carlson, Lauri: 1982, "Plural Quantification and Informational Independence", *Acta Philosophical Fennica* 55, 163-174.

Carlson, Lauri: 1983, *Dialogue Games*, D. Reidel, Dordrecht.

Carlson, Lauri: forthcoming, "Reference in Dialogue Games".

Chomsky, Noam: 1980, "On Binding", *Linguistic Inquiry* 11, 1-46. Reprinted in Frank Heny, ed., *Binding and Filtering*, MIT Press, Cambridge, 1981, pp. 47-103.

Chomsky, Noam: 1981, *Lectures on Government and Binding*, Foris, Dordrecht.

Chomsky, Noam: 1982, *Some Concepts and Consequences of the Theory of Government and Binding*, MIT Press, Cambridge.

Cooper, Robin H.: 1979, "The Interpretation of Pronouns", in Heny and Schnelle 1979, pp. 61-92.

Davidson, Donald: 1973, "Radical Interpretation", *Dialectica* 27, 313-328.

Donnellan, Keith: 1966, "Reference and Definite Descriptions", *Philosophical Review* 75, 281-304.

Donnellan, Keith: 1970, "Proper Names and Identifying Descriptions", *Synthese* 21, 335-358.

Dougherty, R.: 1969, "An Interpretive Theory of Pronominal Reference", *Foundations of Language* 5, 488-519.

Dowty, David: 1980, "Comments on the Paper by Bach and Partee", Bach and Partee 1980, in Kreiman and Ojeda 1980, pp. 29-40.

Evans, Gareth: 1980, "Pronouns", *Linguistic Inquiry* 11, 337-362.

Evans, Gareth: 1977, "Pronouns, Quantifiers and Relative Clauses (I)", *Canadian Journal of Philosophy* 7 467-536. Reprinted in Mark Platts, ed., *Reference, Truth and Reality: Essays on the Philososphy of Language*, Routledge & Kegan Paul, London, 1980, pp. 255-317.

Evans, Gareth: 1977, "Pronouns, Quantifiers and Relative Clauses (II): Appendix", *Canadian Journal of Philosophy* 7, 777-797.

Geach, Peter: 1962, *Reference and Generality*, Cornell University Press, Ithaca, New York.

Geach, Peter: 1972, "Referring Expressions Again", in *Logic Matters*, Blackwell, Oxford, pp. 97-102

Geach, Peter: 1975, "Back-Reference", *Philosophia* 5, 193-206.

Gödel, Kurt: 1980, "On a Hitherto Unexploited Extension of the Finitistic Viewpoint", *Journal of Philosophical Logic* 9, 133–142.

Grice, Paul: 1969, "Vacuous Names", in Donald Davidson and Jaakko Hintikka, eds., *Words and Objections: Essays on the Work of W. V. Quine*, D. Reidel, Dordrecht, pp. 118–145.

Hankamer, Jorge, and Ivan Sag: 1976, "Deep and Surface Anaphora", *Linguistic Inquiry* 7, 391–426.

Harada, S. I. and Saiko Seito: 1971, "A Non-Source for Reflexives", *Linguistic Inquiry* 2, 546–557.

Hausser, Roland: 1979, "How Do Pronouns Denote?" in Heny and Schnelle 1979, pp. 93–139.

Hawkins, John A.: 1978, *Definiteness and Indefiniteness: A Study in Reference and Grammaticality Prediction*, Croom Helm, London.

Helke, Michael: 1971, "The Grammar of English Reflexivization", Ph.D. Dissertation, MIT.

Heny, Frank and Helmut Schnelle, eds.: 1979, *Selections from the Third Groningen Round Table* (*Syntax and Semantics*, 10), Academic Press, New York.

Higginbotham, James: 1980, "Pronouns and Bound Variables", *Linguistic Inquiry* 11, 679–708.

Hintikka, Jaakko: 1956, "Identity, Variables, and Impredicative Definitions", *Journal of Symbolic Logic* 21, 225–245.

Hintikka, Jaakko: 1969, "On the Logic of Perception", in *Models for Modalities*, D. Reidel, Dordrecht.

Hintikka, Jaakko: 1973, *Logic, Language-Games, and Information*, Clarendon Press, Oxford.

Hintikka, Jaakko: 1975a, "Knowledge by Acquaintance – Individuation by Acquaintance", in *Knowledge and the Known*, D. Reidel, Dordrecht.

Hintikka, Jaakko: 1975b, "Objects of Knowledge and Belief", in *The Intentions of Intentionality*, D. Reidel, Dordrecht.

Hintikka, Jaakko: 1976, *The Semantics of Questions and the Questions of Semantics* (*Acta Philosophica Fennica*. 28:4) Societas Philosophica Fennica, Helsinki.

Hintikka, Jaakko: 1979, "Quantifiers in Natural Language: *Game-Theoretical Semantics*, D. Reidel, Dordrecht, pp. 81-117.

Hintikka, Jaakko: 1981, "Semantics: A Revolt against Frege", in G. Fløistad and G. H. von Wright, eds., *Contemporary Philosophy: A New Survey*, Vol. 1, *Philosophy of Language / Philosophical Logic*, Martinus Nijhoff, The Hague, pp. 57-82.

Hintikka, Jaakko: 1983, "Semantical Games, the Alleged Ambiguity of 'Is', and Aristotelian Categories", *Synthese* 54, 443-468. Reprinted in Hintikka and Kulas 1983, chap. 8.

Hintikka, Jaakko: 1984, "A Hundred Years Later: The Rise and Fall of Frege's Influence in Language Theory", *Synthese* 59, 27-49.

Hintikka, Jaakko: forthcoming(a), "Abstract Meaning vs. Strategic Meaning".

Hintikka, Jaakko: forthcoming(b), "Game-Theoretical Semantics as a Synthesis of Verificationist and Truth-Conditional Semantics", in Ernest LePore, ed., *Semantics, Theories, and Natural Languages*, Academic Press, New York.

Hintikka, Jaakko: forthcoming(c), "Logic of Conversation as a Logic of Dialogue", in R. Grandy, ed., *Philosophical Grounds of Rationality: Intentions, Categories, and Ends - A Festschrift for Paul Grice*, Oxford University Press, Oxford.

Hintikka, Jaakko, and Lauri Carlson: 1977, "Pronouns of Laziness in Game-Theoretical Semantics", *Theoretical Linguistics* 4, 1-29.

Hintikka, Jaakko, and Lauri Carlson: 1979, "Conditionals, Generic Quantifiers, and Other Applications of Sub-games", in Saarinen 1979, pp. 179-214.

Hintikka, Jaakko, and Jack Kulas: 1982, "Russell Vindi-cated: Towards a General Theory of Definite Descriptions", *Journal of Semantics* 1, 387-397.

Hintikka, Jaakko, and Jack Kulas: 1983, *The Game of Lan-guage*, D. Reidel, Dordrecht.

Hintikka, Jaakko, and Jack Kulas: forthcoming, "Different Uses of the Definite Article", *Communication and Cognition*.

Hintikka, Jaakko, and Esa Saarinen: 1975, "Semantical Games and the Bach-Peters Paradox", *Theoretical Lin-guistics* 2, 1-20. Reprinted in Saarinen 1979.

Jackendoff, Ray: 1968, "An Interpretive Theory of Pro-nouns and Reflexives", Indiana University Linguistics Club, Bloomington.

Jackendoff, Ray: 1972, *Semantic Interpretation in Genera-tive Grammar*, MIT Press, Cambridge.

Janssen, Theo: 1980, "Coreference and Interreference in Anaphoric Relations: Grammatical Semantics or Pragmatics?" in Johan Van der Auwera, ed., *The Semantics of Determiners*, Croom Helm, London, pp. 67-80.

Jespersen, Otto: 1933, *Essentials of English Grammar*, Holt, Reinhart and Winston, New York.

Kamp, Hans: 1983, "A Theory of Truth and Semantic Inter-pretation," in J. A. G. Groenendijk et al., eds., *Formal Methods in the Study of Language* (Mathematical Centre Tracts 135), Mathematisch Centrum, Amsterdam, Part I, pp. 277-322.

Karttunen, Lauri: 1969, "Pronouns and Variables", in R. Binnick, A. Davison, G. Green, and J. Morgan, eds., *Papers from the Fifth Regional Meeting of the Chicago*

Linguistic Society, University of Chicago, Department of Linguistics, Chicago, pp. 108–116.

Klemke, E. D., ed.: 1970, *Essays on Bertrand Russell*, University of Illinois Press, Urbana, Illinois.

Kreiman, Jody and Almerindo E. Ojeda, eds., *Papers from the Parasession on Pronouns and Anaphora*, Chicago Linguistic Society, Chicago, 1980.

Kuno, Susumu: 1983, "Reflexivization in English", *Communication and Cognition* 16, 257–272.

Lakoff, George: 1968, "Pronouns and Reference", Indiana University Linguistics Club, Bloomington.

Langacker, Ronald W.: 1969, "On Pronominalization and the Chain of Command", Reibel and Schane 1969, pp. 160–186.

Lasnik, Howard: 1976, "Remarks on Coreference", *Linguistic Analysis* 2, 1–22.

Lasnik, Howard: 1982, "On Two Recent Treatments of Disjoint Reference", *Journal of Linguistic Research*, 48–58.

Lees, Robert B., and Edward S. Klima: 1963, "Rules for English Pronominalization", *Language* 39, 17–28. Reprinted in Reibel and Schane 1969, pp. 145–159.

Leisenring, A. C.: 1969, *Mathematical Logic and Hilbert's Epsilon-Symbol*, Macdonald Technical and Scientific, London.

LePore, Ernest and James Garson: 1983, "Pronouns and Quantifier-Scope in English", *Journal of Philosophical Logic* 12, 327–358.

Mates, Benson: 1973, "Descriptions and Reference", *Foundations of Language* 10, 409–418.

McCawley, James: 1982, "How to Get an Interpretive Theory of Anaphora to Work", in his *Thirty Million Theories of Grammar*, Croom Helm, London, pp. 128–158.

Moore, Samuel, and Thomas A. Knott: 1965, *Elements of Old English*, 10th ed. (revised by James R. Hulbert), George Wahr Publishing Co., Ann Arbor, Mich.

Partee, Barbara: 1972, "Opacity, Coreference and Pronouns", in Donald Davidson and Gilbert Harman, eds., *Semantics of Natural Language*, D. Reidel, Dordrecht, pp. 415–441.

Partee, Barbara and Emmon Bach: 1980, "Quantification, Pronouns, and VP-Anaphora," in J. A. G. Groenendijk et. al., eds., *Formal Methods in the Study of Language* (Mathematical Centre Tracts 135), Mathematisch Centrum, Amsterdam, Part I.

Postal, Paul: 1969, "On So-called 'Pronouns' in English", in D. A. Reibel and S. A. Schane, eds., *Modern Studies in English*, Prentice-Hall, Englewood Cliffs, N.J., 1969, pp. 221–224.

Postal, Paul: 1970, "On Coreferential Complement Subject Deletion", *Linguistic Inquiry* 1, 439–500.

Radford, Andrew: 1981, *Transformational Syntax: A Student's Guide to Chomsky's Extended Standard Theory*, Cambridge University Press, Cambridge.

Reibel, David and Sanford Schane, eds.: 1969, *Modern Studies in English: Readings in Transformational Grammar*, Prentice-Hall, Englewood Cliffs, N.J.

Reinhart, Tanya: 1974, "Syntax and Coreference", in G. Reisse and J. Hankamer, eds., *Northeastern Linguisitc Society Proceedings* 5, 92–105.

Reinhart, Tanya: 1976, "The Syntactic Domain of Anaphora", Ph.D. Dissertation, MIT.

Reinhart, Tanya: 1978, "Syntactic Domains for Semantic Rules", in Franz Guenther and S. J. Schmidt, eds., *Formal Semantics and Pragmatics for Natural Languages*, D. Reidel, Dordrecht, pp. 107–130.

Reinhart, Tanya: 1981, "Definite Anaphora and C-Command Domains", *Linguistic Inquiry* 12, 605–635.

Reinhart, Tanya: 1983a, *Anaphora and Semantic Interpre-tation*, Croom Helm, London.

Reinhart, Tanya: 1983b, "Coreference and Bound Anaphora: A Restatement of the Anaphora Questions", *Linguistics and Philosophy* 6, 47–88.

Richards, Barry: 1979, "Pronouns, References, and Seman-tic Laziness", in Jonathan Dancy, ed., *Papers on Language and Logic*, University of Keele Library, Keele. Reprinted in Frank Heny, ed., *Ambiguities in Intensional Contexts*, D. Reidel, Dordrecht, 1981, pp. 191–230.

Ross, John: 1967, "Constraints on Variables in Syntax", Ph.D. Dissertation, MIT.

Ross, John: 1969, "On the Cyclic Nature of English Pro-nominalization", in Reibel and Schane (1969), pp. 187–200.

Russell, Bertrand: 1905, "On Denoting", *Mind* 14, 479–93. Reprinted in Russell 1973, pp. 103–19.

Russell, Bertrand: 1973, *Essays in Analysis*, edited by Douglas Lackey, Allen and Unwin, London.

Shopen, T.: 1972, "A Generative Theory of Ellipsis", Ph.D. Dissertation, UCLA.

Solan, Lawrence: 1983, *Pronominal Reference: Child Lan-guage and the Theory of Grammar*, D. Reidel, Dordrecht.

Stenning, Keith: 1978, "Anaphora as an Approach to Prag-matics", in Morris Halle, Joan Bresnan, and George A. Miller, eds., *Linguistic Theory and Psychological Reality*, MIT Press, Cambridge, pp. 162–200.

Stockwell, Robert P., Paul Schachter, and Barbara Hall Partee: 1973, *The Major Syntactic Structures of English*, Holt, Rinehart and Winston, New York, chap. 4 ("Pronominalization"), pp. 161–229.

Strawson, P. F.: 1950, "On Referring", *Mind* 59, 320–44.

Strawson, P. F.: 1964, "Identifying Reference and Truth Values", *Theoria* 30, 96-118.

Vlastos, Gregory, ed.: 1971, *Plato I: Metaphysics and Epistemology*, Doubleday, Garden City, N.Y.

Wasow, Thomas: 1975, "Anaphoric Pronouns and Bound Variables", *Language* 51, 368-379.

Wasow, Thomas: 1979, *Anaphora in Generative Grammar*, E. Story-Scientia, Ghent.

Webber, Bonnie Lynn: 1979, *A Formal Approach to Discourse Anaphora*, Garland Publishing, New York.

Wiese, Bernd: 1983, "Anaphora by Pronouns", *Linguistics* 21, 373-417.

Zribi-Hertz, A.: 1980, "Coréférence et pronoms réfléchis: Notes sur le contraste Lui/Lui-Même en française", *Linguisticae Investigationes* 4, 131-179.

abstract meaning, 29, 139, 142-145, 147, 150, 219
acquaintance
    identification by, 95, 214, 216
adverbial prepositional phrases
    (See "prepositional phrases")
ambidextrous quantifiers, 24-25
ambiguity, 28
anaphora
    different kinds of, 110
    in general, 35
    propositional, 221
    is deixis in a semantical game, 147
anaphoric pronouns, 25,28
    anaphoric "the"-phrase, 90, 92, 95
        behave essentially alike, 90, 92, 95
        parallel with, 98-104, 133
    bound-variable account of, 80-82
    deictic pronouns and, 96
    coreference accounts, 81-84
    differences with anaphoric
            "the"-phrases, 95, 116
    different kinds of, 84, 147
    discourse determinanats, 217
    as free terms, 109
    in discourse, 85
    logical model of, 94
    placeholder account of, 79, 80, 222
    pragmatic context used in
            interpretation of, 135-140
pragmatically controlled, 220-222
quantifier phrases and, 129
repeated-reference account of, 80, 86
syntactically controlled, 220-222
uniform vs. nonuniform
            treatment of, 84
    uniqueness requirement, 117, 133-135
anaporn, 147-148
"any", 17
antecedents, 55
    (see "head-anaphor")
applications of game rules
    (See "rule application")

applied language, 3
atomic sentences, 4, 22–23, 27
　　truth conditions for, 22
Austinian "if", 101
Bach–Peters sentences, 36, 38, 39, 42, 75
backwards anaphora, 131, 161–162, 193
branching quantifiers, 10, 18, 28
category of entities, 26, 37, 88
c–command, 19, 198, 200, 203, 208
c–dominate, 19
"certain, a", 190–191
choice set, inductive, 62–64, 87, 88, 95, 96, 119, 191
　　importance in pronominal
　　　interpretation, 146
　　(See also "I (Discourse set)")
class of individuals as
　　choice of a player in a
　　　　　　semantical game, 92
clause, 61
command, 16
competent speaker, 30
comparative (vs. positive), 72
compositionality, 4, 39
conditionals
　　game rule for, 11–12, 89
conditionally connected subgames, 105–106
conjunction, 104–105
conjunctively connected subgames, 105–107
context–independence, 4
contextual identification, 215–216
contextually prominent individuals, 95
conversational
　　expectation, 118
　　principles, 60
coreference
　　accounts of,
　　　provide no genuine theory, 84
　　　yield only empirical
　　　　　generalizations, 83, 158, 162
　　actual–identity account of, 82, 150
　　assignments, 81–84
　　　the uses of indexing in, 82, 192
　　　pragmatic element in, 82
　　　syntax determines, 82, 83

concept of, 62, 81-84, 170
  criticisms of, 81-83, 122, 146-147, 150-155, 215
  explanatory value of, 83
conditions on, and scope, 158
not a grammatical notion, 150
indefinite NP's and, 151-152
intended-identity account of, 82, 151
optional vs. obligatory, 82-83, 191-193, 202
possible-impossible, 157, 191, 193-194
        interpretability and, 171
relativized to a play of
        a semantical game, 157
relative to rule ordering in GTS, 157
restriction (See "(CR)")
restrictions cancellable, 161
as a semantical primitive, 83, 150, 153
syntactic structure and, 180, 189-191, 197-198
(CR) [coreference restriction], 203-205, 208
crossing anaphoric relations, 75, 93, 114
      (See also "Bach-Peters sentences")
  problems with generative accounts of, 36
cross-identification, methods of, 214
definite article, 25
  and indefinite article, 70
definite descriptions, 33-76
      (also see "the")
  existential force of, 42
  discourse and, 43
  existence requirement, 46, 55
  Mates-type uses of, 62-63
  referential and attributive, 44-45
    possible-worlds treatment of, 44
  Russellian use of, 66-68, 71
  uniqueness requirement for, 46-47, 55, 102
deixis, 84-86
  assimilation of anaphora to, 147
demonstratives, 65
  as archetypal ways of reffering, 65
  etymological connection with pronouns, 103
denoting phrases (Russell), 75
descriptively identified individuals, 45, 214
dialogue games, 85
Dictionary of National Biography, 214
discourse, 17, 49, 95, 104, 108-109, 136

anaphora, 85, 102
  and subgames, 104-108
  application of GTS in, 51
  environment, 96
  logic and semantics of, 43
  ordering principles and, 43
  presupposition and, 43
  theory, 15, 44, 57, 108, 217
  and human memory, 91
domain, 152-153, 200
donkey sentences, 99-100, 106-107, 112,
  130-132, 190
  and "bound pronouns" view, 130
dynamic vs. static accounts, 170
ellipsis, 221
epistemic logic, 23
epithetic
  (See "the")
epsilon terms (Hilbert), 94, 129-130
exclusion, quantifier, 58-62, 113-114, 212
exclusion
  phenomenon, 60-61
    in predicate calculus, 60
  principle, 60-61, 113-128, 142, 151, 159,
  163-164, 168, 172, 180, 193-195
      counterexamples to, 172-173
      clause-bound, 208-210
      identity and, 210-212
      knowledge and, 212
      semantical nature
        of exceptions, 211-212
      semantical nature of, 213
  rules for quantifiers, 61
existential quantifier, 7
explanatory strategies, 28-30, 211-212
false sentences, logically, 28
falsification, games of, 5, 85
Falsifier, 6
first-order languages and logic, 3, 6, 7, 15
  extensions of, 9
  representations of English, 17, 18, 85
  Russell's campaign for, 33
Frege-Russell paradigm, 75
functional interpretations, 12, 28

(G. about), 206
(G. an), 14, 51, 53, 92, 93, 114, 189
(G. anaphoric the), 48–58, 61–68, 87–90, 95,
    102, 113
(G. anaphoric nu x), 50
(G. and), 12, 121, 170
(G. any), 15, 18
(G. ask), 124, 182
(G. believes), 122
(G. believes to), 186, 187
(G. cond), 11–12, 18, 89, 131, 189
(G. each), 15, 19, 122, 174
(G. every), 14–15, 107, 129, 174, 187
(G. genitive), 26, 51, 62, 75, 76, 160, 164–170, 172,
    178, 198–199, 206–207
(G. he), 90, 92–94, 98, 102, 104, 113, 115, 116, 118,
    129, 133–135, 141, 143, 149, 158–159, 167, 169–171,
    174, 176, 182, 190–191, 198, 205, 209
(G. himself), 120
(G. in), 178
(G. ʝ), 37, 39
(G. it), 92, 189, 218
(G. knows that), 24
(G. knows who), 24
(G. name), 25, 59, 75, 88–89, 113, 159, 161, 167,
    170–171, 187–188, 192, 198, 205, 209
(G. near), 27, 172–174, 175, 180, 206–208
(G. necessarily), 23
(G. neg), 41
(G. not), 18
(G. or), 12, 18, 121
(G. only), 123–124
(G. promise), 124, 181–182
(G. remember), 165
(G. Russellian the), 37–38, 40–45, 162
(G. she), 92, 94, 102, 116, 141, 164, 167
(G. some), 13–14, 16, 107, 190, 209
(G. the), 64, 160, 171
(G. the only), 41
(G. wants to), 184
(G. when), 132, 205
(G. with), 173
(G. v), 5, 12
(G. &), 5, 12

(G. E), 5
(G. E ex), 61
(G. U), 5
(G. U ex), 61
(G.~), 5, 6
games of exploring the world, 30
game-quantifier languages, 23
games
    two-person zero-sum, 4
      and natural-language sentences, 12
gender attributions, 98–99
generative rules, 29
generative semantics, 39
generic force, 152
genitive, 26, 219
    reflexive
      in Swedish, 168–169
      why none in English, 168
Godel's interpretation of
    first-order logic, 11
governing category (Chomsky), 199
government (Chomsky), 199
GTS
    applied to natural language, 12–15
    applied to logic, 3–12
    tool of linguistic explanation, 27–30
    forte of, 36
head-anaphor relation, 54–55, 56, 79, 81, 86, 87, 94, 98,
    110, 120, 135, 141–142, 171
    irrelevance in GTS, 56–57, 102–104, 117, 146–150
    possible use of, 144
    problems with, 58, 122–123
higher-order
    functions, 11
    sentences, 7
    translations
Highland use of, 12, 28
    "himself", 71, 145
    "the", 71, 73
I (discourse set), 48–49, 56, 59, 63, 66, 67, 87–90, 94
    structure on, 54–55
identification, methods of, 210–218
identity statements, 210
indefinite article, 70

ambiguity of, 130
as existential quantifier, 107, 110, 112
as universal quantifier, 99-100, 107, 108, 110
indefinite NP's and pronouns, 190
indexicals, 214-215
individuals
"too old", 90, 137
infinitary games, 22
infinitely deep languages, 23
indexing in coreference assignments, 82, 193
informational independence, 9, 15, 28
inside out, 4, 39
intensional
operators, 12
concepts, 23
contexts, 45
interpretability, 29
interpretation
for a language, 3-4
interpretative semantics, 81
intuitive evidence, 167
"is", alleged ambiguity of, 33, 152
knowing that, 23
knowledge, 223-224
(See also "exclusion principle")
labelled-tree form, 14, 20
Langacker-Ross Restriction, 161-169, 173, 179, 181,
187-188, 193-195, 197, 200
differences with GTS, 162-163
language as universal medium, 68
lawlikeness and generic "the", 69
lexical theory, 22,31
lexicalist-functionalist approach, 22, 31
linearly ordered quantifiers, 9-10, 28
linguistic theory, recent, 84
logical form, 17-18
machine translation, 136
meaning
different kinds of, 29
memory
human short-term, 91
methodological considerations, 127
modal concepts, 23
modal rules in semantical games, 18

Montague semantics, 3, 81
"museum scenario" for generic "the", 70–71
Myself, 4, 6
natural language, 3
    translations into logical notation, 12
        differences with formal language, 15, 22–23, 24, 115
Nature, 4, 6
necessity (and semantical games), 23
negation
    game rules for, 12
"never", 17
Nominative Island Constraint, 200–201
nonanaphoric pronouns
    (See "pronouns": nonanaphoric)
(O. any), 18, 162
(O. comm), 16, 17, 19, 20, 21, 88, 131–132, 159,
    161–163, 167, 170, 190, 191–192, 200, 209
(O. CR), 20–21, 203–204, 207
    wrong predictions by, 204
(O. each), 19
(O. LR), 16, 17, 20, 21, 89, 122, 159, 161, 171,
    190, 192, 201–202, 206, 208–209
Old English forms of "the", 65, 103
"only", 41
Opacity (Chomsky), 200–203
Operationalist theories of meaning, 29
Optimal strategy for Myself
    determining pronominal reference, 56
ordering principles, 16–22, 31, 157–197
    discourse and, 43
    explanatory value of, in GTS, 40–41
    general, 16–18, 159, 162
    for (G. genitive) and (G. she/he), 164–165
    for pronominal game rules, 160
    special, 16, 18–19, 31, 159, 162, 180–181, 191,
    197–198
    syntactic structure and, 21, 180–181, 203, 207, 212
output of rules
    order of, 27, 91, 106–107, 173, 188, 206–207, 209
outside-in semantics, 4, 39
partially ordered quantifiers, 9
perceptually identified individuals, 45, 65, 214
plural pronouns, 92
pointing, 104, 214–216

positive (vs. comparative), 72
possible-situations semantics, 44
possible-worlds, 213
    semantics, 23, 44
pragmatic
    account of generic use of "the", 68–69
    interpretation of anaphoric pronouns
        (See "anaphoric pronouns")
    "axiom of choice", 69
    deduction, 69
    factors, 142
    treatment, 66
    pressures, 67
    wastebasket, 138
prepositional phrases
    in atomic sentences, 22, 27
    nested, 178–179
    ordering principle for, 16–17, 176, 179, 180
    quantifier-like nature of, 27
    reflexives and, 127, 176
    rules for, 172–179
    semantics of, 174–175
    sentential (adverbial), 175, 178–179, 206
    verb phrasal, 175–176, 178–179, 206
presuppositions, 43, 55
primary occurrences (Russell), 39–40, 42
principle of charity, 64, 66–67, 190
progression principle, 16, 84, 131, 161
pronominal anaphora
    essentially semantic, 146–150
pronouns of laziness, 79, 84, 217–220
    and subgames, 217
    cancellability, 220
    rely on remembered strategies, 218
    strategic meaning and, 218–220
pronouns
    assimilated to bound variables
        (See "variable-binding account")
    as choice terms, 94
    deictic, 95, 96, 97, 102
        vs. anaphoric pronouns, 96
    different uses of, 97
    nonanaphoric, 95, 96
    unified semantical behavior of, 97

proper names, 66, 75, 88, 110, 116
    interpretation in semantical games, 25, 59, 159
propositional rules in semantical games, 19, 209
pseudo-clefting, 175
psycholinguistic
    plausibility of game rules, 30
    realism: GTS vs. pure syntax, 208
purposes in language use, 15, 85
quantification theory
    (See "first-order logic and language")
quantifier rules
    for natural language, 12-16, 19, 90, 157
quantifier phrases in natural language, 129
    treated as terms, not quantifiers, 130
question-answer relations, 15
questions, 212
    presuppositions of, 44
    the semantics of, 23, 108
    subordinate, 31
range restriction for quantifiers, 46-48, 52, 65
recursive functions
    restricting strategies to, 11
reciprocals, 200
referential dependency (Evans), 194
reflexive pronouns, 83, 92, 119-125, 153-154, 204
    acceptability of, 119-120, 207, 216
    distribution not complement
        of nonreflexives, 120-121, 176
    game rules for, 119, 122, 183, 186
    with identity, 210-211
    and direct targets (Kuno), 176
    direct relationship (Zribi-Hertz), 177
reflexivization transformation
    not obligatory, 127-128
relative pronouns
    in quantifier phrases, 13
remembered strategy, 52, 63, 64, 88, 89, 91, 100-102,
    105, 106, 108, 110-111, 217, 219
replacement
    quantification theory with and without, 61
representativeness
    generic use of "the", 69, 71
role switching,
    in semantical games, 5

in subgames, 10, 11, 99
rule application, 143
    coordinated, 118
        pronouns and tenses, 118
    and sentence generation, 183–184
    simultaneous, 118, 137
    timing of, 163–172
rule ordering, 158
    (See also "ordering principles")
Russellian "the"-phrases, 35, 36, 171
Russell's theory of descriptions, 33, 65, 87
    applicability to natural language, 34
    difficulties (prima facie) with, 38–45
    primary and secondary occurrences, 39–40, 42
    epsilon terms and, 94
    a GTS codification of, 37–38
    localization of, 45–49
    notation for, (iota notation), 34
        problems with crossing anaphora, 36
    Strawson's criticisms of, 42–45, 55, 75
scope, 17, 18, 28, 91, 108–112, 116, 130, 152, 158
    no indicators of, in natural language, 18, 80, 94
    duration of individuals (membership in I), 111–112
    quantifier – and ordering, 203
    relative priority of logical operators, 111–112
    stress and, 41
s-command, 19, 158
s-dominate, 19
"se" (Old English), 65, 103
second-order logic, 10
secondary occurrences (Russell), 39–40, 42
semantical game, 5
    finiteness of, 6, 23
semantical paradoxes, 22
semantical representation, 3
semantics
    first-order logic, 3
    modal logic, 3
    and pragmatics, 138
sentence
    concept of, 108–112
    as a unit of discourse, 109
sentence vs. discourse semantics, 84–86
"seo" (Old English), 65

Skolem functions, 7–9
sloppy identity
  (See "pronouns of laziness")
species–characteristic properties
  in generic "the", 69
strategic meaning, 30, 117, 147, 150, 152
  with lazy pronouns, 218–220
  syntactic indicators of, 141–143
  determining "head" of pronoun, 142
strategies, 4
  functions or functionals, as, 7, 63, 89–90, 101
  knowing a, 29
  partial, 9
  subgames, in, 10, 63
  winning, in GTS, 4, 64
stress, 134
  and scope, 41
subgames, 10–12, 15, 28, 49, 52, 54, 63, 85, 86, 89,
  95, 99, 111, 190
subject position, 200–202
Swedish, 168–169
supergames, 15, 85, 104, 136
syncategorematic notions, 27
synonymy, 28
syntactic analysis
  of inputs to game rules, 14
  and rule ordering in formal languages, 15
  and rules for semantics, 185
syntactic anomaly, 29
syntactic theory, systematic, 80
tenses, 25, 52
  past, 118
temporal
  concepts, semantics of, 214
  particles, 25
  stages, 214
"the"-phrases, 34
  (See also "definite descriptions")
  anaphoric, 35, 45, 48, 54, 58, 71, 87–113
    analogous to pronouns, 98
    in formal languages, 50
    as a semantic phenomenon, 56–58
    as semantically basic, 46, 64–66, 88
    similarity to pronouns, 35
    context-independent (Russellian), 35

counterepithetic, 53
    spithetic, 53, 55, 66, 134
    generic, 35, 45, 68-69, 71, 73-74
    Platonic use of, 72-73
    "preeminent" sense of, 72
    "species" use of, 73
theoretical explanations, 167
time-structure
    forward-branching, 25
transformational grammar
    pronominalization in, 80, 127
translations with Skolem functions
    of first-order to higher-order, 8-9, 10
truth-conditional semantics, 3, 30
truth
    in GTS, 29
truth conditions, 3, 30
truth definition
    game-theoretical, 4, 6, 138
        equivalence with Tarski-type, 6-7
        for sentences of English, 12
    Tarski-type, 3-4, 6-7
uniqueness requirement for
    anaphoric pronouns
    (See "anaphoric pronouns")
universal medium, language as the, 68
urn model, 61
variable-binding account of pronouns, 18, 80, 82, 84,
    94, 109-110, 117, 129-130, 146-147
variables of quantification theory, 146
verification,
    games of, 5, 15, 85
    strategies of in subgames, 11
verificationist theory of meaning, 29
Verifier, 6
wh-movement, 14
wh-question, 107
Who's Who, 214
winning, 15
    atomic sentences, 22
    inifinite games, 22
    strategies, 4-5, 12
        existence of, 29-30, 138
        actually having one, 138
word order and scope, 201

Name Index

Arid, C., 212
Aristotle, 72
Bach, E.,
   and B. Partee, 60, 115, 155
Beth, 73
Bolinger, D., 160, 167
Bresnan, J., 31, 79
Carden, G., 207
Carlson, L., 26, 43, 49, 85, 92, 114, 197, 217
Chomsky, N., 33, 80, 81, 82, 84, 115, 127, 162,
   198-203, 208
Clark, E., 71, 145
Clark, H., 72
Clinton-Baddely, 35, 101
Davidson, D., 33, 66
Donnellan, K., 44-45
Dougherty, R., 82, 148
Evans, G., 194, 223
Filmore, C., 72
Grancis, D., 137, 193, 216
Fraser, A., 159, 216, 223
Frege, G., 33
Geach, P., 153, 223
Gilbert, M., 140
Godel, K., 11
Grice, P., 88
Hankamer, J.
   and I. Sas, 220-222
Harada adn Seito, 185
Hare, C., 223
Hawkins, J., 46
Helke, M., 127
Higginbotham, J., 80, 82, 158
Hilbert, D., 33, 94, 129-130
Hintikka, J., 3, 29, 43, 49, 60, 68, 75, 80, 88,
   113, 114, 118, 214-215
Hintikka, J.,
   and L. Carlson, 52, 63, 75, 79, 92, 99-100, 131,
   160, 217
Hintikka, J.,
   and J. Kulas, 4, 9, 10, 23, 26, 31, 46, 87, 88, 90,
   92, 118, 153

Hintikka, J.,
  and E. Saarinen, 38
Hintikka, M., 210
Jackendoff, R., 81, 178, 185–186, 193
Jacobson, P., 75
James, 55
Jespersen, O., 70
Kamp, H., 111
Karttunen, L., 57, 75, 223
Klemke, E., 33
Kulas, J., 87
Kuno, S., 167, 176–177
Lackey, D., 33
Lakoff, G., 33
Langacker, 82, 161, 209

LePore, E.
  and J. Garson, 130–131
Mates, B., 62
May, 158
McCawley, J., 75, 125
Moore, S.
  and T. Knott, 103
Moyes, P., 97, 137, 140
Parker, R. B., 126
Plaidy, J., 202
Plato, 72–73
Postal, P., 92, 190
Quine, W., 33, 114, 202, 214–215
Radford, A., 82, 171
Ramsey, F., 33
Rathbone, J., 149, 223
Reinhart, T., 20, 81, 82, 155, 158, 175–188, 190
  192, 193, 195, 203–208, 211–212
Ross, J., 161
Russell, B., 33–45, 75
Saarinen, E., 90
Shopen, T., 82
Strawson, P.F., 42–45, 75
Van Lehn, 18
Vlastos, G., 72
Wasow, T., 80, 84, 120, 149, 176, 192
Wittgenstein, 60
Zribi-Hertz, 177